Prison and
Social Death

CRITICAL ISSUES IN CRIME AND SOCIETY

RAYMOND J. MICHALOWSKI, SERIES EDITOR

Critical Issues in Crime and Society is oriented toward critical analysis of contemporary problems in crime and justice. The series is open to a broad range of topics including specific types of crime, wrongful behavior by economically or politically powerful actors, controversies over justice system practices, and issues related to the intersection of identity, crime, and justice. It is committed to offering thoughtful works that will be accessible to scholars and professional criminologists, general readers, and students.

For a list of titles in the series, see the last page of the book.

Prison and Social Death

JOSHUA M. PRICE

RUTGERS UNIVERSITY PRESS
New Brunswick, New Jersey, and London

Library of Congress Cataloging-in-Publication Data

PRICE, JOSHUA M.
   Prison and social death / Joshua M. Price.
     pages cm.—(Critical issues in crime and society)
   Includes bibliographical references and index.
   ISBN 978–0–8135–6558–3 (hardcover : alk. paper)—ISBN 978–0–8135–6557–6
   (pbk. : alk. paper)—ISBN 978–0–8135–6559–0 (e-book (web pdf))
   1. Imprisonment—United States. 2. Prisoners—United States—Social conditions. 3.
   Prisoners—Deinstitutionalization—United States. 4. Social isolation—United States.
   5. Marginality, Social—United States. I. Title.

   HV9471.P72 2015
   365'.6—dc23   2014035929

            A British Cataloging-in-Publication record for this
               book is available from the British Library.

              Visit our website: http://rutgerspress.rutgers.edu

            Manufactured in the United States of America

To Constanza and Rozann, with tremendous gratitude

To the innumerable whose lives are touched by prison . . .

I didn't realize the social death that we were given at the sentence. This wasn't a five to fifteen or five to ten; this was a life sentence, a death sentence, in a sense.

—Raymond Santana, member of the "Central Park Five," in an interview with journalist Amy Goodman (2012)

Contents

Acknowledgments

I owe a profound debt of gratitude to the members of the Southern Tier Social Justice Project—Rozann Greco, Cheryl DeRosa, Saleem Díaz, and Lawrence Parham. Rozann, thank you, thank you, thank you. I would also like to express my appreciation to the Broome/Tioga (New York) NAACP for their initial invitation to collaborate in creating the Broome County Jail Health Project in 2004, especially Billie Anderson and the indomitable Stan Gluck, mensch and revolutionary, who was crucial for his support and conversation throughout this project. *Consigliere* Edmond Victor Pickett advised me. Kathy Pierre, Candis Henderson, Mary DeGroat, Felicia Jennings, George Moon, and Nancy Jennings each taught me an enormous amount. Brave and thoughtful Keith Hoover, whistleblower extraordinaire, encouraged and guided me. Ray Roe, Shahin Rashid, Ron Benjamin, and many other community members and students, too numerous to name, participated in or otherwise contributed to this project at various points.

Through INCITE!, Critical Resistance, and the New York Prison Justice Network, I have met many activists from around New York State and the country who make me feel hopeful even in the depths of despair, including Karima Amin, Judith Brink, and many others.

Daniel Schugurensky arranged for a visiting appointment at the Ontario Institute for Studies in Education at the University of Toronto in 2007, where I composed the first ideas for this manuscript.

During a 2008–09 fellowship at the James Weldon Johnson Institute directed by the late Rudolph Byrd, Robbie Lieberman, Trimiko Melancon, Tekla Agbala, Ali Johnson, Eunjung Kim, and Calinda Lee deepened my understanding of race and civil rights history. Martha Fineman invited me to the Vulnerable Populations Working Group. Barry Simms made me rethink punishment and race in hemispheric terms.

As a self-identified external reviewer, Jodie Lawston made incredibly helpful suggestions and deeply engaged critiques that made the argument stronger. Comments from an anonymous reader for Rutgers University Press were also useful. Peter Mickulas was a terrific and strong editor. Each chapter, and the overall organization, bears the mark of his detailed comments. Raymond J. Michalowski supported an early draft of this manuscript for this edited series and supplied encouragement at each step. John Raymond's editing and helpful queries improved the book.

Aníbal Quijano, María Lugones, and Nicholas De Genova have inspired me politically throughout, and at times provided much-needed moral support. María and Aníbal confronted me with a decolonial framework that forced me to rethink my work in salubrious ways. Kym Clark interrogated my taken-for-granted assumptions in several drafts. I rely on Shai Lavi and Lubna Chaudhry for the lifeblood of companionship. Shai helped me refine the ideas basic to this book.

Ongoing dialogue with William Martin has been a source of sustenance; so has his friendship. He and other members of the Binghamton Justice Projects, including Kelvin Santiago-Valles, Brendan McQuade, Brian Zbriger, and Andrew Pragacz, have offered continued interlocution on incarceration, surveillance, and social control.

A number of other colleagues and friends provided crucial intellectual conversation, guided me with their wisdom, and refined my thinking. I include Patricia Clough, Denise Ferreira da Silva, Michael Moon, Juanita Diaz, Mecke Nagel, Kathy Boudin, Robin Levi, Debbie Mukamal, Denis O'Hearn, Ellen Boesenberg, Carmen Pimentel, and Linda Basch. Jenna M. Loyd and Mohamed Aly developed my thinking on the link between advocacy for the incarcerated and advocacy for detained immigrants, especially those facing deportation. In the late '90s, Joel Copperman set me down the road of considering alternatives to incarceration.

I've been blessed with truly exceptional students who have been inspiring companions in the research and politics that form the basis of this book. Noelle Paley was more of a colleague than a student. Andre Massena, Willa Payne, Jillian Lyons, Alycia Harris, Dorothy Soleil Agustin, and Austin Sanders were fantastic. Numerous conversations with Olivia Santoro developed my thinking on the implications of heteronormativity and the gender binary for the organization of the prison.

Provost Donald Nieman, Dean Ricardo Lauremont, and Dean Anne McCall of Binghamton University, along with Michael Pettid, Bill Martin, and Associate Deans Anna Addonisio and Florence Margai, arranged for support of this book project at every stage.

I would like to express my deep appreciation to the anonymous artist responsible for the cover art, *Me, Myself & I*. I am grateful to the Koestler Trust for art by offenders, secure patients, and detainees and to Fiona Curran for permission to use it.

Aimée Brown Price and Monroe Price meticulously reviewed the manuscript. Their detailed comments sharpened the text. Thanks, Mom and Dad. They, along with Asher Price, continue to exemplify for me disciplined research and inspired writing. Vivian Price was radical company throughout.

And finally, to María Constanza Guzmán, near or far, last—and most. Thank you for the daily gift of joy. Thank you also for your patient encouragement and conversation when I was at my nadir.

I would like to say to all the people above, I hope you're proud of me. I hope you're proud of this book. Though I take responsibility for any errors, I count the content, just as the politics on which it is based, to be a collective achievement.

PART ONE

Elements of Social Death

CHAPTER I

Crossing the Abyss

THE STUDY OF SOCIAL DEATH

May 2007. The woman comes through the security door into the visiting room. She glances around the room and looks a bit startled when the corrections officer motions her to a stool opposite me. She is surprised to see me at first. I am accustomed to this reaction. Even though she had written me personally and asked me to come to interview her (she must have gotten my name through a jail grapevine), we had never met before and she did not know we were coming today. Rosie, one of my students from New York City, sits at my side.

The jail has started restricting our access, so now, instead of a pre-arranged private room, we must conduct our interviews in the public visiting room. The staff at the NAACP interprets this as the jail administration trying to obstruct our research and our attempts to monitor jail conditions. The practical consequence is that we are now allowed no pens, no papers, no recording devices, no privacy, and our interviews are conducted in the presence of correctional officers. Especially significant, however, is that our visits are now docked from each person's allotment of two hours of visiting time per week. Docking their time forces the people incarcerated at the jail to balance their desire to report abuse to a civil rights organization (us) against their need to see family and friends.

We go through a few preliminaries, buffeted by the chaotic sounds all around us—lovers chatting, holding hands over the dividers, babies bouncing, guards roaming around, half bored, alternating between staring indifferently beyond all of us and glaring from time to time. I introduce myself to her formally and I explain that we are from the NAACP. I tell her she does not have to answer any of our questions. Would she still like to talk with us? I ask. She nods. Then she gives us her narrative. She is self-possessed and emotionally self-contained though her rage at the jail is clear and her grief hovers at the margins. (In order to protect people's privacy, I have changed names and identifying details throughout.)

"I entered the jail on October 27th and I thought I might be pregnant. I have three children, and so I know what it is to be pregnant. I was a little happy." This time when she entered, "I felt some pain on my side. On my right side." She was allowed to see a nurse, but the nurse dismissed her fears. She awoke one night with tremendous pain in her side and started banging on her cell door. It took fifteen minutes for the guard to come and another fifteen minutes for the nurse to come, who had her transferred to the medical unit. Her experience there was not much better. She started bleeding from the vagina, but the nurses incorrectly told the doctor it was from her anus and generally treated her complaint lightly. She awoke the following night and her panties were caked in blood. When she showed the doctor, he told her this was serious and sent her to an outside hospital. It was a tubal pregnancy and she had to have her right fallopian tube removed.

As I listen, I try to stay composed. I try not to react strongly to anything she says or reveal shock or disbelief. And I am not in disbelief. She is the third woman I have met in as many months who has miscarried at the jail. She is not the first who has suspected a tubal pregnancy but could not receive medical attention. Through speaking with incarcerated women and with my students in the project who are themselves mothers, I have learned that an undiagnosed tubal or ectopic pregnancy is potentially fatal for the mother. If it is not diagnosed, the tubal pregnancy can rupture the fallopian tube, leading to internal hemorrhage and possible sterility.

As always, I ask if we can come back for a follow-up visit, just to check on her and to make sure the jail has not engaged in recriminatory treatment against her for speaking with us. I also ask permission because we do not want to compete with other people's visits. "You don't have to worry about that," she replies, a bit dryly. "Ain't nobody coming to visit me."

I change key. "How are you? How have you been emotionally?" I ask. She has been through a lot of trauma recently. Her bearing cracks a bit. "I'm all right. I'm facing a lot of time, you know? And I already have two kids in foster care and so this one would have faced the same thing. So maybe it is for the best."

"Is there discrimination involved? Or do they treat all prisoners this way, do you think?"

"I wouldn't say there's discrimination," she responds. "They're just assholes."

Later, Rosie remarks this confirms a lot for her: women are often left to self-diagnose any health problem; the system is chaotic.

For me, her story of acute suffering that edged its way out under the fluorescent lights is a bit hard to take. She will not, in all probability, receive any of what has come to be known lately as "grief counseling." I do not know how she adjusts emotionally—or physically—to her condition and her experience given that she is facing a long period of incarceration (I never learn her crime).

She does not think racism is involved. Others provide examples of racist treatment. Most of the people we interview are African American, and I hear so many, many stories of reproductive horrors. So much death, so many separations, undiagnosed conditions, so many worries and festering wounds. It is hard for me not to see a link between prison, reproductive health, and race. (Fieldnotes, 2007)

To BE SENTENCED to prison is to be sentenced to social death. Social death is a permanent condition. While many people integrate themselves back into the society after imprisonment, they often testify that they permanently bear a social mark, a stigma.

The term "social death" comes from Orlando Patterson's analysis of slavery. In analyzing the social status of the slave, Patterson argued that slaves were rendered noncitizens, social nonentities (Patterson 1982).[1] They were condemned to social death. Social death comprised three aspects: the slave was subject to systematic violence, to generalized humiliating treatment, and to "natal alienation." Natal alienation meant severance from ancestors and children. Even when a family was together, as on a plantation, each had to be made powerless vis-à-vis the others. An enslaved person could be whipped or sold off at any time, and other slaves were in little position to do anything. The institution of slavery made it difficult, moreover, to transmit one's heritage to one's progeny. In effect, one's family and community ties had little or no legal or social standing. Natal alienation under slavery meant a radical kind of separation from others. This was an essential part of the structure of slavery. It is why Patterson deemed the slave a "genealogical isolate."

Similarly, the prison separates people from communities of support, and from their parents and children. The isolation of people in prison renders them vulnerable, moreover, to other forms of violence, including sexual violence (see Levi and Waldman 2011; B. Smith 2003, 2005). Natal alienation forces people in prison into a structure of vulnerability, subject to direct and indirect violence and humiliation. Calling the condition of prison "natally alienating" allows us to bring together many forms of state intervention that otherwise may seem disparate and unrelated. For example, it allows us to

explain the implications of incarceration for reproductive health and reproductive justice.

While people's experiences vary significantly, the interviews I have conducted consistently revealed three basic qualities of incarceration: generalized
humiliation, institutional violence, and natal alienation. The conjunction of
the three yields the peculiar contours of social death.

People who have been sentenced to prison are not the only social dead.
Immigrants facing deportation are subject to social death (De Genova and
Peutz 2010). Social death is also a central part of genocide (Card 2003). People
undergoing genocide are often first dehumanized through social death. The
connections among different forms of modern social death are complex.
This book, however, focuses on the social death of incarceration. In the case
of the United States, social death is also a racial mark.[2]

In arguing that they face social death, I am not claiming that incarcerated people are enslaved. Nor am I arguing that in facing social death, resistance is thereby forgone. Acknowledging any kind of potent social category
or oppression does not imply that people give in to that oppression or that
they do not create important bonds of solidarity and survival. I do not see the
woman above as passive. If I thought that resistance was futile, I would not
engage in participatory research.

PARTICIPATORY RESEARCH
ON JAIL HEALTH CARE

The research for this book is drawn in large part from grassroots participatory research and activism around health care of incarcerated people in upstate
New York. Between 2004 and 2007, working with community members, my
students and I interviewed over 150 people at the Broome County Correctional Facility. We also conducted over twenty interviews with formerly incarcerated people in the offices of the local NAACP. After the jail administration
restricted our access in 2007, I focused on the challenges facing the formerly
incarcerated when they try to reintegrate into society.

This is how it happened. I live in Binghamton, a deindustrialized
working-class town in upstate New York. In July 2004, I came on a small
item in the *Reporter*, a local progressive newspaper. The local branch of
the NAACP, the article read, had received numerous letters from people
held at the county jail who complained of poor health care. The NAACP
was calling a meeting to discuss the complaints and what could be done.
I decided to attend the meeting, mostly because I thought this was an
important issue and because I wanted to get more involved in the community. At that time, the NAACP met in an industrial section of the city,
amid the factory ruins, a block from a Coca-Cola plant, in an old building

abutting the tracks of the freight train. The meetings were held around an office table.

Only about seven other people attended that first meeting, most quite a bit older than I, septuagenarians from the civil rights movement who were still active in the community. We started the meeting by introducing ourselves. I said I was from the university, but this felt almost unnecessary. Since I was sporting a rumpled, blue oxford shirt and short hair, they took me for a student. Once they learned I was a social scientist, they invited my participation in documenting the prisoner abuse. We decided that I would follow up on complaints and interview people. It turned out that later they asked around about me. Several colleagues vouched for my political commitment.

I returned a few days later. Stan, the NAACP branch secretary, presented me with a folder full of letters and documents on the health care provider at the county jail. The Sheriff's Department runs the Broome County Correctional Facility. Like most jails, it is county run. County jail inmates are generally people being held before trial, people arrested but who have not made bail, or people sentenced to less than a year. (Conventionally, prisons or penitentiaries hold people sentenced for more than a year and they are under state or federal jurisdiction.) The jail houses more than five hundred people. At the time I began this research, the county contracted Correctional Medical Services (CMS), a private health care corporation, to provide medical care at the jail. In 2006, possibly due in part to scandals and lawsuits facing CMS nationally and in part to local pressure, the jail contracted with a new, smaller organization, Correctional Medical Care (CMC). Yet CMC soon came under state scrutiny as well, after a series of suspicious inmate deaths around the state.[3] The size of the county jail's medical contract is more than two million dollars per year (Reilly 2012). The financial transactions of even a small jail in a provincial town are sizeable.

Over the next few years, as I researched medical care at the jail, I served as a member of several NAACP delegations that met with the sheriff to express our concerns about conditions at the jail and the treatment of the incarcerated, especially their health care. In each of these meetings, the sheriff assured us that everything was fine: "You'll always find complainers, but . . ." his office had not received many complaints. (I learned only later of a series of lawsuits pending against the jail that alleged poor medical treatment.) On the other hand, he touted the revenue the jail generated for the county. Keeping someone incarcerated in a New York State penitentiary costs around $60,000 a year per person, the most expensive per capita cost in the nation (Henrichson and Delaney 2012). Jails cost significantly less, perhaps in the range of $26,000 per person (Schmitt, Warner, and Gupta 2010, 11). The sheriff told us he "rents" cell beds to other agencies—federal agencies, including immigration authorities and the Federal Bureau of Prisons, and county jails as far away as Long Island. He charges them per diem rates. This, he argued, generates enormous revenue to the county. This practice is widespread in prisons and jails (see Barry 2009). To put this in context, the scale of the corrections economy nationally exceeds $74 billion a year, up from $22 billion in 1982.[4]

Soon after I began, I realized how useful it would be to involve my students in conducting the research. With NAACP staff, we developed a research protocol, including a set of interview questions and steps to ensure everyone's welfare and safety, including students, community members, and people held at the jail. I am trained as an anthropologist and ethnographer, so I taught student volunteers from my classes how to do interviews and supervised them as we took statements from people who wished to register concerns about their treatment. Other students did research on Correctional Medical Services and other aspects of privatizing correctional medical care.

The project evolved to the point where it became a collective effort, centered on weekly meetings at the NAACP to discuss what we were learning from the interviews and plan next steps. At its height, about twenty-five people attended the weekly meetings at the NAACP. White people, African Americans, Latinos, Muslims, Roman Catholics, immigrants from the Caribbean and the Middle East, currently and formerly incarcerated people, working-class and middle-class students, and civil rights activists participated. These groups overlap. Some of the people who had been incarcerated had served short stints in jail, while others had spent most of the last thirty or forty years in state or federal penitentiaries.

Those involved worked together to explore the depth and size and character of the abuse. People who were currently in the jail, formerly incarcerated men and women now at home or in shelters, as well as the relatives of people who had died or who had children or spouses still incarcerated, came forward and identified themselves to us, sometimes in great fear and sometimes without fear. We were not funded and did not seek funding. No one was paid. The research was participatory and activist in the sense that the motivation for the work was to stop abuse of incarcerated people.

Many we interviewed at the jail were confident and calm. Others were terrified, or despondent. Some were in physical pain during the interview itself. Though almost everyone we interviewed was lucid, sober, and direct, I interviewed a few who were obviously mentally ill—who heard screams and voices in their heads, or who did not have a clear sense of how long they had been incarcerated, or who genuinely did not seem to understand what they had been charged with or why they were in jail, or who were desperate for their medication.

The stories the people in jail told me were often harrowing. We interviewed someone who had gone into a diabetic coma when denied his insulin shots; a woman who showed me her scarlet, swollen limb, whose skin was peeling, and who told me she was worried she had gangrene but could not get medical attention. I interviewed people forced to languish in their cells for days with a burst appendix or a fractured vertebra before they received anything other than Pepto-Bismol or Advil.

We found many examples of neglect or abusive treatment that interfered with incarcerated women's reproductive freedom, including denial of prenatal care and lack of access to abortion (resulting in, for example, unwanted births, tubal pregnancies, and other added health risks to women with problem pregnancies), and no routine preventive care.

We saw patterns emerge from interviewing women about their gynecological and other health care needs, women who needed pap smears, breast exams, prenatal care and counseling, who suffered from untreated yeast infections, who had not been given their HIV cocktail or their hepatitis medication, who were worried they had a problem pregnancy but could not receive a medical exam, who had swollen limbs, open wounds, or who simply lacked a diagnosis. Their health seemed to be treated with indifference and sometimes with antipathy. To be in prison is to be ignored, shunted aside, and "treated as garbage," as one long-termer remarked.

People in jail generally recognize suffering in solitude and without recourse as violent and humiliating. Poor health care, or withholding adequate health care, can be in effect a form of punishment (see Farmer 2003). This is especially true when poor health care is rampant, routine, and even institutionalized.

Prison violence thus cannot be limited simply to intentional physical abuse by other incarcerated people or by a specific guard or guards. It involves institutionalized forms of mistreatment, including poor health care.

Prison violence also includes other routine practices that are arguably abusive, such as pat-downs and cavity searches (see chapters 2 and 3; also see A. Davis 2003; George 1993; Shakur 2001). Shackling pregnant women is one such practice. After interviewing a pregnant woman who was shackled, one of my students, Noelle Paley, herself a mother, commented on how dangerous it could be to make a pregnant woman walk unassisted. Pregnancy, she pointed out, changes one's center of gravity and equilibrium. If the woman we interviewed had fallen, she would have had no way to break her fall, since her hands were shackled to her waist. Shackling is difficult and humiliating for anyone. But it is dangerous to make pregnant women walk unassisted if they are shackled at the wrist and ankle (Paley and Price 2010).[5]

The public erasure of institutional abuse against incarcerated women in particular is buttressed by the shame and silence associated with women's incarceration. As we saw in the story that opened this chapter, even grief is disenfranchised (the phrase is Marie Gottschalk's; personal communication). These variegated forms of violence, especially institutionalized sexual violence against women, have not received the scholarly or public attention they merit (but see Buchanan 2007; Diaz-Cotto 2006; Dignam 2008; Price 2012b; Levi and Waldman 2011; B. Smith 2003).[6]

As a project of solidarity, civil rights activism, and social research, collaboratively documenting the health care of incarcerated people provides an important entry point to understand the social condition of incarceration more generally. Sick or healthy, able-bodied or not, we all rely on one another. However, one may never feel quite so alone as when one's health is at risk and one has no one to help, no family, no friends. Studying health care throws into relief questions of isolation and support (see Berkman 2005).

Although most people we interviewed pointed to examples of racial discrimination, some argued that all incarcerated people are treated badly. Even if jails and prisons treat all people the same (and this is hotly contested by many we interview), the same treatment may be disparate in its effects. For a man or woman to be separated from his or her newborn is natal alienation, but if a woman is still lactating, then this can be particularly onerous and painful, physically and psychologically, to both mother and child.

The consequences of separation reverberate long after a person gets out, even after a short stint. We met with one woman once a week for months while she was pregnant in jail with her second child. The whole time she was in jail, she was trying desperately to get prenatal care for a problem pregnancy. She finally gave birth in jail, a day before the DA dropped charges and she was let out. When she was arrested, she lived with her first child, and had a job and a fully furnished home. By the time she was released, she had lost her job, all her furniture had been stolen, her landlord had canceled her lease, and her child was in someone else's custody. She worked hard to get back on her feet and regain custody of her child (see Price 2012b, 149).

RESEARCH ON PAROLE AND REENTRY

In 2006–2007, several events led me to shift my focus from health care and conditions at the jail to issues faced by people once they got out. Over the protestations of the NAACP, the sheriff began requiring that we have advance written permission from people's lawyers before he granted us space for a private visit. But many people did not have lawyers, and for those who did, often the lawyers were unresponsive. The jail administration imposed other restrictions on time, access, and confidentiality that I described in the opening paragraphs of this chapter. Together, these constraints made the interviews no longer feasible.

With our access blocked, we were forced to reevaluate what direction to take. Around this time, a parole officer revoked parole for one of the most active participants in our research, sending him back to prison for at least a year. The abruptness of his disappearance, the arbitrary reasons given by the parole office for the revocation, and his wife's desperation and anger convinced me to try to understand the structural and institutional reasons parole officers send people back to prison. I asked around and found widespread frustration and indignation with the parole office. Together with several community members, we initiated an organizing effort to stop abuse of authority by parole officers (see chapter 7). We started a petition protesting against many of the parole office's practices. This petition drive, which was covered in the local press, led to meetings with local politicians. Through this effort, I learned a lot about parole conditions, including how people are obligated to waive their First and Fourth Amendment rights as conditions of their release.[7]

As we were gathering signatures, two of my former students, L. and T., who themselves had been incarcerated, urged me to work with them to start a local drop-in and resource center for people who were getting out of prison or jail. In 2006, five formerly incarcerated people and I formed the Southern Tier Social Justice Project to advocate for the formerly incarcerated and their families. One significant element of this organizing and advocacy was ongoing research on housing, employment, child custody, barriers to education, as well as the psychological and emotional well-being of the formerly incarcerated.

After they are released, people with a felony conviction frequently find it difficult to find housing and employment. In many places it is legal to discriminate on the basis of a criminal record. Depending on their offense, they may also be banned from many social welfare benefits, including food stamps, federal student aid, and public housing (Allard 2006). In most states they lose voting rights, sometimes permanently (Chung 2013; Ewald 2002; Fellner and Mauer 1998). But these are only the legal aspects; the mechanisms of excluding people who have been incarcerated are also informal and reflect widespread cultural aversion. People who have been to prison experience distrust in the society at large. "I got a mark," one man told me. The stigma is practically indelible. It haunts a person for decades after he or she is released and manifests itself in both the public and private spheres of one's life. "I can put a sticker on it," this man continued. "I can camouflage it. But they'll take that sticker off. Anything you think is in your past is going to bite you in the ass" (Fieldnotes, 2012). Another man reflected on how unforgiving the society is: "I did my crime thirty years ago, but it might as well have been yesterday."

If you go to jail but not to prison, you experience many of the conditions I describe, but the legal and social consequences of going to prison differentiate it from serving a term in jail. Dealing with parole, looking for work and trying to explain a large gap in your résumé, or trying to get back into school with a felony conviction are some of the features that make the prison tantamount to permanent social excommunication. After having interviewed dozens of people who have been to prison or to jail, I have come to share the perspective of people who have served time in prison that there is something singular and irreducible about having served time in a penitentiary.

METHODOLOGY

The accounts of the criminal justice system by those caught within its maws hold a fundamental place as a resource for this book (Price 2008). Even if people who have been to prison usually lack credibility or authority, in this book the knowledge they produce sets the compass. In chapter 4, I delve deeper into the problem of testimony as evidence.

The narratives give a textured understanding of humiliation, institutionalized violence, and natal alienation. These were common threads throughout the narratives, but not everyone experienced these three qualities the same way. The abominably poor health care at most facilities exposes older prisoners and the chronically ill to particular misery and the possibility of an early death. Solitary confinement, with its "slow and daily tampering with the mysteries of the brain," as Charles Dickens (2001 [1842]) once put it, makes for a peculiar sort of hell that people in the general prison population are spared; people in the general population experience another kind of hell. People who identify as transgender or who otherwise do not conform to gender expectations are particularly vulnerable to abuse and mistreatment. And racism, as one man remarked to me, "is a given"; I heard many examples of discriminatory treatment.

The forcible separation of family members evoked slavery in an immediate and embodied way for many African Americans we interviewed. In this way, new research questions emerged from the interviews. Is the practice of separating family members a legacy of slavery? This is the subject of chapter 5 (also see Esposito and Wood 1982; J. James 2005; B. Smith 2005; Wacquant 2002).

In order to gather the narratives, I caromed back and forth across this small town in my little Honda Civic, learning its geography anew. People wrote me, called me, sent messages through loved ones, or contacted me through NAACP members. People left messages on my phone at the university: "My whole family is on pins and needles. Come to my home. I'll have a former employer come. They'll tell you what I'm saying is true." Other people called the NAACP to request that they look into their case or to complain about their treatment.

When I went to the jail to do an interview, I introduced myself and mentioned my NAACP credential. That was usually sufficient to convince people I was there to listen to their story and to advocate for their well-being. For others, simply representing the NAACP was not enough:

> "Who sent you?" The man addressing me behind the glass seems almost too big for the small room. It is my first interview at the jail and I am a little nervous. I launch into the statement I had been practicing, glancing down at the oral consent form I had before me. Then I say, looking up, "I am here from the NAACP. We have received word that you are having a problem with health care here at the jail. Would you like to speak with us?" The man looks at me guardedly through the glass and speaks loudly so that I can hear him through the metal grates on the side of the glass. "Who do you know at the NAACP?" I reply with a name. "Ah," he relaxes and sits back easily. "She's my auntie." (Fieldnotes, 2004)

We were always conscious that people could face repercussions for speaking with us, and so we took special safeguards, including checking up on people after we first interviewed them. Many people told us that they appreciated the follow-up. Every so often, people sent me their own follow-up letter. The following excerpt from such a letter was typical in its tone and content:

> Dear Joshua,
> How are you? It will surely please me to know, by the time this letter reaches you, it finds you in the very best of spirits, both mentally as well as physically. You were right! I have definitely been getting some dirty looks [from corrections officers] since after you left.

Some reported to us in the follow-up meetings that they received no change in treatment. Others told us that their medical treatment improved after our visit. Some told us that the staff treated them more roughly after they spoke with us, but at the same time provided better medical treatment, as if the staff were providing it grudgingly.

One purpose of the visits was to put the administration on notice that outsiders were observing them. "Oh yeah, they know you're watching them. Believe me, they know," I was assured by a former corrections officer, a whistleblower fired by the sheriff after he had exposed the abuse at the jail. He encouraged me to continue as best I could. People who had served time at the jail also thought this work was worth continuing and ultimately helped protect the people we met with. A man who had served countless stints at the county jail and in state penitentiaries told me as much in an interview.

B: You know, they discriminate against black inmates . . . that's a given. . . . But the ones that get discriminated against the most are the ones that got nobody outside looking out.

JOSH: And that's the important distinction for you?

B: Yeah.

JOSH: It's really the people on the outside.

B: If you ain't got nobody on the outside, where you writing to consistently or calling consistently, your ass is out. You are a lizard. You are less than nothing and that's the bottom line. I mean, I can't get no more plainer than that. You are a lizard. (Fieldnotes, October 2004)

This man, whom I will call Byron, thought monitoring conditions at the jail, and especially interviewing people currently imprisoned, was a crucial form of solidarity. Most important, his view was supported by the vast majority of the people who contacted us from the jail and who seemed relieved to see us when we appeared.

During this first interview, Byron also quizzed me. "Who are you? Why are you doing this?" I told him I am a university professor, an anthropologist—a social scientist. I am originally from Los Angeles, but I've been in Binghamton for about five years teaching at the university. As for my motivation, "I think that the issue of prisons and prison growth is an issue for our times," I proclaimed a bit grandly, and then, "I think the conditions at the local jail are terrible and . . ." I hesitated, "I was looking for a way to get involved," I ended lamely. He scrutinized me. "But who are you? Who are you really?" I was not sure what he was getting at, but I was uneasy all of a sudden. He looked at me probingly. I felt on the spot. My motivations, at least the ones I was conscious of, seemed trite. I felt as if I were dissimulating despite myself, leading me to speak in clichés. I repeated myself, almost muttering, "No, just a university professor. . . . It's a fundamental moment to fight against the prison and advocate for the incarcerated . . ." I trailed off. After a beat, I backed up. I told him I have conducted ethnographic research on the legal system and on structural and interpersonal violence against women, and I have facilitated participatory research with youth who have been involved in the criminal justice system. I admitted this was my first experience interviewing, or even interacting, with adults who have been to prison. This was definitely new terrain for me and so I was trying to enter slowly and carefully.

He told me soberly, "If you keep pushing this thing, do not think your white skin is going to help you. They'll do you just like they try to do me." I took his comment seriously, a warning on the limits of skin privilege for someone investigating jail conditions. He was a man in his sixties who had survived the Jim Crow South as well as more than two decades in the New York penitentiary system. I would do well to heed what he said about survival, especially in this small town. But I also took it that he was marking his support for our project and for our investigation.

For a while, at least, the jail administration gave us access to private rooms to interview people held at the jail. NAACP members and community members like Byron were instrumental in arranging interviews with currently and formerly incarcerated people. They also gave advice and made suggestions.

The research meant that I sometimes conducted as many as three interviews a day, but usually it was just one. Over the next three years, I went frequently to the jail, often with as many as six students in tow, but most of the time I was by myself. We would sign in, present our letter from the NAACP, and then sit in the fixed chairs in the waiting room and wait to be called. Jail staff varied in the way they treated us; corrections officers were especially unpredictable. At times, I would wait two hours at the jail just to find out that the person I had come to interview had been transferred or that visiting hours were now over. Once I recognized the corrections officer who frisked me on the way in. He was a former student! Though he surely recognized me, he gave no indication he knew me as he quickly patted my back and belly, and ran his hands up and down my legs, including along the trouser inseam. I was a bit unnerved by how he failed to acknowledge me at all. The memory of that short interaction has stayed with me as emblematic of something important in this period.

I also conducted interviews in public housing, homeless shelters, anonymous downtown coffee shops, or the shared office space of the local branch of the NAACP near the railroad tracks. We met wherever people wanted to meet. I was surprised the first time I met people who had multiple generations incarcerated. Then I met more and more people like that, and then more and more. I saw three generations of women in a family tied up in the criminal justice system, routinely stopped and searched by parole officers or police, separated from one another, sometimes losing custody of children, sometimes evicted from their homes, and I started to wonder, How far back does it go? How many generations?

THE ABYSSAL DIVIDE

After conducting an interview, I left the people at the jail, or at the homeless shelter, in their despair and their suffering, and traveled by car the ten minutes to the university campus, its academic chitchat in the halls, cappuccinos and graduate students, classes and department meetings, undergraduates and e-mail.

The experience was one of crossing back and forth across seemingly incommensurable worlds. I was undergoing this shift every day, sometimes several times a day. The shift was from seeing massive social suffering up close and then moving to the norms and phenomenology of everyday university life. How did these worlds exist simultaneously and so close together? In the university setting, the horror of incarceration, if present at all, was highly abstract. The concerns were different; the reality was different. Social death names the distance between one reality and the other, the yawning gulf between the apparently civilized world of daily university life and the utter incivility, organized chaos, and terror rampant in jails and prisons throughout the United States.[8]

Boaventura de Sousa Santos (Santos 2007, 2014) has called this phenomenon, or a related one, the abyssal divide. Civility, civil society, public deliberation, liberty, and the rule of law are characteristic of only one side of the divide. Degradation, untrammeled sexual violence, and outright physical domination mark the other side.

The divide originated in the moment of European colonial expansion into what is now called the Americas. On the one side, the Conquest initiated European modernity, and with it modern notions of citizenry and the dawning of rights; at the same time, coterminous but at its underside, modernity was marked by rapacious greed, multiple genocides of indigenous peoples, the burning of centuries of accumulated wisdom in the name of the Christian God, and wholesale enslavement (also see Dussel 1993, 2000; Gilroy 1995, 44, 53–54). Ever after, this divide has lain at the root. "Today as then," argues Santos, "the legal and political civility on this side of the line is premised upon the existence of utter incivility on the other side of the line" (Santos 2014, 124).

The abyssal divide contains a racial component. On the one hand is that which became "Europe" and "white." On the other, there is Caliban, the despised, the heretic, the wicked, the witch, the "Negro," and the "Indian" (see Mignolo 1995). The racial distinction is implicitly hierarchical, with the superior race on one side and the inferior, dominated race on the other (Quijano 2000, 216). Racializing the distinction makes the hierarchical arrangement seem natural.

The key aspect of race is devaluing and subordinating one group; skin color is just a rationale (Mignolo 1995, 81; Spillers 2003, 207). Those who rule on "this side" reduce those on the "other side" of the line to modern subhumanity. "Subhumans are not conceivably candidates for social inclusion." Modern humanity is not conceivable without modern subhumanity. But the negation of one part of humanity is sacrificial, in that it is the condition for the affirmation of that other part of humanity that considers itself universal

(Santos 2007, 52). As part of this process, the abyssal divide eliminates whatever realities are on the other side of the line. "The other side of the line comprises a vast set of discarded experiences" (Santos 2007, 48).

Incarcerated people and their families are forced to the other side of the abyssal divide. Recuperating their narratives is a way of recuperating those discarded experiences. It is important to point out, however, that the dehumanization of incarcerated people is only one facet of a larger process of colonization where others are also dehumanized, whether through ethnic cleansing, child labor, sweatshops, or sex trafficking (Mbembe 2003; Santos 2007).

Placed in terms of the "abyssal divide," the racism of the prison system is anchored in the very structure of the colonial experiment that began over five hundred years ago. The evidence of the colonial legacies is all around us. For example, the Louisiana State Penitentiary is still known as Angola, a racially marked name it inherited from when the site functioned as an antebellum slave plantation. That the lines of men hoeing in the sun work for pennies a day seems to reflect more of a continuity with their enslaved forebears than a disjunction (see chapter 5; also see M. Alexander 2010, 12–13, 21–22; Huckleby 2002; J. James 2005, xiii).

As the name Angola reminds us, slavery was a colonial practice of global dimension. Placing mass incarceration in colonial history helps to check the tendency to think of the United States as exceptional. And yet the United States is exceptional, as even a cursory glance at our incarceration rates attests (see, e.g., Mauer 2006; Pettit 2012; Western 2007). As many commentators have observed, the U.S. rate of incarceration is the highest in the world at 714 people per 100,000. Our prison population has exploded over the last forty years to just over 1.5 million in 2012 (Carson and Golinelli 2013). If one includes people in jails, the number swells to around 2.3 million people (Pettit 2012, 1). Other groups are held behind bars but are often not counted among the incarcerated, including people incarcerated in U.S. territories (over ten thousand); military facilities (over one thousand) (Sabol, West, and Cooper 2010); jailed in Indian country (seventy-eight thousand) (Minton 2012); and detained in juvenile facilities (almost one hundred thousand). The U.S. Immigration and Customs Enforcement arrested or detained over three hundred thousand people in 2012, and deported over four hundred thousand people, a record high.

The overall prison population has fallen slightly since 2010, and the number deported dipped slightly in 2013. Yet we may simply be moving from mass incarceration to mass supervision (Miller 2014). "Even if you get out of prison still living / Join the other five million under state supervision," singer Yasiin Bey (formerly Mos Def) put it in 1999. Things have only gotten worse since he sang that lyric fifteen years ago. According to the Bureau of Justice

Statistics, almost seven million people were under some form of adult correctional authority supervision in 2011 including probation and parole (Glaze and Parks 2012). This is practically 3 percent of the population, or more than one of every thirty-one adults, an astronomical figure (Pew Center on the States 2009).

The criminal justice system affects some communities more than others. One in forty-five whites was under correctional control in 2009, but this number jumps to one in twenty-seven Latinos, and one in eleven African Americans (Pew Center on the States 2009). More than 3 percent of all African American men were imprisoned in 2011. This is six times the proportion of white men and more than twice the rate of Latino men (Carson and Sabol 2012).

The United States is a statistical outlier not only in rates of incarceration. We also lead in terms of cruel, harsh, and dangerous punishment, including imprisoning and executing the mentally ill and mentally disabled, trying children as adults, and shackling women giving birth. We lead the world in the number of people we place in solitary confinement, including minors, the mentally ill, and pregnant women, and the number we sentence to life imprisonment, including nonviolent offenders and minors (Simon 2001; Whitman 2007). The United States is unusual in employing punishment intended to humiliate publicly, such as chain gangs or making convicted felons carry signs that read, "I stole mail. This is my punishment," or "Sorry for the Jackass Offense," and so on (Huschka 2006; Simon 2001; *United States v. Gementera* 2004; Whitman 2007). Many countries have moved away from public humiliation, at least in terms of official penology; few retain the death penalty.

The U.S. penitentiary and the criminal justice system, then, has special features that distinguish it as particularly dreadful and unforgiving, even as it is characteristic of this global coloniality of power (Quijano 2000).

And here is one of the ironies of using statistics. Numbers give some sense of the magnitude of the prison juggernaut and lend visibility to an otherwise overlooked and largely invisible population. But they shed little light on the historical context, or on the prison as a colonial institution. Statistics obscure the meaning of incarceration in the lives of those most affected, such as what it is like to suffer through solitary confinement, or to negotiate life under the trying conditions of parole. Focusing narrowly on the numbers of incarcerated people overlooks the incalculable damage to daughters, sons, brothers, mothers, grandparents, spouses, and partners whose lives are also torn apart when a person goes to prison. This social cost is not easy to quantify. This is why narratives are so important.

SOCIAL DEATH VERSUS CIVIL DEATH

I describe incarceration and its mark as "social death" instead of using the more common expression "civil death." Civil death implies the lawful abrogation of legal rights (Dayan 2011, 39–70; Ewald 2002; Manza, Brooks, and Uggen 2003). Social death goes beyond the legal realm. It is wider and more substantive, and in some ways more ineffable, but no less powerful, than simply a question of rights accorded to citizens, although social death includes the suspension of those rights. Social death is not only a legal condition. It is a social condition. The social dead are not merely formerly full citizens who have temporarily lost some of their freedoms. Instead, their social status has changed much more radically, and in some ways permanently. This distinction is crucial for the methodology, since the narratives uncover the meanings of this condition.

Ending civil death would entail restoring (or granting) the rights accorded to citizens. It would mean conferring individual rights. The remedy is consistent with liberal individualism and a civil rights agenda. Ending social death is not so easy or straightforward. Overturning social death would require changing social categories such as "felon" and "ex-con." It would mean transforming the social relationships on which these categories depend, including relationships that have been institutionalized not only by law but also encoded in language and sanctioned by custom.

Civil death is a symptom of social death. To end civil death, social death—the fear, contempt, the vengeance, and the dehumanization that compose it—must end. The tangible, legal, and objective aspects of citizens' rights are important to address, though they alone do not account for the full depth of social death. Other social practices and cultural representations are also responsible for a criminalized, racialized, stigmatized other. (In order to take a small step towards a change in language, I have generally followed the practice of Eddie Ellis and others of using the terminology of "incarcerated person" or "formerly incarcerated people" instead of "felon," "prisoner," "parolee," or "ex-felon" [Ellis 2013]).

CHAPTER SUMMARY

The next two chapters detail the constituent elements of social death: natal alienation, humiliation, and violence. In chapter 2, I argue that the natal alienation engendered by incarceration is inconsistent with full reproductive justice. Entire communities suffer because of the wedge forced in women's lives by prison—women and children and neighborhoods suffer when a person of any gender is incarcerated. In this sense, the experience of forced isolation fans outward through time and space: through time by affecting the trajectory of women's lives, and through space by rupturing the lives of people in widening circles.

Chapter 3 considers whether prisons are intrinsically humiliating. They involve stripping one of pride, honor, and dignity. Formerly incarcerated people are treated as damaged goods and as permanently tainted. The prison accomplishes the goal of communicating that the social dead have been thrown out of society. In reviewing what one criminologist terms the current enthusiasm for inflicting cruel punishments, I look at practices that aim to debase or dishonor.

Natal alienation and humiliation both imply violence. The prison is an institutionalized and state-sanctioned set of violent practices that includes poor health care and exposure to premature physical death (see Burridge and Loyd 2007; Gilmore 2007). Social death means the systematic limitations in nearly all spheres of life.

Part II offers a methodology and a genealogy of social death. People in prison are constantly accused of exaggerating, omitting, lying, hiding, or twisting the facts. These charges evacuate them of credibility. Since this book relies on testimony, the charge presents a fundamental challenge. Rather than simply countering these claims (though I think they are vastly overstated), I acknowledge that deception, dissimulation, and silence can be useful tools in the face of hostile treatment and oppressive conditions (Hine 1989; Kelley 1994; Scott 1992). This chapter outlines a methodology for research and advocacy across lines of difference under stark, trying conditions.

Chapter 5, "Racism, Prison and the Legacies of Slavery," takes up a genealogy of racial debasement. Is the institution of prison the genealogical descendent of the institution of slavery? The ravages of slavery intersect with the stain of racism to yield a story of contemporary practices of dehumanization. Slavery was predicated on a hierarchical divide. The modern prison is a contemporary expression of this divide. This chapter thus places modern forms of dehumanization within longstanding structures of racial oppression basic to the United States since its founding.

The contemporary penitentiary, however, is not simply modern-day slavery. The history of the prison reflects the influence of social movements for social reform and the changes wrought by the industrial revolution. By retracing this history in chapter 6, I show that psychic violence has been intrinsic to the environment of the prison from its beginnings through the present day.

The third part of this book focuses on the postincarceration experience of social death. Chapter 7 is entitled, "Doesn't Everyone Know Someone in Prison or on Parole?" Staging the chapter at a community meeting on abuse by parole officers, I look at a misunderstanding between a community member and one of my students. The misunderstanding exemplifies the abyssal divide.

Chapter 8, "Spirit Murder: Reentry and the Dispossession of Rights," delves more deeply into the postincarceration experience. Upon reentering society, formerly incarcerated people are still consigned to social death, even if the terms and the circumstances have changed significantly. Their social reception amounts to spirit murder, to use Patricia Williams's expression (1991). Spirit murder is the disregard shown for others who qualitatively depend on our regard. It is a sociological, institutional, bureaucratic, and cultural phenomenon that thrusts the formerly incarcerated out of the society. I review the formal restrictions placed on people when they come out of prison that mitigate their full civic participation and their freedom. In order to understand, and to counter, spirit murder, I describe how people maneuver and sustain themselves despite their experiences of being scorned.

Chapter 9, "States of Grace: Social Life against Social Death," continues in this vein. People consciously "live a life," in the words of one incarcerated man, to overcome the social fragmentation and isolation engendered by prison. This chapter is based chiefly on three examples. In each case, I want to see how they understand and strive against social death and how it is imposed on them and their loved ones.

This book ends on an ambivalent note. We didn't make any lasting changes in our community—certainly not to jail practices, nor to parole officers' treatment of people on parole. Nevertheless, the project was educational for the students and it was useful for the NAACP and the community in some limited ways. Were our attempts worth the effort? By way of conclusion, I take stock of our failure, and inventory briefly the lessons I learned as well as the contradictions we were unable to resolve. Then, drawing on W.E.B. Du Bois's understanding of what he termed "abolition democracy," I consider whether the abolition of prisons is a useful and practical goal when confronted with social death.

CHAPTER 2

Natal Alienation

I went into the Broome County Jail in November 6, 2006. I found out I was pregnant when I got in there, when they did a test. Immediately, I said, "I need to have an abortion. I need to have an appointment to have an abortion." A week went by, and I asked them again; another week went by. I told them again and tried to get appointments with the nurse, or anything, appointments outside. I tried to get an appointment with a doctor outside. I put in a grievance with the sheriff. And the sheriff or someone had come to see me. I'm not sure. But someone had to come see me and take down what was wrong, what was my complaint. Still, nothing was done. At this point, you're realizing you have no control, that you can't do anything about it, like, you're so helpless. You can complain all you want and nothing is happening. Two weeks later, this is about a month in, I put another grievance in. So, this time what I did, they had a doctor in medical that felt my stomach and said, "Well, she's pregnant." Well, we already know this. He thought I was about ten weeks or something.

At that point I knew time was running out because you can only have an abortion up to so many months or so many weeks. So, at about the sixth week, they came, and they told me I had an appointment, and then I was too far along to have an abortion. So, after that, I put in to have a late-term abortion somewhere else, and then I got dismissed from jail.

Q: You were released from custody altogether?

A: Yes. When I went in, I was using drugs before that. So, naturally I wanted to have an abortion. It was irresponsible to get pregnant in the first place, but I didn't want to bring a child into the world whose mother was in jail. What could I really do at that point? So I wanted to have an abortion. And I couldn't. It was too late. So then I got released, and I thought about the late-term. And I just couldn't do it because the baby's too far along at that point. So, my other option was adoption or raising the child and having my mother take care of yet another child of mine. So I chose to go with adoption.

Q: How many requests for an abortion did you put in?

A: Like ten. But I only put two grievances in. Like, every other day, I was saying "I need to have an abortion. I need to have an abortion." (Fieldnotes, 2008)

INCARCERATION UPENDS women's reproductive decision making. This woman describes her helplessness and vulnerability as the jail restricted her reproductive choices and denied her proper medical attention. Her account places separation and reproductive justice at the center of the discussion of incarceration.

But true reproductive justice goes far beyond abortion on demand. Women of color activists have argued that thoroughgoing reproductive justice requires that women and girls have the economic and political resources to make decisions for themselves about not just reproduction but also their sexuality and whether and under what conditions they wish to parent (Ross 2008; Shen 2006). They also suggest that full reproductive justice is directly linked to living in healthy communities. Under this expanded notion of reproductive justice, no amount of prison reform would be enough to ensure reproductive freedom. Seeing jail, prison, and other criminal justice institutions as factories of natal alienation allows us to expand the particular meanings associated with reproductive freedom and genealogical continuity.

Natal alienation provides a paradigm for describing how jails and prisons offer substandard and indifferent prenatal care, shackle pregnant women, and separate mothers and their children. It offers a framework to explain how the state dictates whether and how one is allowed to parent. It helps make clear why prison and jail conjure images of slavery for so many. Tracing the history of natal alienation shows how the forced separation of incarceration echoes that of slavery.

The gendered structural violence of prison disproportionately affects women of color and poor white women. Although this chapter focuses on how natal alienation holds consequences for women, parenting, and reproductive justice, the separation shakes and undermines men's lives, too. Entire communities suffer because of the wedge forced in women's lives by prison— women and children and neighborhoods suffer when a person of any gender is incarcerated. In this sense, the experience of forced isolation fans outward through time and space: through time by affecting the trajectory of women's lives, and through space by rupturing the lives of people in widening circles. If this book makes any contribution at all, it is to argue that natal alienation is intrinsic to the modern penitentiary system.

While the most obvious state-imposed physical separation may begin with incarceration, the social separation, and the attempts and threats of separation begin before, and continue long after, a woman goes to prison. Though it goes beyond the scope of this chapter, our research shows how the parole office, child protective services, drug treatment programs, schools, the law courts, and other institutions are empowered to, and do in fact, separate women from their children and from other people to whom they are tied by social and affective bonds. The prison, in other words, is nested within other institutions that harm women through separation and the threat of separation. Incarceration, the linked parole office, and other institutions are instruments of gendered social destruction. The effects of the separation are intergenerational. Mothers, fathers, children, grandmothers, even great-grandmothers, have their lives cast a-kilter by the interventions of these institutions. It is a crucial ingredient of social death.

This makes for ironies not lost on those most affected. The mother of a minor incarcerated in an adult prison tells us: "They say you can't beat your child, but they take them away and beat the hell out of them. They put them in the hole for thirty days. Why isn't a [child protective services] worker in there to protect them like when they come into my home to protect her from me?" (Fieldnotes, 2007).

Two brief clarifications before I go further. First, natal alienation is a structural condition and an institutional arrangement. The violence does not depend only on the feelings of a particular person about parenting. Plainly, incarcerated women, just like any group of women, have a range of attitudes toward their kin in general and their children in particular. Not all mothers feel connected to their children, for example. Nevertheless, prison organization entails systematic separation and as such is violent, even if a particular mother (or child) does not experience the separation as a rupture.[1]

The second caveat has to do with research ethics. This chapter is based in large part on interviews with incarcerated mothers, including several women who have given birth while incarcerated. Since the interviews were undertaken as part of solidarity work in which we were trying to identify problems with health care and health care delivery, we kept to questions about health care, and documented whatever harm people described. I avoided asking questions I felt were prurient or voyeuristic, and I have not included descriptions of suffering or humiliation if they serve no purpose other than putting suffering on display. When I have had doubts, I have opted to cite published texts by incarcerated women since the authors intended their accounts to be shared and read by others.

NATAL ALIENATION AND SOCIAL DEATH

The paradigm case of natal alienation is watching one's kin whipped by the slave master and being unable to intervene. A former slave, Mr. Reed, encapsulated the injustice of natal alienation in a Works Progress Administration oral history project interview conducted in 1930: "The most barbarous thing I saw with these eyes—I lay on my bed and study about it now—I had a sister, my older sister, she was fooling with the clock and broke it, and my old master taken her and tied a rope around her neck—just enough to keep it from choking her—and tied her up in the back yard and whipped her I don't know how long. There stood mother, there stood father, and there stood all the children and none could come to her rescue" (Rawick 1972, cited in Patterson 1982, 8). Relatives cannot protect each other. One faces the corrosion and loss of ties to ascending and descending generations. (Chapter 5 explores the slave origins of natal alienation.)

The condition of social death is peculiarly individual, individualized, and individualizing. The person who is socially dead has the solitude and solitariness of existence impressed on her. "You know that my family has never understood me very well before, they are trying to now, but for years I had no line, at all, to the outside. . . . It was almost like being held incommunicado. Incommunicado, it's almost destroyed me" (Jackson 1970, 22).

According to a commonsense view in the United States, implicitly upheld by liberal individualism, prison harms only the incarcerated person. The condemned is the one punished. If one conceptualizes incarceration as social death, then one moves away from seeing prison as a punishment visited only upon the bodies of the incarcerated. One of the consequences of incarceration is that people otherwise connected are isolated from one another. If incarcerated people are isolated from kin and community, then reciprocally the people on the outside are isolated from those who are incarcerated. The harm is borne by all of them. This obvious truth is suppressed given the centrality of individualism in the United States. As a result, the fundamental harm, predicated on connection and continuity, cannot be theorized *as* harm:

> Martha leaves a tearful message on my machine. "Call me, Frank is in trouble!" When I call her back, I can hear in her voice that she is beside herself. Frank has been "violated," or has had his parole revoked, by his parole officer. So, he's back in jail. "I don't know what I'm going to do," she remarks. Martha has severe arthritis, her lungs fill with fluid, and she has had several heart attacks. Frank is her son. "He cleans, cooks, and bathes me." She also relies in part on his salary. "He's been so good," she tells me pointedly. I know why she says this: I've seen him yell at and harangue her. "He's been so good lately. Why can't they just leave us alone?" Frank served five years in prison for assault. "We were on our way

to the supermarket and they swooped down on us." Parole officers had discovered THC in a urine test. For this and for other minor violations of his parole conditions, his parole officer decided to arrest him, and he is now facing at least a year in prison. None of the violations amounted even to a misdemeanor.

When we go up to visit him in the jail, he puts on a show of confidence and strength, but admits he has not had his psychotropic medication for the week he's been in jail. He is also having trouble getting his insulin. They are palpably, acutely scared. "I don't know what I'm going to do," she says again. "Okay, Mom," Frank says. "Hang in there." (Fieldnotes, 2011)

At a subsequent parole hearing, the administrative judge from the parole office finds Frank in violation of his parole conditions. The judge revokes Frank's parole, effectively sentencing him to at least a year in the penitentiary. Frank's lawyer notes to me that the Board of Parole appoints the administrative judge who tries his case, and so the judge does not have judicial independence (see New York State Parole Handbook 2010).

Like many incarcerated people, Frank is shipped hundreds of miles away to a prison in a rural part of the state, far from public transportation. Martha is stuck, vulnerable, her health insecure, her financial situation precarious, and she faces alone the full emotional tonalities of having her life ripped asunder when her son is incarcerated. She tells me,

Last time they sent him to Clinton, way up next to Canada. They call it Siberia. New York State's Siberia. They sent him way up there. I could visit him only once because I was on chemo for breast cancer. So, I was in and out of the hospital. There were days so bad I couldn't even get to the phone. And I lay there for, like, seven days. I was so sick. Twice. They had to stop the chemo because they said it was killing me. Thank God it worked before it killed me. It just seems that if they find out something's up with the family, that's the time they try hardest to violate the person [revoke his parole]. (Fieldnotes, 2011)

They do the best with the situation they confront, but the situation puts both of them in imminent danger:

A couple of months later, I drive to the New York–Canadian border to visit Frank. Checking the map, I pull into the parking lot beside a group of vast, impressive, but staid nineteenth-century buildings ranged behind the telltale high chain-link fences topped with spiraled concertina wire, cameras, and guard towers. This must be the place. I get out and make my way past the security doors and into the gothic facility. "No," corrections officers in the receiving area tell me, "You have the wrong one. The prison you want is a few miles down the road." A bit embarrassed, but also off-balance, I go out again and drive on. I pass another prison, and then another one, and then another one. Each one is enormous, spread over acres. Attica, Wende, Buffalo, Groveland, Livingston, and Wyoming can all be found within a few minutes of each other in the far northwest part of New York State, a short distance from the frontier with Canada. Hundreds of miles east, I know, other prisons are ranged along the northeast corridor of New York and Canada.

The reality of the place—of the region—slowly dawns on me, accompanied by a queasy feeling deep in my belly. The economy, the scale of these structures, and the necessary infrastructure to keep them functioning must be massive. They jut out from a country landscape otherwise populated by an occasional filling station, a clapboard house, and fields of green.

Once I get to the one I'm looking for, I make my way through the many gates to a dingy reception area directly before the metal detectors. I sign in and wait a bit impatiently for my name to be called. I sit in a fixed plastic chair in the waiting area, along with all the others. I am surrounded by women and small children, most of them African American. The children, some of them babies, must, like their mothers, remove their shoes and outer garments before being marched through the metal detectors. Women with underwire bras set off the beeping alarm and so they must go to the bathroom, remove their bras, and put them in paper bags.

Guards openly scrutinize hemlines and cuts of clothing. If an article is deemed too tight or revealing, a corrections officer might refuse a woman entrance. This happens to the woman before me in line. She is elegantly dressed, painstakingly made up, and has layered necklaces around her neck and gold earrings dangling from her many ear piercings. The first time through the metal detector, she sets off the alarm. A corrections officer brusquely orders her to take off all of her necklaces, rings, and earrings. She looks smaller, somehow, without the jewelry. Shorn of her accessories, she walks through again. The corrections officer, a man, notes from behind her form-fitting white capris and points at them, commenting, "Too tight. I can't let you through." She turns and purses her lips. She beats a mortifying retreat, back to the bus, though she may have traveled hours and hours to arrive in time for a visit. I think about saying something to defend her. But I don't think it will make any difference. Also, I think, I've come too far to be turned away for starting an argument. I keep silent and feel guilty for keeping silent. I see another woman set off a buzzer as she walks through the metal detector with a small child. The corrections officer reaches for the child's booties; instinctively, the child recoils against her mother. Because of the demographics of prisons, I figure most of these visitors will have made the ten-hour commute from New York City to come to this very rural location on a country road.

When the loudspeaker finally calls out my name, I pass through two more sliding doors with my cohort of visitors and we fan out to our assigned tables in the visiting room. I sit and wait. Frank comes in about ten minutes later with a group of other men. He laughs when he sees me across the room and comes right over to me and gives me a big hug. Then he stands back and examines me. He tells me I look a bit worn. "You need to give yourself a rest." I came prepared with a pocket full of quarters for the vending machines and I buy coffee for both of us. We sit at the square table at right angles to one another. He has to face the corrections officer who sits on a raised dais at the front of the large room. We relax into the time together. For a while, it's almost as if we create our own space, as if we are in a coffee shop again, at least that's how I experience it. We even laugh too loud and too long. After the visit, I call Frank's mom, Martha, to tell her about the visit and how Frank looks to me. She tells me that she has just been evicted. (Fieldnotes, 2011)

Those who remain on the outside are faced with new caregiving tasks, economic challenges, and forced to pay expensive telephone bills if they wish to stay in contact with loved ones. Parenting from a distance is particularly difficult (Boudin and Greco 1988).

My relationship with my children is gone. It will probably gather when I get back out there but it's gone now. First the shock of the eight years, them not having me around for eight years. They write at the beginning, they tell you how much they love you, "Stay strong"; "God is with you." But eventually you won't hear from them no more. The cost to make the phone calls is so expensive to where families' phones are being cut off or blocked with an MCI outlandish bill. Because it's like fifteen dollars and something every time you call with those minutes. And it builds up for people on fixed incomes. I'm not fortunate to have a family with a lot of money. So, I don't have communications from the phone. So I can actually say I don't have a family right now. (incarcerated woman, "The We That Sets Us Free/Building a World Without Prisons," Justice Now!, 2008)

The difficulty of visiting can in turn be the first step to losing contact and control of one's children. The results are sometimes dire.

I was receiving reports that my son's father was out of control and that my son's wellbeing was in jeopardy. I was considering having my son removed from that environment. The situation worsened and I was out of my mind with worry. I was totally aware of the crisis building around me. The feelings of hopelessness and helplessness overtook my ability to reason and rationalize. I pleaded with my brother and a close friend to consider taking custody of my son. Afraid of reprisal from his father, they denied my plea. I was Frantic! A few weeks later I was told my son was hit by a van and killed instantly. (cited in Boudin and Greco 1988, 2.12)

The prison engenders vulnerability. The mother was helpless to stop an impending tragedy when her child was left exposed and undefended. In what must be the limit-experience of natal alienation, the social death of the mother translated into the premature death of her son.

When I first met Letty a few years ago, she was a teenager. The administration had shackled her wrists and ankles to a security belt fastened around her pregnant belly. The shackles made her walk with a shuffle and she could not raise her hands. She always entered her side of the visitor's room alone and unassisted. Whenever I saw her she always seemed chipper and energetic. On the day I met her, I felt particularly rumpled and frazzled. Beneath her shackles, she was dressed in the special striped uniform that signified that she was in the special housing unit [SHU]. She looked at me, and in an irony that still makes me feel abashed, she commented sincerely, "You look tired." In fact, I am often asked, solicitously and carefully by incarcerated people how I am doing. They are regarding of me, often more so than my students or colleagues.

"I've been in the SHU for fighting with a white girl. She punched me in the face," she told me that first day. Later, another incarcerated woman spoke to us of Letty. She posed to us rhetorically, "Now, how are you going to put a pregnant woman in solitary?"

That day, Letty was frustrated with her lawyer. "Could you contact my public defender? He keeps missing my court dates." She had to wait, delay after delay, to go to trial. She was worried about her young daughter, somewhere out there. When her parole officer sent her back to jail, the Department of Social Services took her child away. The court subsequently took away custody, and her daughter was sent to live with her father, who has moved out of state. "Could you call my mother? Could you ask her about my daughter—how she is doing?" I took down the number.

I asked after her health. Was she getting proper prenatal care? "They're giving me vitamins and folic acid, but I haven't seen an OB/GYN, and I need to see someone. They told me 'soon.' I'm concerned because I was getting Depo[-Provera] injections before I got pregnant but I got pregnant anyway and I'm worried that the Depo will affect my baby."

The Depo caused her to lose weight and lose her hair (see Paley and Price 2010).

Letty worried because if they didn't release her soon, she faced the prospect of giving birth in jail and then being separated from the baby, her second child. (Fieldnotes, 2006)

SEPARATING WOMEN FROM THEIR CHILDREN

What are the reproductive issues that center on the image of a pregnant woman in solitary confinement? A woman giving birth in shackles (Roberts 1998)? A woman separated from an infant child? Letty's situation involves a dense cluster of questions about her civil rights, custody rights, adequate representation, right to proper medical attention, and exposes an overreliance on solitary confinement. She makes charges of racial discrimination. She has been taking Depo-Provera, furthermore, a potentially dangerous contraceptive marketed to and disproportionately used by women of color (Roberts 1998).

Natal alienation ties these separate strands together and puts them in the context of reproductive health, state violence against women, racism, and structural oppression. It puts antiracist activism together with feminist antiviolence work and the antiprison movement. Thinking of reproductive justice as an issue of institutional violence against women requires coalitional thinking.

Months later, I go with Noelle Paley, a student, to interview Letty's mother, Dana. She offers us coffee in the living room. Her daughter was first incarcerated when she had a one-year-old child. Though Letty is now out on parole, her mother tells us that Letty's parole officer repeatedly revokes her parole for minor violations that do not amount to crimes. The parole officer regularly searches through the mother's things, though he has no right to. Dana submits to the parole officer's illegal searches of her house to avoid antagonizing the parole officer, and because she is not sure of all her rights. In any case, neither Dana nor Letty feels she has much recourse or alternative (Paley and Price 2010). They are afraid. "When you knocked at the door today, I wasn't sure who it was going to be, even though I knew you were coming, and so I almost didn't open the door," she tells us, as if to underscore how afraid she was. Letty adds, "I'm not going to run from parole—but I don't answer the door until after curfew. I'm off balance, tense all the time."

When the parole office puts her daughter back in jail, the violent separation fragments all their lives. "It's not only affecting her, it's affecting me. It's making me sick. Leticia had her child [became a mother] very young, I lost her then. She was imprisoned and I couldn't do my job as a mother and it hurts. I want my baby back. I couldn't take Letty's daughter to see her mother because the father had custody."

Dana tells us that Letty has had trouble getting over the trauma of her first lengthy prison sentence. "They get no counseling for what they experienced in jail. She will never be the same. She has nightmares about demons coming after her." Letty listens and looks at her mother without commenting.

The federal authority for Housing and Urban Development (HUD) also plays a role in fragmenting the family. "HUD told me they had trouble with Letty staying with me because of her felony. I told them I will drop HUD so Letty has someplace to live. You will not come between myself and my child." Dana is using her own money to support Letty. The institutions that isolate them from one another also endanger them and threaten their survival in a very real way.[2] (Fieldnotes, 2007)

The parole office and housing police do not simply monitor her, they divide her family. Policies and practices of state and federal agencies that are gender neutral on their face have a disparate impact on women.

Official commitment to sameness and gender neutrality can lead to absurd measures. "We have to treat everyone the same," commented the executive director of the Idaho Commission for Pardons and Parole. "There's no consideration given to mothers of newborn babies or nursing mothers" (Brodwater 2007). She was defending a policy that does not allow incarcerated mothers to express milk for their infants. Shouldn't some women, in this case pregnant women or new mothers, be treated differently, or at least with discernment? Doesn't the commitment to sameness have clear adverse consequences for women's reproductive freedom and reproductive health, not to mention the health of their fetus or newborn? Aren't there implicitly discriminatory implications in applying an ethic of "sameness," or nondiscrimination, indiscriminately, so to speak? The rigors of incarceration pointedly put at risk connection with one's children.

One of the most enraging things that I had was being separated from my child, was being forbidden to hold her, to touch her, to breastfeed her. The condition of women in prison in the United States is unbearable. I have seen women who have given birth and they have not been able to even see their children. Social workers can tell women if their children can visit them or not. (incarcerated woman, "The We That Sets Us Free/Building a World Without Prisons," Justice Now!, 2008)

The separation holds clear psychological consequences. Kebby Warner describes the emotional affects of losing newborns for some mothers: "I've seen women come back in a total state of shock and confusion after giving birth. One woman turned to pills, getting high by taking others' psychotropic medication to dull her pain. One night she OD'd and was rushed to the hospital, barely surviving. Later she was put in segregation, placed on suicide watch" (Warner 2010, 91–92). The institutional practice of separating mothers and children, backed by a set of beliefs about child welfare, fetal and infant health, state paternalism, histories of state intervention in the private sphere, racial regimes, and the social organization of incarceration, has come to us from generations of past practices, especially, but not only, the institution of slavery.

In her influential book, *Killing the Black Body* (1998), Dorothy Roberts locates the separation or the split in the haunting image of a pregnant slave forced to dig a hole and then compelled to lie down and place her belly in the hole to protect the fetus—legally the future property of the owner—before she is flogged (Roberts 1998, 40). This was a widespread practice, as slave narratives from throughout the South testify (Grandy 1843, 28; also see Jefferson, cited in Cook and Poteet 1979, 285). Chapter 5 will recount other legacies of slavery for the prison system.

Imagining, and then institutionalizing, a metaphysical, social, economic, and legal division between a fetus (or a baby) and its mother is a founding moment in the American experience, argues Roberts. It puts in place the possibility, in the sense of the intellectually conceivable idea, of the state acting in the interest (or supposed interest) of a fetus as separate from the interest of the mother. Looked at from another perspective, making this separation might not make any sense, or it might be morally abhorrent to imagine a legal distinction of this kind. Roberts suggests that only after this innovation could one possibly argue the rights of a fetus in opposition to the rights of a mother (1998).

In recent years, prosecutors around the United States, but especially in the South, have charged pregnant women who test positive for drugs with child endangerment (Roberts 1998, 172–202; Stone-Manista 2009). In these cases, prosecutors understand themselves to be acting on behalf of the state and the supposed health of the fetus, against the mother. Roberts suggests this prosecution enforces the split between the mother and her progeny, including her fetus (1998, 40–42).

It is worth remembering that the practice of separating African American parents from children and from other kin continued after the end of slavery, often under the guise of the well-being of minors. Laws throughout the South forced poor and orphaned African Americans into apprenticeships with white people until they reached legal age. In her book on Reconstruction, *To 'Joy My Freedom*, the historian Tera Hunter details the agonizing efforts by formerly enslaved African Americans to reunite despite these institutional efforts to pull them apart (1998, 35–36). Subsequent Progressive Era reforms, including empowering state agents to place children in foster care, in detention, or in orphanages, are part of this history of intervening in families and taking away the children of people of color and poor whites. The "child-snatching" tradition, still with us in the practices of social workers, also reflects a legacy of white Protestant suspicion of contemporaneous waves of immigrants from eastern and southern Europe and the corresponding state attempts to intervene in the private sphere (see L. Gordon 2002; Roberts 2003). Institutionally separating children from parents and communities can also be interpreted as a contemporary residue of the residential school movement, whereby government agents and missionaries spirited away Native American and First Nations children and placed them in abusive boarding schools, splitting families and threatening Native sovereignty and cultural survival (see A. Smith 2005).

Although it is disproportionately women of color who suffer these racial legacies, they affect white people, too, whenever state agents intervene in the decision making of a woman over the fetus. For example, in the opening passage of this chapter, the jail administration in effect forced a white woman to carry her pregnancy to term.

New ideologies, rationale, and practices also evolve. For Susan Rosenberg, who served more than a decade in a federal penitentiary, the separation of a mother and her child is linked to the war on drugs and the war against women, but with racial overtones:

> The war on drugs has become a war on women in the drug trade: the wives and girlfriends of the drug dealers, the runners, mules, and drug users. In the long-termer's unit at Danbury FCI [Federal Correctional Institution] for women, many prisoners are serving lengthy sentences with no hope of parole. For the most part, these "losers" are first-time, non-violent offenders whose convictions are related to drug conspiracies. The majority are black or Latino. They leave their children and families on the outside in ruin. (Rosenberg 2005, 93)

A majority of people in prison are parents (Glaze and Maruschak 2010). Under the federal Adoption and Safe Families Act (ASFA), signed into law by President Bill Clinton, if a child is in foster care for fifteen of the last twenty two months, the foster care agency is almost always required to file a proceeding to terminate parental rights (Lee, Genty, and Laver 2010, 77). This law adversely affects incarcerated women.

> Intimidated by the Administration for Children's Services and the long court process, and believing that ultimately I would lose my son and not be allowed to see him again, I agreed to an open adoption. My cousin and I agreed on visits at the convenience of both parties, which would

include holidays and summer vacations. But soon after the adoption went through, my cousins moved to Virginia, so I see my son much less frequently than the agreement provided. (Carol E. 2010, 84)

Child welfare agencies can seek to terminate parental rights if they deem the parent does not maintain consistent contact or fails to "plan for the future" of the minor. If the parent loses parental rights, the child may be put up for adoption. If the child is adopted, the parents lose all rights to see the child. In that case, birth-parent access to the child is at the discretion of adoptive parents:

> I have considered going back to court time and time again, but I don't want to put my son through a custody battle. Also, I loathe riling the adoptive parents, which might mean seeing him even less. So I'm patient and humble, and I wait. He recently started calling me Mom instead of Carole. Yesterday, he asked me if he could come live with me in New York. I told him maybe someday. (Carole E. 2010, 85)

Kebby Warner lost her baby involuntarily to adoption. In fact, she never got to see the child again after she left the hospital. Warner discusses the visceral disbelief she had that prison guards—really prison policy, backed by child protective services, the judicial system, and, ultimately, federal law—could truly separate her from her child:

> I was given a chance to say good-bye to my baby before they put on chains and handcuffs. How do you say good-bye to your newborn child? These people could not really be telling me I had to leave her! I couldn't leave her. The guards began rushing me, telling me it was time to go. What did they mean? Time to go? Where were we going? . . . Then I heard the guard say, "Come on, Warner." I gave her to the nurse. With every click of the handcuffs and the sound of the chain being locked, my heart shattered. Before I was escorted out in a wheelchair, the nurse took Helen out of the room. My heart and soul went with her. (Warner 2010, 92)

Laws that putatively protect children, along with agencies that are supposed to protect children from harm, that on the surface do not discriminate, act as a fulcrum between incarcerated mothers and their children. Another woman comments on how hard it is to part from her child:

> Every time my son came, I still had to say good-bye and give him to somebody else, who would walk out with him, and it never got any less wrenching to do the good-byes. I cried every time, and I can't even count how many times I was yelled at by officers for crying: "What are you crying for, you get visits, a lot of people don't." That was true, and I was grateful for it. But it didn't make it any less difficult when he left.

When the visit ended, you had to get strip-searched. So I couldn't just go back to my cell and be by myself and think about the visit. . . . There's a line. It was always so awful in that line. You didn't chitchat or ask, "How was your visit?" Mostly we were so into the pain of seeing our people walk away again, that it was usually just really quiet. And you didn't even look in anybody's eyes, you just kind of closed off. We had to stand in this line, but we were leaning against the wall, and everybody was in their own pain. (Archibald 2010, 58–59)

Archibald paints a picture of each woman alone, in her own fresh grief.

Incarceration particularly affects the children. Chesa Boudin's parents were incarcerated from the time he was fourteen months old (Boudin 2007). He asks:

Concern over crime has been mounting, as have the number of prisoners in this country. What about their children? We outnumber the total number of convicts in the US, yet are not guilty of any crime. Is it time for our government to take a more holistic, long-term approach to reducing crime, one that considers the effect of parental incarceration? The war on crime, and drugs in particular, has effectively created a generation of parentless children. Many of us will become incarcerated at some point ourselves. (Boudin 2007)

For Boudin, it is obvious that the state harms and punishes the children of the incarcerated. He argues the need for a new approach, a new manner of conceiving and responding to crime. Without a new approach, the prison shatters the lives of people who have not been convicted of any crime. Laura Whitehorn, who spent many years in prison, also frames vulnerability to state incarceration as intergenerational. At the point of race and gender, she sees structural and systematic separation as a war on women of color, their right to reproduce, and their children.

A huge number of the women [in prison] are mothers. It means that, on the outside, there are basically a lot of orphans. I consider that prison system today to be a form of genocide. Prison has been used against third world populations inside the United States, in particular African American and Latino populations. These women are very young when they come to prison. They have sentences that will go through their childbearing years. Their children are either farmed out to relatives, or they become wards of the state. It means that the women, who would form some sort of collective bond when there's a need for struggle, are gone from the community. And it means that their children may well go to prison themselves. Those of us who grew up *with* mothers have complaints that we didn't get enough love. What does it mean to have your mother in prison? (White-horn in Buck, Whitehorn, and Day 2005, 263; emphasis in original)

The San Francisco Children of Incarcerated Parents, an advocacy organization, gathered stories of children left in the wake when a parent is incarcerated. The accounts underscore how imperative it is to see to children's needs as well.

When I was 16, the police came. They kicked the door in and took my mom to jail. They told me, "Call someone to come and watch you." They were so busy trying to take her out, they didn't care about me. I had to take care of myself for almost six months while she was in jail. It got lonely and scary. Using drugs, she's hurting herself. Take her away from me and now you're hurting me. (Terrence, twenty-four years old, San Francisco Children of Incarcerated Parents Partnership 2010, 40)

Danny, eighteen years old, alludes to the long-term consequences of having an incarcerated mother.

It really messed my head up, 'cause you can only see your mom through a gate, and that's supposed to be your blood relative. The last thing I remember is I had to turn my back to her and leave. It was hard. That was the last time I saw her until I was 13 or 14. If there had been some time set up where I could talk to my mom consistently on a one-to-one basis, I think my life would be completely different. Just knowing I had a mother that cared. You're living life solo, but there's a mother out there that you came from. (San Francisco Children of Incarcerated Parents Partnership 2010, 42)

Based on the interviews, the San Francisco Children of Incarcerated Parents Partnership developed a "Bill of Rights," which includes, "I have the right to be kept safe and informed at the time of my parent's arrest," and "I have the right to speak with, see, and touch my parent." They also include a useful series of policy recommendations (see http://www.sfcipp.org/index.html, accessed April 2014).

PUBLIC VIOLENCE AND PRIVATE VIOLENCE

A gender analysis of social death shows how prison violence complements violence in the home. Angela Davis has theorized how both work to discipline and subordinate women (see A. Davis 2003; Bhavnani and Davis 2000; Price 2012b). We can take that same insight and see how public or state violence and private violence work in tandem toward natal alienation. A woman in a parenting workshop at Bedford Hills had to fight in court to maintain contact with her son.

I couldn't call because there was a block on the phone. I thought I'd never see [my son] again. I heard that when my son asked why can't I go see my mother anymore, his father told him I had died. I finally pushed myself to go to the law library. I did the work in the law library on my own, and I filed a petition for visitation. It took almost two years to go to court and have a trial. His father was opposed to my son seeing me, and he argued my time (25 to life), against me, saying I was civilly dead and therefore shouldn't see my kid. The judge made the decision and I won my rights to see him. It took five months after the court decision to see my son and I've only seen him 3 times since the court decision. . . . I get to talk to him about 4 or 5 times a year. It makes a big difference because if he didn't forget me from ages 3 to 8, he's not going to forget me from ages 8 to 18. He knows where I am. (cited in Boudin and Greco 1988)

The tie between public and private violence buttresses the tendency of the state to condemn women to the isolation of social death. Beth Richie sees a disturbing continuity in the abuse of some incarcerated women. She writes that they "continued to be controlled, manipulated, threatened, and even stalked by their abusers" (Richie 2001, 375). This may be counterintuitive. Incarcerated women themselves sometimes think that incarceration would at least end partner abuse. "I thought here [in jail] would keep me safe, at last," one woman says. "But no, he is still controlling me. . . . He has threatened to hurt my mom if I say anything in court about him. . . . I am totally alone here . . . isolated from my people when I need them most. It's like double prison" (forty-year-old woman detained in protective custody, cited in Richie 2001, 375–376). Richie cites another woman she interviewed:

My kids have told me that he is messing with them [sexually abusing them] while I am gone. It made me sick, but at first I was afraid to tell because he said he'd really take them if I report him. Well, I did anyways. And I hear nothing has been done. I just hope I get home soon because even though he beats me, that's better than him messing with my babies. I can't talk to anyone here about it because it would get me in trouble for not looking out for them. So I just got to beat my case and hurry home to the madness. (thirty-one year old; cited in Richie 2001, 375–376)

Natal alienation captures this state of helplessly witnessing harm done to one's parents and children. Unfortunately, even as the mainstream reproductive rights movement puts at the margin the fight for reproductive freedom for incarcerated women, the mainstream antiviolence movement, not to mention the victims' rights movement, marginalizes their related right to live free of violence. The harm of being isolated from one's children can be connected to, or reinforced by, violence in the home, including sexual violence. In a later chapter, I describe a case of a battered woman who is not allowed to stay at a shelter because of past criminal involvement.

FIGHTING FOR REPRODUCTIVE JUSTICE

Forced separation of children and mothers is only the most potent moment in a range of social ruptures that harm entire communities. Law enforcement increasingly collaborates with immigration officers in surveillance, detention, and deportation.

Two cases of women detained on minor immigration violations illustrate the tie between natal alienation and community harm. Federal agents placed Sayda Umanzor in jail in Cleveland on October 26, 2007, since she was an undocumented immigrant (R. Smith 2007), and police jailed Danielle Ferreira on a shoplifting charge in Charlotte in November 2007 (Manware 2007), but she was kept on an immigration hold for overstaying her visa. Jail administrators denied both women the chance to breastfeed their newborns. They were required to get court orders to express milk.

In both cases, immigrant communities—pastors, immigrant organizations, and other community members—publicly demonstrated to oppose the harm done to them when incarceration splits mothers from children. These cases, which may appear as little more than brief entries on a police blotter, encapsulate how immigrant communities see jail as restricting reproductive freedom. For these communities, the fight for immigrant rights is tied to protesting jail conditions, anger at overzealous immigration officials, and concerns over policing of their communities, including the increasing collusion between immigration authorities and the police (also see Bhattacharjee 2002 for extensive analysis of interagency collaboration). Public attention to the situation of jailed immigrants is voiced in the idiom of reproductive justice. In this way, these stories point to the need for coalition between groups, including anti-prison activists, immigrant rights activists, feminists, and others.

Two of the most compelling organizations that advocate for the reproductive health of women of color in the United States use a human rights approach. Justice Now! in Oakland, California, conducts participatory research on women's health in California prisons. They were instrumental in documenting and publicizing how prison doctors sterilized hundreds of women in California prisons without obtaining proper consent from the women or authorization from the state (Howle 2014; Johnson 2014). SisterSong in Atlanta holds that every woman has the human right to:

1. Decide if and when she will have a baby and the conditions under which she will give birth.
2. Decide if she will not have a baby and her options for preventing or ending a pregnancy.

3. Parent the children she already has with the necessary social supports in safe environments and healthy communities, and without fear of violence from individuals or the government.

Organizations like Justice Now! and Sistersong go beyond a narrow focus on abortion on demand to tie women's reproductive justice to community autonomy, and to coalitional struggle against intersecting oppressions. Neither organization proposes a ready-made, universal approach. Rather, they are projects forged by women of color in a struggle for reproductive justice.

In these cases, the language of human rights permits, I think, the public naming of social harm that is otherwise disavowed (cf. Lowe 2006). It allows for the denunciation of certain kinds of degradation as wrong and unacceptable. Unlike the Eighth Amendment injunction against "cruel and unusual" punishment, human rights covenants are broader in their approach and they do not depend on any one governmental structure or judicial system for interpretation (Dayan 2007; Schorsch and Levi 1998; A. Smith 2004). In the conclusion to this book, I explore human rights approaches more fully as a response to the problems prisons present. The consequences of natal alienation weave their way through subsequent chapters.

CHAPTER 3

Humiliation

"When I came in, I was taking my cocktail for HIV. I told them what I was taking and gave them my doctor's name, and told them my prescription was at the CVS pharmacy on Court Street." Janie is in jail for a minor drugs charge. Jail administrators and medical staff have refused to dispense her medication despite her increasingly desperate requests. Consequently, her viral load has skyrocketed and her T-cell count plummeted. I see the cost quite vividly unfold before my eyes over the course of months. As I meet with her over that time, her face has become splotchy, though her almond eyes remain crystal clear. She is understandably morose. She looks into my eyes, into my soul, really, or so it feels like to me, and tells me, plainly, without drama or self-pity, "I do not want to die in jail. A prison sentence should not be a death sentence." So, that becomes an organizing point—a prison sentence should not be a death sentence. When she complained too much, she was put in the medical unit, which functions for her as punishment, because a doctor still does not see her but she is locked in 24–7. This is medical care as punishment (Farmer 2003). Each time I see her she seems more tired, fatigued, listless. I visit her one week and she has been put into shackles. She tells me she has been chained to a chair for a time. "The nurses and guards were talking and now everyone knows I have AIDS." In violation of the law, the jail authorities and medical unit breached confidentiality so now staff and other incarcerated people taunt her. She is despondent. The next week she tells me that she made the mistake of commenting out loud, "I can't take much more of this." The corrections officers took this as a suicide threat, perhaps seizing the opportunity to punish her again. "They grabbed me, ripped off my headcovering (she is a practicing Muslim), stripped me, and put me, naked, into the suicide watch room." Sexually humiliating and traumatizing poor, beaten down, tired people who cannot defend themselves. Racial and religious discrimination. This is what I see. Many mornings, now, Janie's face bobs up to my mind's eye first thing in the morning. That image of her keeps my eyes pinned to the ball. (Fieldnotes, 2007)

COURT RECORDS FROM her subsequent lawsuit against the jail confirm that Janie repeatedly tried to obtain her medication from nurses and doctor during the eight months she was held at our county jail. They continually rebuffed her. They refused to give her an official diagnosis of HIV positive, which would have obligated them to treat her. She testified at trial that a nurse told her, "It's not our fault you have AIDS. There's nothing we can do about it." She filed several grievances. In its ruling, a federal court held that, "There is no evidence that any of Plaintiff's claims, formal or informal, were investigated by the grievance officer or any other officer at the facility." Nevertheless, the court dismissed her lawsuit.

Janie's account congeals many of the elements I will explore in this chapter, including institutionalized sexual harassment and other state conduct that is humiliating, cruel, and jeopardizes the mental and physical health of incarcerated people, even to the point of exposing them to the risk of an early death.

Humiliation involves stripping people of dignity, honor, or pride, rendering them helpless, and making them the object of contempt. Humiliation, along with natal alienation, is a key component of social death. To face social death, in other words, is not merely to be thrown out of society. It is not merely to face indifference. For social death to work, it is important that the social dead are demeaned and ridiculed.

Humiliation differs fundamentally from shame. It is an exercise of domination. "Humiliation involves being put into a lowly, debased, and powerless position by someone who has, at that moment, a greater power than oneself," writes psychologist Susan B. Miller (1988, 44–45). Shame, on the other hand, revolves around taking responsibility for one's actions. Shame involves "a reflection upon the self by the self," as Miller puts it. We feel shame when we perceive in ourselves a moral failing or a lapse in judgment. Humiliation, on the other hand, is forced on us (Mendible 2005, 7). "People believe they deserve their shame; they do not believe they deserve their humiliation" (Klein 1991, 117; emphasis omitted).

The distinction between shame and humiliation is crucial, even if they sometimes coincide. I leave aside the question of whether people in prison feel or ought to feel shame for what they have done.[1] Instead, this chapter focuses on humiliation as intrinsic to the modern penitentiary.

In prisons and jails, the state through its agents, practices, and policies exercises its power to humiliate. When people are incarcerated, they are forced to depend on the institution for their well-being. If the institution does not see to their needs, or if they are subject to ill-treatment, then the institution is at fault, especially if the mistreatment is systematic or rampant. Thus, the prison cannot let its employees humiliate people in prison with impunity. One could go further: if people in a prison are allowed to humiliate each other, then a prison bears some responsibility (see Ripstein 1997, 91).

Humiliation in prison is not merely pervasive; it is organized, institutionalized, routine, and largely legal, though illegal forms of humiliation are also ubiquitous and perhaps inescapable. It is well known that sexual harassment and sexual assault are widespread, including assault by corrections officers. Attempts by prison and jail staff to break prisoners (as in breaking their will) is another primary form of humiliation in prison. But degrading treatment takes many other forms. Cruelty and *Schadenfreude* is a familiar coin to anyone who has been incarcerated.

INSTITUTIONAL HUMILIATION IN A DECENT SOCIETY

A decent society is one whose institutions do not humiliate people. So argues the philosopher Avishai Margalit in *The Decent Society* (1998, 1). Humiliation is any sort of behavior or condition that constitutes a sound reason for a person to consider his or her self-respect injured (Margalit 1998, 9). This account of humiliation is normative rather than psychological. One may be humiliated, in other words, without necessarily feeling oneself to be.

This normative test is useful because we will be able to conclude that prisons humiliate if we can establish that the institutional practices include treatment most would consider humiliating, even in cases when a particular person does not believe herself to have been humiliated, or believes she deserves it. As the philosopher Arthur Ripstein puts it, "Just as the person whose self-esteem is so low that they supposed they deserved whatever treatment they got is still humiliated, so too the person who refuses to take humiliation seriously is still treated in an unacceptable way" (Ripstein 1997, 99). This normative test provides methodological advantages as well: it is difficult to interpret someone's subjective state; it is easier to assess norms.

Evaluating whether an institution harms people's self-respect, moreover, permits an analysis that does not rest on intention to humiliate or whether an institution was designed to humiliate. This is different from the criteria the Supreme Court has used for establishing "cruel and unusual punishment" under the Eighth Amendment to the Constitution, according to some legal theorists. Since its landmark ruling in *Estelle v. Gamble* (1976), a case involving denial of medical care to prisoners, the courts have required a showing of "deliberate indifference" to prisoner well-being in order to find a violation of the Eighth Amendment. In subsequent rulings, the Court has held that the test has both objective and subjective components. Legal scholar Alice Ristroph has argued that the subjective component includes intent, which is notoriously difficult to prove (see Ristroph 2008, 1356–1357, 1381).

Although prison staff often intend to humiliate, many of the indignities imposed on the imprisoned spring from the very organization of the modern penitentiary, independent of any individual intent.[2] Institutionalized forms of sexual harassment are a good example.

Are Strip Searches Institutionalized Sexual Harassment?

Prisons and jails are rife with sexual abuse, according to all available data (see, e.g., Beck and Johnson 2013; Levi and Waldman 2011, 226–228). Estimates vary, but according to one recent study by the Bureau of Justice Statistics, an estimated 9.6 percent of former state prisoners reported one or more incidents of sexual victimization during their most recent period of incarceration in jail, prison, or postrelease community-treatment facility (Beck and Johnson 2013). According to all studies to date, the rates of sexual violence against women, the mentally ill, and people who identify as LGBTI (lesbian, gay, bisexual, transgender, intersex) are significantly higher.

But even the reported rates are probably underestimates. Sexual abuse is generally underreported wherever it occurs, but incarcerated people in particular may fear stigma or retribution for reporting abuse. Another factor that suppresses accurate reporting is that many forms of harassment are often not counted as abuse in official statistics since they are legal, administrative, and a daily occurrence at most facilities. In this latter category fall pat searches, strip searches, and cavity searches.

This kind of abuse begins on arrival. Corrections officers strip and search the bodily cavities of inductees. In a 2012 case that challenged the practice as degrading, the Supreme Court included a description.

> At the first jail, petitioner, like every incoming detainee, had to shower with a delousing agent and was checked for scars, marks, gang tattoos, and contraband as he disrobed. Petitioner claims that he also had to open his mouth, lift his tongue, hold out his arms, turn around, and lift his genitals. At the second jail, petitioner, like other arriving detainees, had to remove his clothing while an officer looked for body markings, wounds, and contraband; had an officer look at his ears, nose, mouth, hair, scalp, fingers, hands, armpits, and other body openings; had a mandatory shower; and had his clothes examined. Petitioner claims that he was also required to lift his genitals, turn around, and cough while squatting. (*Florence v. Board of Chosen Freeholders of County of Burlington et al.* 2012)

This process is demeaning regardless of the intentions of the staff. M. Grayson Taylor describes the induction from the standpoint of someone forced to undergo it: "Stripped and confused, the prisoner is then sprayed with a harsh chemical solution for lice and other parasites. Just like other beasts of burden used on farms and plantations. Gloved and armed guards then force the humiliated prisoner to consent to full body searches, which include entering his mouth and rectum" (2000, 52). From his perspective, the full body search is part of a ritual that strips people of their previous identity through a kind of profanation or degradation, and initiates them into their new identity (also see Goffman 1958, 49–50).

Part of the difficulty of seeing routine body searches as humiliating is that administrators justify what they do in the name of institutional security. This rationale makes it difficult to see the violence involved (also see Scheper-Hughes and Bourgois 2004, 21). In fact, the United States Supreme Court has sided with corrections officials in holding that routine strip searches are not a violation of civil rights (*Florence v. Board of Chosen Freeholders of County of Burlington et al.* 566 U.S. 10–945 [2012]). The Court granted authorities substantial discretion in deciding who and when to strip search in order to maintain safety and stability at detention centers. "Correctional officials have a legitimate interest, indeed a responsibility, to ensure that jails are not made less secure by reason of what new detainees may carry in on their bodies" (2012).

So, if stripping incarcerated people is legal and routine, can it be humiliating? Taylor sees it as racial and sexual humiliation redolent of slavery.

> [Strip and cavity searches are a] portion of the dehumanization process [that] cause a certain amount of physical discomfort, but the mental anguish is endless. Anyone would feel violated! For the black male, however, this anguish is multiplied a thousandfold. He has doubtless had encounters with racists long before entering prison, and he has heard of many more. Now he must experience the same ritual in which his slave ancestors were forced to participate. (Taylor 2000, 52)

This is not only true for black males. Many African American women also draw a parallel between incarceration and slavery (Buchanan 2007, 48; B. Smith 2005).

The difficulty in seeing strip searches as sexual harassment is due in part to context. As Australian activist Amanda George points out, if people were handled this way any place outside of prison, no one would have any trouble seeing sexual violence. George sees an irony in this. At the same time that "the state deplores 'unlawful' sexual assaults by its employees, it actually uses sexual assault as a means of control" (George 1993, 212).

Former political prisoner Laura Whitehorn frames the effort at resisting the dehumanization of pat searches in prison as part of the daily struggle: "You have to exert an enormous amount of psychic energy to remove yourself from the situation, where this guy's running his hands over your body. You end up exhausted at the end of the day, and your nerves are shot. Your only life is resisting these situations" (Whitehorn in Buck, Whitehorn, and Day 2005, 262). The struggle against harassment is a struggle not to be made into an object, a rag, waste. "The struggle inside prison is to refuse to be victimized. Once you allow yourself to be a victim, you lose your ability to stand up and say, 'I'm a person; I'm not a piece of garbage.' But over the years, when you have to put up with that again and again, you avoid situations because you just don't want to go through it" (Whitehorn in Buck, Whitehorn, and Day 2005, 262).

If pat searches can be harassment, so much the more so for cavity searches. Susan Rosenberg describes how prison officials ordered a physician's assistant to conduct a cavity search (her account is graphic):

Five COs pushed me into an examining room. The physician's assistant came in and said, "We can do this easy or hard. It's up to you."

I went crazy. I started hitting and kicking with every ounce of my being. I might have to do it, but I would not do it easy. They overpowered me, pushed my head down onto the examining table, pinned me there, and pulled down my pants. I kept kicking backward until they held my legs. I was cursing and yelling. "This is rape. You're fucking raping me! You could do an X-ray. You know we don't have contraband!"

The physician's assistant took his fist and rammed it up my anus, and then he took it out and did the same thing up my vagina. He didn't "look" for anything. (Rosenberg 2011, 70)

Assata Shakur describes a cavity search she was forced to undergo: "The 'internal search' was as humiliating and disgusting as it sounded. You sit on the edge of this table and the nurse holds your legs open and sticks a finger in your vagina and moves it around. She has a plastic glove on. Some of them try to put one finger in your vagina and another one up your rectum at the same time" (Shakur 1987, 85). For Angela Davis, this carries consequences for the nature of citizenship in a democracy.

We acknowledge the fact that women in prisons all over the world are forced, on a regular basis, to undergo strip searches and cavity searches. That is to say their vaginas and rectums are searched. Any woman capable of imaging herself—not the other, but rather herself—searched in such a manner will inexorably experience it as sexual assault. But since it occurs in prison, society assumes that this kind of assault is a normal and routine aspect of women's imprisonment and is self-justified by the mere fact of imprisonment. Society assumes that this is what happens when a woman goes to prison. That this is what happens to the citizen who is divested of her citizenship rights and that it is therefore right that the prisoner be subjected to sexual coercion. I want to urge people to think more deeply about the very powerful and profound extent to which such practices inform the kind of democracy we inhabit today. (Davis 2005, 47)

The routine strip searches and cavity searches, as organized forms of sexual assault, cut to the core of citizenship in a democratic society. As a social practice, these searches, and their invasive, assaultive character, are at once well known to all and socially invisible. Davis suggests the strip search corrodes the nature of our political process in deep ways. Giving sound reasons for a person to feel disgraced, mortified, and vulnerable in systematic and deep ways is a way of communicating that the society can visit whatever horror upon him or her with impunity.

ILLEGAL SEXUAL ASSAULT

In addition to legal practices, an entire set of otherwise legal administrative conditions give rise to widespread illegal abuses (Buchanan 2007; Dignam 2008). Male correctional officers are often in positions of authority over women, for example. Human Rights Watch has cited this practice in American prisons as contributing to sexual misconduct, especially when male staff members are allowed to have physical contact with imprisoned women (Human Rights Watch 1996, 2; also see B. Smith 2003).

The call for a ban on male staff in female facilities is not new. Almost two hundred years ago, influential prison reformer Elizabeth Fry argued that men should not be allowed to supervise women (1827, 26). In the ensuing generations, legal scholars, policy-makers, and successive waves of feminists have echoed her call against male jailors in women's facilities (Freedman 1984). But male jailors still oversee women at many facilities.

The constant surveillance in prison can shade into voyeurism, creating conditions where digital peeping toms can flourish. Incarcerated women often comment on how correctional officers watch them through cameras when they are on the toilet or taking a shower. When male officers are given direct access to women, the mistreatment is more direct.

Part of the intake was a shower. Her wheelchair did not fit into the stall. "They made me strip naked and put me in the middle of the room in my wheelchair." Her eyes well up with tears. "And they forced me to bathe in front of all of them!" She is crying openly now. "There were male guards, female guards, and they were laughing. They were talking about how I

smell, how I stink, and they refused to touch me." As she recalls the incident, she seems to relive it. She looks at me imploringly. "I think about it
even now." (Fieldnotes, 2008)

It would be a mistake to attribute the pleasures of taunting and jeering to
the perverse desires of a few bad apples. Potential for abuse exists whenever
male correctional officers have unfettered access to incarcerated women as
they shower or perform other intimate, private functions.

Taking pleasure in viewing incarcerated people at their most vulnerable
moments is only one facet of correctional officers taking advantage of their
position and access. Robin Levi and Ayelet Waldman's oral history of women's
prisons is a virtual compendium of sexual abuse (Levi and Waldman 2011).

Pat searches can veer into intentional sexual exploitation. One woman
says, "When he would give me shakedowns, he'd cup my breasts or say things
about my butt, like 'I'd like to lick that butt'" (Levi and Waldman 2011, 79).
Another woman makes a similar comment: "He would stand out of the camera's view and he'd put his hand through the bars and touch my breasts, or put
his hands down my pants and finger me. Sometimes he'd take me to another
room without a camera and 'pat search' me, feeling all over me and inside
me, but the room was right by other officers so we didn't have sex" (Levi and
Waldman 2011, 194). Pat searches provide the idiom, the envelope, for the
sexual assault.

Most women who are incarcerated have survived physical or sexual abuse,
or both (Beck and Johnson 2012; Beck et al. 2013; Browne, Miller, and Maguin
1999; McDaniels-Wilson and Belknap 2008). The sexual violence inside may
rekindle previous trauma.

> If I was standing in the counselor's door talking to the counselor, he
> would come up behind me and squeeze my butt cheek. I couldn't say
> anything. I just started thinking, *I killed a man who was trying to sexually
> assault me, and I've been gang-raped before by three men. This is what I deserve.* I
> started not caring. . . . He would come into my room on a midnight shift
> and I would be asleep and he would wake me and say, "I want you to suck
> my dick." In the beginning I was like, "Ah, no." but he would grab me by
> the back of my hair or something and I would do what he wanted me to
> do. (Levi and Waldman 2011, 113, emphasis in the original)

Even if she thought she deserved the abuse, it is still humiliating.

Sexual abuse frequently goes unreported, legal experts and incarcerated
people agree, because prison personnel operate with near total impunity.

> Everyone knew that you couldn't go to the prison officials and give
> a report, because the prison officials wouldn't do anything other than

retaliate against you. That officer sexually assaulted me for years. Then he got fired from the Department of Corrections. He wasn't fired for sexual harassment, even though I later learned that he'd sexually harassed and assaulted many inmates, not just me. He was fired because he had missed too many days of work. Can you believe that? I later learned that there were several reports written about him by his bosses at the Department of Corrections, and in one of the reports they said that he should not be working at a women's facility. But nobody did anything to stop him from working there. Nobody forced him to work at a men's facility. Nobody did anything. (Levi and Waldman 2011, 79)

Another woman comments, "I didn't tell anyone because they had seen us talking, so I thought. *If I go and try to tell them something, they're going to say 'Oh, you were asking for it. You wanted that to happen'*" (Levi and Waldman 2011, 113, emphasis in the original). Another women echoes, "If you ever get involved with staff, it's always your fault. You did it. You manipulated" (Levi and Waldman 2011, 204).

An additional reason not to report abuse is that correctional officers and other prison employees can retaliate. As another woman put it, "Incarcerated people are often afraid to report out of fear of being blamed, or fear of repercussion from other officers or from other prisoners." These are not idle fears. "When you're a prisoner in that environment, you don't feel like you have the power to say no. Your life, your every move, is controlled by these people. When you eat, when you sleep, everything is known." This condition is exacerbated by an internalized belief that prisoners have no rights. "At the beginning of your prison term, I didn't feel like I was a human being. I didn't feel like I had any rights. I didn't feel like anyone cared. I never felt like I had the power to say no, until I met my lawyer" (Levi and Waldman 2011, 82).

Often, however, a lawyer is not enough. "An edifice of near-insurmountable constitutional, statutory and common-law obstacles to prisoner litigation immunizes correctional authorities against enforcement of constitutional protections, criminal and civil laws, and prison policies intended to stop sexual abuse by prisoners," observes one legal scholar (Buchanan 2010, 6–7). The legal standard to find against corrections officials is extremely high. The Prison Litigation Reform Act of 1995, passed under Bill Clinton, made it even harder for incarcerated people to appeal successfully against prison or jail administration.

Janie, whose case I described at beginning of this chapter, lost her federal lawsuit against the jail precisely because of the Prison Litigation Reform Act. She had filed grievances, but when the initial grievances met with no institutional response, she failed to exhaust other administrative remedies. As a result, the federal court ruled, she had no basis for her lawsuit.

THE GENDER BINARY AND THE
HUMILIATION OF TRANSGENDER PEOPLE

In the late summer of 2013, a military court sentenced Chelsea Manning, formerly known as Bradley Manning, to thirty-five years in military prison. The next day, she announced her name change and declared her intention to change her gender, thrusting the issue of incarcerating transgender people in male facilities onto the national stage. The military responded by announcing that they did not offer hormone-replacement surgery or gender-reassignment surgery and had no intention of offering it in the future. Advocates for transgender rights responded that Manning had a constitutionally protected right to treatment. As of this writing, the issue is unresolved.

At root is a basic dilemma. Our prison system is organized on a binary model: there are prisons for men and prisons for women (I explore the history of this arrangement in chapter 6). Since prisons and jails institutionalize this binary, any other gender or gender expression is hard for correctional facilities to countenance. "I am what you call a gender-non-conforming lesbian. . . . They were confused with where to place me because I looked like a boy," Krystal Shelley writes (2011, 165). Transgender people are systematically written out of the prison schema, but at the same time they are at the mercy of prison authorities. The very presence, let alone the experiences, of transgender and transsexual people reveal the structure of the prison as humiliating.

> I was arrested at the Parole Office in *full* female attire and appearance. Taken to Williamson County Jail for in-processing. A male lieutenant there had me lean against the wall so *he* could "pat search" me as cameras and other officers watched. He squeezed my breasts so hard that tears came to my eyes and my knees buckled. He screamed "What *gender* are you?" I replied, "Female." He screamed, "This paperwork says you are a *male*." I replied, "My gender is female, my sex is male, and my orientation is *certified* Transexual Woman." He stepped back, looked me up and down, and said, "I don't know how to handle *this*." (Witherspoon 2011, 210–211; emphasis in the original)

The lieutenant's befuddlement encapsulates the dilemma. But as we see, his perplexity is not harmless. In this case, routine practices, such as the pat search, mix with sexual harassment and even physical assault: "He squeezed my breasts so hard that tears came to my eyes and my knees buckled." This recalls the way staff harass other women.

Transgender people testify that correctional officers and administrators try to demoralize them, mock them, expose them to danger, and force them into traditional gender norms. These are not incidental excesses. Charlie

Morningstar, an indigenous transgender person, comments, "There was the 'she/her' thing that's like scratching on a blackboard, when you've lived all this time being called by masculine pronouns. Since the staff knew about the newspaper articles about 'the woman who lived as a man,' they would talk about putting a dress on me in an attempt to humiliate me" (Levi and Waldman 2011, 180). The coercion to conform to gender norms can be explicit: "I met this one sergeant that wanted me to shave my face every day, because of my strong male appearance. Every time I saw her, I dreaded life in that place. She made me lock in until I shaved, or she would send me back from work and threaten me with a 115 [disciplinary document]" (Shelley 2011, 166). One of the recurrent battle lines is transgender people's access to hormone therapy. This is at issue in Chelsea Manning's case. But she is hardly alone in her struggle.

> A nurse looked at all the medications that came with me from Williamson County Jail, which I paid for, and said, "Well, I'm not sure I'll let him have these," referring to my hormone medications. The nurse had ALL my medications, except my Prozac depression medication, destroyed, and I have been fighting ever since to get allowed to have access to take my hormone replacement therapy medication again. We are routinely denied [a diagnosis of Gender Identity Disorder][3] and hormone replacement therapy treatments. That's why there is such a high suicide rate among the transsexual women in [prison], which is covered up. (Witherspoon 2011, 212)

Humiliation can extend to other aspects of gender presentation, such as clothing. Responding to a prohibition against wearing boxers in a facility for women, one transgender person comments, "It's forced feminization, they're going to make us wear these panties. They've determined what women wear and that's it" ("Cookie" cited in Girshick 2011, 198).

Gender nonconformity is often linked, directly or indirectly, to why they are in prison in the first place. For example, many police assume that transgender women and transvestites are sex workers. In other cases, transgender people engage in illegal activity to sustain themselves given their social exclusion. This may involve everything from property and drug crimes to defending oneself against homophobic and racist attacks on the street. Sometimes, the offense is violating the gender binary itself. Witherspoon, who identifies as a transsexual woman, was arrested and placed in jail for using a women's bathroom. In general, police and prison authorities often see transgender people as lawbreakers. Lori Girshick cites "Cookie": "They just feel that this is part of my delinquency. You know, they attribute it to my delinquency" (2011, 191). The various trajectories to prison for transgender people led one of my students to name a "transgender-to-prison pipeline," playing on the expression a "school-to-prison pipeline."

Putting man-to-woman transgender people in male prisons invites sexual abuse, even though the practice is routine. The institutionalization of a strict gender binary is part of the violence. Witherspoon writes of the danger in which prison administrators placed her after she was booked:

> I was put in a caged area where over 200 men witnessed, gawked, and made fun of me. Some made passes, some made lewd comments, and others made known their desire to have sex with me. The officers shouted comments at me like, "Yea, now you got to pull your nuts back out and be a man," "your cellie is going to REALLY be glad to see you," and "Are those REAL tits or silicone?" Then I was forced to strip off my clothes, bra, panties, and stand nude in front of them while I changed clothes. This generated a lot of "cat calls," whistles, and more lewd comments. (Witherspoon 2011, 211)

Corrections officers then handcuffed Witherspoon to one of the men for transport and placed them on a bus. Blocked from view by others, the man forced Witherspoon to fellate him during the trip. The assault continued for so long her gums bled. When they arrived, a corrections officer asked her, "How did you get that blood on you?" "I look around at all their stern warning faces and replied, 'My gums bleed.' The sergeant looks at me, then them, and says, 'Right.' He un-handcuffs me and puts me in a cell by myself for the night" (Witherspoon 2011, 212). On a segregation/safe unit, Witherspoon was housed with other transgender people. She comments that some were forced to cell with their rapists. They may ask to be moved, but often to no avail. "The administration and staff here are made up of typical Texans that they call 'BUBBAs' who are proud Southern Baptist Homophobes first and guards second" (Witherspoon 2011, 213; capitalization in the original).

Clifton Goring/Candi Raine Sweet describes herself as a "transgender black woman," but is incarcerated in a male facility in New York. "While in prison, I have been cut by other prisoners for refusing to perform sexual acts for them, and I have been beaten and sexually assaulted (sodomized with a nightstick) by correctional staff. I see first-hand the very issues that the system needs to change" (Goring/Sweet 2011, 185). She lays blame in particular on prison administrators and correctional officers. "We all have one very strange fear in common, which is the fear of being harmed by the very ones who are there to protect us: the staff. . . . These very same prison staff do not even get punished for their violating actions. Nothing usually happens to the staff, which really compounds an already unsafe atmosphere and makes it an even less safe place for gay persons, transfolk, or two-spirited persons" (186).

Though all incarcerated people face treatment that gives them good reason to think their dignity has been injured, transgender people face uniquely debasing treatment. The violence is gendered and sexualized in multiple, complex ways. "Straight people, or ones who are not of trans nature, do not face the same kind of violence or the same negative aspects of prison as much as gay persons, queer persons, bisexual people, two-spirited people, femme queens, non-femme queens, femme men, gender variants, gender-non-conforming people, or us transfolks have to face" (Goring/Sweet 2011, 187). Cholo echoes Goring/Sweet and Ruth Gilmore (2007, 28) when she describes prison as state-sanctioned vulnerability to premature death. "Prison is possessed by hatred and violence. This hatred leads to violence that oftentimes results in death, and death after rape is what transgender people and queers are subjected to in prison. Transgenders and queers in prison are enduring inhumane treatment and their cries are not really being heard during their walk through the valley of the shadow of death" (Cholo 2011, 215). Another transgender person describes the intense sexual abuse: "I was arrested one day regarding something minor. Due to my gender being marked as male, I was put in with the men. Within 15 minutes, I was raped by 3 different men" (cited in Grant et al. 2011, 168).

The Supreme Court has come close to ruling that placing transsexual women in male prisons is a violation of their civil rights. In *Farmer v. Brennan* (511 U.S. 825 [1994]), prison officials placed Dee Farmer, a transsexual, in general population where she had been raped. Finding for Farmer, the Supreme Court held that, "A prison official may be held liable under the Eighth Amendment for acting with 'deliberate indifference' to inmate health or safety only if he knows that inmates face a substantial risk of serious harm and disregards that risk by failing to take reasonable measures to abate it" (*Farmer v. Brennan*, 511 U.S. 825). Yet the binary organization of prisons itself puts transgender people at risk.

CRUELTY

Many students who engage in community-based research with me feel that publicizing the abuse and neglect we uncover will lead to public outrage. I am not so sure. The awful conditions persist for many reasons, but it is hard to chalk it up to public obliviousness, given the hypervisibility of prisons, prisoners, crime, and the criminal justice system in the media.

A casual glance over contemporary television entertainment reveals the proliferation of programs that celebrate or at least provide the viewer with voyeuristic pleasure in seeing people arrested and incarcerated. Reality programs follow police and document arrests, booking, and incarceration. Comedies with scenes in prison almost invariably play on themes of sexual violence and coercion. Hollywood films, advertising, political campaigns, humor on late night television, and the nightly news are stocked with images of mug shots, guard towers, people behind bars, suspects in interrogation rooms, hopeless people with their faces pixilated, and so forth.

The spectacle of prison violence is a clue that some part of the dominant culture wants to watch the pain, disgrace, and degradation of the criminal. Popular culture reflects a thirst for cruelty, but it also feeds that craving. Humiliation in jail and prison operates against this cultural backdrop, a set of shared meanings that organizes and institutionalizes the desire for punishment (Mendible 2005, 2). Conventional penology usually justifies punishment in terms of deterrence, retribution, or incapacitation. But criminologist Jonathan Simon has argued that this conventional approach overlooks these darker impulses to take pleasure in the pain of the convicted (Simon 2001).

Gail Palone exhibits this satisfaction in the punishment of her son's killer. Trevor Jones was seventeen when he tried to swindle Palone's son Matthew during an illegal sale of a handgun. Jones ended up firing the gun and killing Matthew, though he claims he did not intend to. Jones was convicted of felony murder and is serving a life sentence without the possibility of parole. Jones's punishment serves as partial compensation for Gail Palone. "When Trevor was found guilty, they promised us that he would get life in prison with no chance of parole," Palone comments. "The state promised us that, and the state should see to it that that's what happens" (*When Kids Get Life* 2007). Her grief, and her sense of justice, is channeled into the desire to see the young man spend his natural life in a cage for a crime he committed when a minor. In a documentary, Trevor Jones reflects on his punishment, "That's about really what they want. . . . You're put out in a box somewhere in the middle of nowhere, and that's where they're going to keep you until your life is over" (*When Kids Get Life* 2007).

The United States leads the world in the number of people serving life sentences without the possibility of parole; it may be unique in sentencing minors this way.[4] Jones received a "life-trashing" sentence, to use Simon's apt phrase. "Prison sentences of forty or fifty years, with no possibility of early parole, operate just like the death penalty in shattering any possibility of common ground between agents of punishment and subjects of punishment. Such sentences are also cruel in the sense used here because they are undisguisedly aimed at causing pain and despair in their targets" (2001, 129). Simon concludes, "What judge could realistically say, 'And I hope you come out a better person' to a twenty-year-old receiving a fifty-year sentence for drug trafficking? They might as well say, 'You have forfeited your right to live among us'" (129). Life-trashing sentences (three strikes laws, consecutive life sentences, life sentences without parole, and sentences over fifty years) are one further manifestation of social death. Sometimes sentences verge on the absurd. Jared Loughner, who was convicted of killing six people and injuring Rep. Gabrielle Giffords in a 2011 shooting in Tucson, Arizona, was sentenced in November 2012 to seven consecutive life sentences plus 140 years in prison. The term "life-trashing" captures this kind of hyperbolic sentencing. The despair this kind of sentencing can provoke is what makes these sentences humiliating. Trevor Jones, serving a sentence with no possibility of parole, says, "Sometimes the actual weight of it all really comes down on you, comes down on me, and you know, [I] get real upset about being stuck here forever" (*When Kids Get Life* 2007).

The sentences must not only be long, the conditions must also be awful. From my students' comments and papers, I see that some percentage of them relish the fact that, for example, people convicted of sex crimes will be raped in prison. Like many others in the society, these students want to know that people in prison are suffering. Their suffering brings gratification.

The violence of prison is thus a desirable social goal, and not just incidental, accidental, or an unfortunate side effect. It is essential that prisons are violent. The violence marks the prison as a prison. Prison violence has a communicative value. It communicates the suffering of incarcerated people to a dominant culture that insists on their suffering.

To be sure, the dominant culture's desire to inflict cruel punishments is not universally shared. The purpose here has not been to represent a social consensus that does not, in fact, exist. Rather, I suggest that indecent and reprehensible conditions are not simply the result of social indifference or lack of awareness, but, to the contrary, reveal an appetite for precisely those hideous conditions that I have described throughout.

BREAKING PEOPLE

For the purposes of the argument so far, it has been useful to hold humiliation separate from violence and from natal alienation as three analytically distinct components that together spell social death. But we have already seen several examples that illustrate how the three frequently coincide in the prison. For example, when staff members sexually assault a person they supervise, cruelty ties together degradation, subordination, and violence. The isolation and the lack of recourse is part of natal alienation, and what makes people in prison vulnerable to abuse.

Violence, humiliation, and natal alienation also work in concert when prison staff try to break the will of incarcerated people. One particularly potent way to break the will is through getting people to inform on others. Susan Rosenberg explains the logic (I cite her at length).

Increasingly, women who have information to trade will use it to get a time cut; others, with no information to trade, end up doing lengthy sentences. The severity of the punishment, the very length of the sentence, is intended to be coercive. As a result, more and more women are targeted by drug agents and pressured into becoming snitches.

The convict code of silence has been dismantled piece by piece by the state. When a woman is a walking "contents under pressure" about to explode, and she finally does, it means she has been broken. She has been bought by the government and can and will be used again and again. Once a defendant gives information in exchange for sentence leniency, the government owns her.

To justify this to themselves, these women end up seeing their captors as all-powerful. It is the government that holds their fate in its hands; it is the government that must be obeyed. Other prisoners are seen as a threat. Building unity among women prisoners becomes close to impossible. Eventually, a more petty form of snitching takes over. The trade of information in prison may not rise to the level of informant trial testimony or "cooperation" as prosecutors euphemistically call it, but it can and does prevent women prisoners from exercising collective power over the actual and difficult conditions of their lives. (Rosenberg 2005, 94)

Through informing, or "debriefing," as it is often termed, a person acts in narrow self-interest in a way that brings him or her into conflict with peers. Getting people to inform is a tactic of divide and conquer. It is humiliating to surrender one's integrity to avoid a lengthy sentence.

It is difficult to imagine how one might face such a choice: eighteen months [in exchange for informing on others] versus life in prison. Belle didn't go for it; and she struggles with this decision every day. I can see it in her face when she thinks no one is looking. When she went back to be debriefed on her own role, and she saw her children in the visiting room, they had grown beyond recognition. At that moment, her beliefs were more deeply challenged than at any previous point in her life. It is the foulest of bribes—your beliefs or your life—an unconscionable action by an all-powerful state. (Rosenberg 2005, 96)

Breaking a person (as a form of humiliation) works together with natal alienation: the prospect of permanent separation from one's children is used to extort information, submission, and concession to the state, debasing oneself and one's principles by informing on others. As Rosenberg frames it, the government communicates to the individual that she is a disposable being in order to leverage compliance. Rosenberg sees this practice as corrupting and undermining the moral integrity of the political system.

Solitary confinement is also used to convince incarcerated people to debrief. To take one notorious example from California, corrections authorities send incarcerated people suspected of gang affiliation to Pelican Bay State Prison until they report on others' criminal activity, especially gang activity, and renounce their gang membership. Pelican Bay (opened in 1989) holds all its prisoners in isolation. People have been held in isolation at Pelican Bay for up to twenty-eight years. Luis Esquivel, a plaintiff in a lawsuit, comments of the thirteen years he has spent in solitary, "I feel dead. It's been thirteen years since I have shaken someone's hand and I fear I'll forget the feel of human contact" (cited by Mariner 2012).

During the administrative hearing that could send them to Pelican Bay, they are denied due process and never come before a judge. In *Ruiz v. Brown*, a lawsuit challenging conditions at Pelican Bay filed in May 2012, the plaintiffs contend that the prison administration "unreasonably condition release from inhumane conditions on cooperation with prison officials" (Center for Constitutional Rights 2012).

In July 2011, and then again in 2012, 2013, and 2014, men held at Pelican Bay staged hunger strikes that quickly spread to other prisons. The hunger strikers issued five core demands, including eliminating group punishment for individual rule violation, abolishing the debriefing policy, and ending long-term solitary confinement. They argue, in short, that the administration, backed by state government, uses the threat of a lengthy sentence or an indefinite period in solitary confinement to intimidate and to pressure a person to capitulate and submit to authority. These techniques are violent and demeaning.

CONCLUSION

I am visiting the jail to interview a woman for the NAACP. A student has come with me and sits beside me. The woman we are to interview comes through a door on her side and sits opposite me on the other side of the thick glass. "I am legally blind and I have diabetes," she tells us. I wonder idly whether her diabetes caused the blindness. "I have a problem with my foot." My student asks to look at her foot. She takes off her sock and shows us a grotesquely long and horribly ingrown nail. Her foot is swollen, the skin is peeling, and the limb has a scarlet cast emanating from the foot, which is even darker. "I am worried that I've got blood poisoning or gangrene. My toes feel like they're burning. They hurt all the time. I can't really walk or even stand on this leg. It won't support any weight. I can't cut my nails. They're too thick." I ask her whether she has received medical attention. "I've asked to see a podiatrist to cut my nails. I'm a little scared because my mom lost her leg and it started the same way, with a toe infection." She continues calmly, "They are supposed to take care of the eyes, the sugar [diabetes], my kidneys, my feet. I've asked to see the doctor many times. I've filed slips. They keep switching my meds." I ask if she is getting her insulin. She says that she is.

She says little more, though she doesn't seem to be in a hurry to leave. She waits, hardly looking in our direction. But then I remember she's blind. I consider whether she is always this laconic, or if it is just that she doesn't hold much hope that this interview will get her anywhere, or maybe she has said all she needs to say in order to explain her condition.

The prospect that she has gangrene is deeply troubling to me. The frustration—your foot that way, the shooting pains, the difficulty walking or even putting weight on it, fearing it will have to be amputated, in a facility that could provide you with the care you need, but doesn't. The uncertainty of living without a diagnosis. The next week she is transferred to another facility and I never see her again. (Fieldnotes, 2007)

Most people would probably agree with the assertion that imprisonment in the United States is a humiliating experience, regardless of how much they know about prison life. The prison is humiliating and not just shaming, where a sense of shame may be an appropriate response to honest reflection on one's past actions. The prison exposes people to sheer, overwhelming institutional power. Many feel dehumanized.

Prisons are cruel places. Sexual harassment is pervasive. Indeed, some harassment is part of everyday prison procedure. Criminal justice personnel and even some prison procedures (such as debriefing) are used to try to break the will.

Incarceration casts a person into a structure where he or she is vulnerable, and risks being turned into a disposable self, a dispensable subject, a thing. On occasion, that person-turned-into-an-object is also sexualized (see Spillers 2003). Social death captures this condition of being cast simultaneously as an object, even a sexualized object and a piece of garbage, a throwaway body (Mignolo 2009; Scheper-Hughes and Bourgois 2004, 19, 21). The prison thrusts people to the other side of the abyssal line, where they are treated abjectly. Any cruelty, small or large, can be visited upon them. Women, transgender people, the mentally ill, and other marginalized populations are particularly vulnerable.

I worry that accounts of the horror men and women face in prison, instead of eliciting sympathy, compassion, moral outrage, or even rank indifference, may evoke glee and gratification or a voyeuristic thrill. Such a reaction fits with the idea of just deserts: people in prison should suffer, should be subject to sexual humiliation, and should be subject to pain and social exile.

This has consequences for advocacy. Simply exposing abuse in prisons is not enough without a public campaign to change a culture that takes pleasure in cruelty.

PART II

Method and a History of Social Death

CHAPTER 4

Dissemblance and Creativity

TOWARD A METHODOLOGY FOR STUDYING STATE VIOLENCE

Hi Josh,

I am a real advocate of this project and decided I can make a more maximum contribution if I break my anonymity, at least with you. I have concerns, as well, and will stop by your office next Tuesday during office hours to discuss them.

There is a saying on the streets, "Game recognize Game" and although I want to believe the best about all human beings, especially in our ability to change and overcome the past and perhaps turn it into something positive. God knows I have worked hard enough to change mine.

I am a former inmate of the Broome County Jail, both this facility and the last. I had horrible experiences with the health care staff.

Much of the information we are collecting is valid, however, as I'm sure you know, probably the same amount is not.

I realized yesterday that Kareem and you seemed frustrated with each other and I believe he is one of the team's most valuable members because like me, he has practical experience and there is no amount of other experience or documentation that can substitute that.

Now that I have come clean with you, so to speak, this opens us up to a lot of people, like myself and Kareem, who have been in jail/prison and who have made great strides in changing their lives. I was afraid to mention my resources because of my own anonymity, but the success of the project means more to me.

Take care, Josh, and we'll talk soon. At this point, I will ask you and Kareem to keep this part of my past between us, as I'm not sure I'm comfortable sharing it with the rest of the team.

[signed "Diane," March 2007]

I RECEIVED THIS LETTER from one of my university students. I must confess that it took me by surprise. Though Diane was a student active in our jail project, I had her down as a bit naïve—not wise to the workings of prisons, jails, and the police. In my class on prisons, I found her comments tended toward the cloying, the sentimental; she often proclaimed the redemptive power of acceptance and love for all.

As it turns out, I was wrong in my assessment of her. She had a cagey, insider's eye that makes her wary of being lied to or hustled. "Game recognize game," as she put it. In fact, she thought it was I, a middle-class white man, who may be the ingenuous one: I have been "gamed," and often, she thinks, and I need to develop more discernment to recognize it. And I realize that the proof is that she gamed me: I had had a totally different perception of her before she sent me this note. Her letter reoriented me in a sudden and powerful way amid all of the jail narratives we had been hearing.

Diane telegraphed a complicated message to me. She marked a central tension between concealment and disclosure. She confided in me for the sake of the project and to open the project to the resources and people she could bring. But she disclosed her status only to me and to Kareem, another student who had also been incarcerated, and she asked that I keep her confidence from other students.

Diane's letter raised a fundamental methodological problem, since our study relied on firsthand testimony. How can we distinguish between truth, half-truths, deliberate fictions, and all that lies in between: urgent information, self-serving representations, rationalization, omission, faithful witnessing, and hyperbole? Discerning evasion and conscious manipulation is not only a methodological issue. It is also a political challenge in documenting social death. In particular, I want to think about careful, critical advocacy aimed at stopping violence and sexual assault of incarcerated people, especially women, when deception, dissimulation, and silence are important tools of their resistance and their daily survival, and an understandable response to hostile treatment and oppressive conditions. Several incidents underscore some of the dilemmas. Ultimately, getting beyond the silences that divided us, and the caution that initially marked our interaction, this chapter is about creativity, theirs and mine.

For the sake of discussing methodology, I focus on the challenge of communicating across a gender divide. This is especially important because so many incarcerated women are survivors of sexual violence (Browne, Miller, and Maguin 1999; Schlesinger and Lawston 2011, 1–2). In most cases I examine here, the gender divide also includes a racial and class divide, since the majority of women we interviewed were African American working-class women. Because of the context, and the histories that divide us, it was difficult for women to talk directly and frankly to me, a white man (see Price 2012b). Other researchers may (or may not) find they confront similar questions. I have interviewed many men, and that poses challenges both similar and different.

Currently and formerly incarcerated women may name state violence in prison in the form of brutal guards, separation from kin, poor health care, and generally abusive treatment. They are often outraged by it. But these things are difficult to discuss frankly. The disgrace of incarceration and sexual abuse are only two of the most obvious barriers to openness to those who suffer from them the most; yet they pose significant stumbling blocks for organizing against that abuse. Fear of public humiliation emerges from our research and activism by, with, and for currently and formerly incarcerated people. Taken together, the fear, the oppressive forces, the high stakes, and the pervasive violence make communication perilous.

DISSEMBLANCE

I met with Karen more than a half dozen times while she was at the county jail. She was speaking to me at some risk. The jail administration retaliated against her for talking with us. Jail guards would pester her to repeat what she had told me. They repeatedly strip-searched her. On the other hand, she felt the ongoing meetings with me also offered her some protection because she had people outside monitoring her. Serving as the eyes and ears of the NAACP, we acted as an implicit check on the jail administration's impunity in its conduct toward her. At the end of every visit, I asked, as I did in all my interviews, if she would like me to come back and check up on her the following week. "Yes, please." she would always tell me simply.

At one point I had to leave town for a couple weeks on a trip, and so I asked Jillian Lyons, one of my students who had been active in the project, to take my place. When I got back, Jillian told me more of what Karen had been through, including that she had been raped at some point. I didn't press Jillian. In fact, I tried not to listen to all the details. I felt that Jillian was beginning to tell me things I didn't have a right to hear: if Karen wanted me to know, she would have told me herself. (Fieldnotes, 2007)

It made sense to me, of course, that Karen felt more comfortable in revealing certain things to another African American woman. But I did wonder at the contrast, since she had already told me so much. Over the course of months she had told me many things she found mortifying and degrading, experiences she had not shared with her family. She had told me how demeaned she felt by the forced strip searches. She took risks to speak with me.

The challenge for me was to understand the silence and social evasion around gendered violence and prison, including the violence that is prison. The silences have a history. They may be due in part to what the historian Darlene Clark Hine has called a "culture of dissemblance" among African American women (Hine 1989). Hine argues that since slavery, rape and the threat of rape contributed to the development of a tendency among African American women "to appear open even as they hide the truth of their inner lives and selves from their oppressors" (Hine 1989, 912; also see Kelley 1994; Young 2012). In an overwhelmingly hostile and menacing society, "Because of the interplay of racial animosity, class tensions, gender role differentiation, and regional economic variations, Black women, as a rule, developed and adhered to a cult of secrecy, a culture of dissemblance, to protect the sanctity of inner aspects of their lives" (Hine 1989, 915). Scholars who wish to document the lives of African American women must develop "an array of analytical frameworks which allow us to understand why Black women behave in certain ways and how they acquired agency" (912).

While Hine is thinking particularly of the historical study of African American women, I will take this question for what it might mean for the contemporary study of violence against incarcerated women generally (also see Bhavnani and Davis 2000). It should go without saying that not all women in prison are African American, the vast majority of African American women are obviously not criminally involved, of course, and not all incarcerated people dissemble. However, the technique of one oppressed group may also be the technique of another (see Scott 1992). It may be that the culture of dissemblance of enslaved women has migrated to serve as a cultural strategy for incarcerated women, but I will leave aside this genealogical question.

If incarcerated people have developed a culture of dissemblance, as my student implied in her letter, then that would hold many consequences for progressive research undertaken in solidarity with imprisoned men and women. For example, it would influence our interpretation of our interviews since dissemblance is interactive: one dissembles before the oppressor. As the case above of Karen illustrates, my students and I would have to consider how we each interact differently with the women, since we are located at distinct points along the axes of race, class, and gender, and we represent a divergent range of experiences with law enforcement and with incarceration.

Dissemblance is a problem only insofar as it poses real difficulties for organizing against the mistreatment of incarcerated people. Dissemblance and dishonor tend to isolate people from each other, including from family members, other incarcerated people, and concerned community members. Since the bedrock of our advocacy was constant visits to people in our local jail, this communicative dilemma was at the core of our work.

Dissemblance is not simply an obstacle to get around; rather, it is a complex question of communication important to understand. Sometimes social scientists, especially anthropologists, speak of earning trust, a trust ultimately used to get the subjects of their studies to speak with candor so they can be recorded. The goal is usually an academic study, or some other end alien to the needs and desires of the research subjects. To that extent, incarcerated women's caution and wariness is justified.

Outsiders are also sometimes motivated by a prurient desire to listen to accounts of sexual violence against incarcerated women. Analogously, Ella Shohat has described the insistence of Western researchers for Asian and Arab women to disrobe or unveil themselves—symbolically or literally—so that the Western researcher can view all (Shohat 2009). In this frame, the researcher is read as voyeur. Though the charge is undoubtedly true of many, I don't think that my desire was voyeuristic; I can point to our progressive participatory-research agenda as justification for wanting to catalog fully the forms of interpersonal and institutional violence the women faced (and face). One consequence of widespread dissemblance means that researchers are left with an incomplete record, and hence cannot make an adequate analysis of gendered violence (see Hine 1989, 916).

But even nonvoyeuristic research tied to advocacy or to campaigns for social justice like our work, as well as other progressive, feminist, and antiracist research, is often of limited utility in improving the lives of incarcerated people in any real way. If telling the truth does not lead to any change, then one's sense of isolation may be merely confirmed.

Clearly, many women were in favor of the research or else they would not have spoken to me—to us—at all, nor would they have asked us to come and speak with them again and again, as Karen did. They would not have collaborated by referring me to other incarcerated women, or recommending to other women that they write me. I would not have received so many letters from women asking me to visit them at the jail. They would not have come to our meetings after they got out. But they did. Some were willing to talk to me, but only me, and not others—not students, not journalists.

Over the ten years I interviewed and worked with incarcerated and formerly incarcerated people, many women like Karen told me things they said they had not told their partners, their families, or friends, including many stories of sexual assault and violence. They divulged secrets that would get them in enormous trouble, or could be a source of terrific embarrassment, and maybe danger, were it to be disclosed to others. From these years of research and solidarity work, I am confident I developed mutual bonds of trust with certain people.

I say I am confident in the mutual trust. But of course this trust and this confidence should be suspect to the reader. If successful dissemblance creates the appearance of openness and disclosure, then I may be deluding myself (Hine 1989, 912). The emotional, linguistic, psychological, and political stakes were weighty, and the situation was ripe for misunderstanding and deception, including self-deception, both theirs and my own. People dissemble for any number of reasons, including to gain advantage, but also, and especially, because of the dishonor and stigma of prison.

THE STIGMA OF INCARCERATION

Stigma attaches to going to prison or jail in several ways. A student who had been convicted of a felony pointed out that the stigma attached to a felony conviction differs slightly from the stigma connected to having served time in prison. A criminal conviction marks a person as dangerous, untrustworthy, and potentially violent, regardless of the crime—he or she is a transgressor (also see Pager 2007). Serving prison time sullies a person's identity and reputation. But these are only two of the stigmas.

Women who are pregnant or who have given birth while incarcerated battle against the perception that they are unfit or undeserving mothers (see Solinger 2009). People who are HIV positive do not always want to release their status to family members, let alone to a larger public or to the prison population. Hepatitis bears a similar, if less marked, stigma. We met people who worried about identifying as having mental illness or suffering post-traumatic stress disorder. Survivors of sexual abuse in prison often had not reported the abuse due to stigma, although they also may not have reported due to a real threat of administrative retaliation. Additionally, they may have feared they would not be believed (Dignam 2008; Levi and Waldman 2011).

Finally, stigmas differ depending on the conviction. People labeled sex offenders are particularly heavily sanctioned socially, politically, and legally. People convicted of murder also bear a heavy stigma, though the aura of menace or of horror is different from the moral revulsion and even violence that is evoked by sex offenders. Other offenses are stigmatizing, but less so.

This basic catalog could be complicated further by distinctions in class and age, as well as other variables in a person's background and social milieu. But there is something artificial about categorizing these forms of stigma separately. Often, they intersect to silence people or lead them to misrepresent what they have been through or are facing. Other times the forms of stigma do not so much intersect as compound one another. Many people we met were ostracized, condemned, or feared condemnation on several counts; some suffered from nearly all the aforementioned sources of public or private humiliation.

A local newspaper columnist contacts me. The columnist often features columns on women's issues. She is doing a story on women who are pregnant or have given birth in jail and she wants to know if I can set up some interviews for her. Because of recent cases of journalists faking sources, the journalist tells me that her paper's editorial policy requires that sources be identified by name. The women have to be ready to be identified publicly. I agree to talk to Gina, who had been imprisoned at the jail for several months while pregnant. I stop by her aunt's house where she is staying since she got out, and she and I have a long talk while she minds her newborn. She asks me what I think, whether I think it's a good idea to speak to reporters. I try to present the decision neutrally. It's impossible to control the story that the journalist will tell, I say. On the other hand, I continue after a pause, an exposé could drum up support for change, for closer scrutiny, and for holding the sheriff and his staff more accountable for jail conditions.

Gina had told me earlier that she would like people to know what is going on at the jail with pregnant women, and that is why I approached her about speaking to a reporter. I know she was angry and terrified when she and other women could not get prenatal care. She told my intern about her experiences being forced to walk in shackles unassisted while pregnant, including up and down stairs.

Yet she balks at going on record. "I just don't know," she muses aloud. In particular, she doesn't want to be named publicly. I understand. It is exposing; as it is, she had to struggle to regain custody of her children. It would become even more difficult if she became publicly identified as a woman who had been incarcerated at the jail. I also wonder whether she is reluctant to display herself as vulnerable, subject to harm, and not as active and strong. Meanwhile, I talk to several other women I know who had been pregnant while incarcerated at the jail. They are also enraged at, and in some cases were traumatized by, the jail conditions. But they will not go on record and speak to a reporter. The journalist drops the story. (Fieldnotes, 2008)

I have already enumerated many reasons why incarcerated and formerly incarcerated women would choose not to speak to a reporter. Here I will add another. Even in the face of a strong desire to speak, incarcerated women may recognize the potential that, like most women experiencing violence, they face social denial of their condition. When they give accounts of their treatment, incarcerated people are usually regarded with indifference, contempt, or fear. Our society has developed a range of psychosocial and cognitive practices so that bystanders (that is, the rest of us), and sometimes even perpetrators, claim not to know the horror visited upon incarcerated people and their families (see Cohen 2001). A dominant common sense treats women convicted of crimes as drug-addled liars, manipulators, selfish, and conscienceless. This serves as a tool to discard or dismiss their opinions and their lives as they live and experience them. What is the point of baring oneself just to be rebuffed?

Although we tried to document testimony without passing judgment on it, we sometimes participated in the social denial.

> I am back at the jail. Initially, I did all the interviews personally or sat in while my more seasoned students took the lead. Because so many people from the jail are starting to come forward to talk to us, I cannot personally meet all the incarcerated people who want to speak with us; my students are conducting the bulk of the eight to ten interviews per week. On the fly, we have instituted systems to check our process: we conduct interviews in pairs and we debrief as a group in the jail parking lot, reviewing what we learned and what we are going to do. Everyone connected with the project must attend weekly meetings at the NAACP.
>
> Today I am sitting in on a follow-up interview. The woman we are interviewing has dark black pockmarks on her face that my intern tells me she did not have a month ago. They are the result of scarring from water-filled corpuscles that dotted her face and that she could not get diagnosed. She is wearing a special jumper that indicates she is in the special housing unit. "I've been here for 45 days and I still don't know my charge. And it's freezing up here! I think they turned off the heat or something." Lots of women have been complaining about the cold this week. They come to their interviews with layers under their jumpers. I ask her if she believes she's seen or been subject to any racist treatment. "Yes, I was put in the SHU [special housing unit or solitary confinement] for fighting, but nothing happened to the white woman I was fighting with." This is not the first time that African Americans have told me they were punished more harshly than white people for the same offense. Afterward, my intern tells me she does not think it was racism, but rather favoritism. Some black women are fussed over by the jail guards, my student says to me, especially if they are young, pregnant, or have a baby. My intern is a grown woman and an African American. I contemplate

her over a coffee at the gas station near the jail: she denies racism when another black woman just told us there is racism. It is true that there is no consensus among the people we interview about whether there is racism at the jail; some African Americans held at the jail say that they do not perceive it. Yet that seems different from denying racism or denying the testimony of a prisoner. At some point later, I know, I will have this one particular thing out with my intern. Maybe she sees or understands something I don't and I need to be open to that, too. (Fieldnotes, 2006)

In reflecting on this incident, I realize now that I never pursued with my intern how she disputed the woman's charge of administrative racism at the jail, and in this way she impugned the woman's credibility. Although I tended to believe the account of discrimination, what if I were wrong? What if, in other words, I was being gamed again?

We never seemed to have enough time for the discussions we needed to have. In trying to get access to people at the jail, arranging for our trips, planning tactics for intervention, organizing a heterogeneous community with deep political splits and factions, operating in a climate of fear, rage, frustration, and crisis, we ended up placing consciousness-raising and overt political education as secondary. In retrospect, we needed to spend more time exploring what we were learning and what it meant in political terms. It is true that the numerous jail visits, the weekly discussions at the NAACP, and our tactic sessions acted as political education, even if obliquely; still, we rarely made enough space for fundamental considerations, for assessment of ends, for analysis of structures of oppression. We tended to focus on practical interventions. We had good justification for this, not least because the problems were pressing and people were impatient with too much talk while friends and family languished in jail. But here too one finds the tension: the lingering questions about the credibility of people in jail, and the racist and sexist abuse they were telling us about, were hardly abstract concerns. How then could we have become more discerning without critical dialogue?

As time went on, many forces—time, money, small-town power, the parole office, the administration at the jail, and the police—began posing obstacles for continuing, each difficult to surmount. Each constantly threatened to fragment our efforts and our energies. The communicative problems internal to the group just added to our difficulties. Taken together, all these forces, tendencies, factors, and institutions jeopardized any possibility of exposing the abuse in a politically powerful way. In a moment of despair, I wrote a political comrade in Massachusetts that I doubted that we could make any political progress. She responded that what I perceived as failure was

a realistic statement not only of how difficult it is to raise awareness of
political contexts and visions of change in local groups experiencing
intense and sustained oppression, but also of their own commitment to
their community, to themselves. That is not a bad thing. They are only
expressing exactly where they are, and that is no failure, it is just fact.
Your failure would only be to alienate them for being where they are, and
it doesn't sound like you have done that. You are having to cross many
violent and entrenched social and political boundaries to do the work
you are doing as a white academic, and they are having to navigate your
boundary-crossings as well as their own, just to work with you. This is
long-term work.

ARTS OF RESISTANCE AND
ARTS OF RECUPERATION

Historically, the gap between the demeaning public representations of
women of color and their actual experiences has offered wiggle room; that
is, it offered a space to maneuver to launch their own forms of resistance to
prying outsiders, even well-meaning outsiders (see Collins 2000; Havis 2009).
The philosopher Devonya Havis has attributed to African American women a
practical capacity to maneuver that she calls "Black women's philosophy." For
Havis, Black women's philosophy is a daily disposition and a skill rather than
an abstract body of thought; it is an "art of resistance." "One can articulate a
certain attitude that can be characterized as Black women's philosophy. As
opposed to a static set of philosophical principles, I posit that Black women's
philosophies are more aptly described as philosophical strategies (arts of resistance) that perform ethico-political interventions. In assuming a posture of
critique, these strategies contest fixity" (Havis 2009; emphasis omitted). For
incarcerated people who are multiply marginalized, doing philosophy in this
sense is a practical activity that provides a method and a means for them to
sustain themselves.

In the stories above, incarcerated women creatively engage in tactics of
everyday survival in the face of massive state violence. This sometimes involves
telling partial stories.

My aspiration to creativity, on the other hand, takes as its point of depar-
ture a remark by Angela Davis (2009). Davis pointed out that the movement
that made Martin Luther King Jr. a spokesman was started by the largely
unknown washerwomen, maids, seamstresses, and dishwashers of Montgomery who decided to boycott the segregated buses and walk to work, bringing
Montgomery to its knees. Davis commented (these are my notes made from
a public lecture): "We don't know how to acknowledge the communities [of

resistance, of struggle], especially without direct visual evidence. The most important part of Black history, women's history, and Black women's history, were performed by people we can only know by the imagination" (Davis 2009). Davis is recuperating an unwritten past, especially a history of resistance to racist, sexist, and sexual oppression. Something like that might also apply to the present, to a history of the present, and to the tens of thousands, hundreds of thousands, now millions who struggle against prison conditions in big and small ways.

Imagination and creativity play signal roles in the project of documenting abuse in order to stop it. In acknowledging the finesse with which people who have been to prison may (or may not) disclose their experiences to me, I see our mutual imagination as a key aspect of building solidarity. This is particularly true when full disclosure is not in the cards, when words fail, or put us at risk.

The challenge for the conscientious social scientist committed to human liberation is analogous to Toni Morrison's challenge in writing of the past. Reflecting on the slave narratives, Morrison comments that, "No slave society in the history of the world wrote more—or more thoughtfully—about its own enslavement. But whatever the level of eloquence or the form, popular taste discouraged the writers from dwelling too long or too carefully on the more sordid details of their experience" (Morrison 1987, 108). "My job," Morrison continues, "becomes how to rip that veil drawn over 'proceedings too terrible to relate.' . . . Only the act of the imagination can help me" (Morrison 1987, 109–111). We can see her "acts of imagination" about the lives of nameless women in the past in, for example, *A Mercy*, or, famously, *Beloved*. Morrison, like Davis, attributes to the imagination a crucial role in reconstructing history. The imagination is key for truth: "I suppose I could dispense with [awe and reverence and mystery and magic] if I were not so deadly serious about fidelity to the milieu out of which I write and in which my ancestors actually lived. . . . It's a kind of literary archaeology: on the basis of some information and a little bit of guesswork you journey to a site to see what remains were left behind and to reconstruct the world that these remains imply" (112). Here, however, emerges a crucial difference between the work of the imagination by someone like Morrison and someone such as me, located at different points along a race and gender divide. Morrison finds a reticence among escaped slaves to speak of their interiority: "But most importantly—at least for me— there was no mention of their interior life" (111). Where Morrison might probe, or reconstruct, that interior life in the service of revelation, for me to do it would be arrogant; given the nature of the dissemblance, it would also lead me astray. Alice Walker has written approvingly of the white southern writer Flannery O'Connor:

That she retained a certain distance (only, however, in her later, mature work) from the inner workings of her black characters seems to me all to her credit, since, by deliberately limiting her treatment of them to cover their observable demeanor and actions, she leaves them free, in the reader's imagination, to inhabit another landscape, another life, than the one she creates for them. This is a kind of grace many writers do not have when dealing with representatives of an oppressed people within a story, and their insistence on knowing everything, on being God, in fact, has burdened us with more stereotypes than we can ever hope to shed. (Walker 1983, 52)

Taking Alice Walker's advice, I ought to retain a certain distance and limit myself to describing what I observed rather than to try and plumb the inner depths of the women, since that would be a suspect desire. These guidelines press themselves as political imperatives in doing research across historically constituted lines of oppressive difference marked by sexual oppression, colonization, and racism. This project implies a restrained approach to the problem of how to translate across an abyssal divide, a divide marked by fear and distrust. Instead, I could attempt to work in solicitous solidarity while valuing uncertainty. This uncertainty is engendered by the dissimulation and maneuver that has historically evolved as a tool or a technique as women of color interact with members of the oppressor class. The methodology can be used as part of the search for new meanings and new social relationships.

CONCLUSION

I referred above to Karen who suffered from a pressing medical condition and whom we followed for several months at the jail. After several months of legal wrangling while she languished at the jail, at length Karen grudgingly accepted an offer from the assistant district attorney to do five years in exchange for a guilty plea in her court case. She decided to give in so that she could be sent to an upstate penitentiary where health care is generally better (although this is a relative statement: state penitentiary health care is also abysmally awful, but she does have the possibility of receiving better medical attention).

After she entered a guilty plea, I went up to visit her one last time before she was transferred to serve out her sentence. The jail administration had taken away our special NAACP visits, which had entitled us to meet in a private room where I could bring in pens and paper. As a result, I could no longer take notes and I had to compete against the noise of the crowded visiting room under the watchful eyes of correctional officers. On the other hand, in the normal visiting room we were able to sit face to face without the glass between us. This was the first time I had seen her without intervening glass. She embraced me when I came in. Her mood had changed visibly.

Instead of despair, she had an air of resignation that left her more pensive and less desperate. She was still frustrated, however. "I pled guilty even though I knew I could have beat those charges. But at least I'll be getting out of here now," even if she was headed to the penitentiary. "I got five years." It was a fixed and finite time. I asked her what she planned to do while in prison, whether she had any projects. "I'd like to write," she said to me. "I'd like to write short stories."

We continued to correspond after she had been sent to a penitentiary across the state.

September 21, 2008

Dear Josh,

I received your letter and of course I was so happy to hear from you . . . I am a facilitator here. I facilitate to prisoners that are soon to be released. I talk to them about how hard the transition may be going back out to their various communities. I tell them about my real life experiences. I am also dealing with a lot of my issues. My health has improved greatly. I play racquetball every afternoon to stay in shape. I do a lot of reading. I have also talked about how you helped me so much. . . . I can't imagine what would have took place with me without your help. I plan on doing something for inmates that are not treated fairly when I get out of here. I would like to apologize for not writing sooner. I will never forget you for the rest of my life. I would also like for you to thank the others that was involved. I will write again soon . . .

I never saw or heard from her again. I never learned whether she followed through with her creative writing project. Nevertheless, I take her impulse as hopeful. Holding in mind the daily drubbings, indignities, and taunts to which she was subject, I see an incommensurable distance between the social death meted out to her and the person she was and aspired to be (see Butler 2004).[1] The distance is not easily bridgeable. I wonder if Karen, as with generations of African American women before her, was able in this gap to exercise self-affirmation, and take it as the grounds for creativity. I do not believe I have some truer or more authentic picture of her than the cruel guards, cavalier nurses, and arrogant doctors have. If I thought I did, I would be falling into that naïveté that the student alerted me to in her letter I cited at the beginning of this chapter.

But I do see a creativity, a creativity she ultimately affirmed to me. Unlike some people who have asked me to tell their story, Karen opted to write fiction. Though I do not know what she will write, I wonder about the character of her writing. It might animate the truth. In that spirit, let me close with the words of Toni Morrison: "Therefore the crucial distinction for me is not the difference between fact and fiction, but the distinction between fact and truth. Because facts can exist without human intelligence, but truth cannot" (1987, 113).

CHAPTER 5

Racism, Prison, and
the Legacies of Slavery

March 2009. During a visit with Daniel at a penitentiary, he tells me that several young men are taunting him. He is serving a new stint in prison after serving a sentence of twenty years. One asked him contemptuously, "Why are you still here in prison after all this time?" He takes it that the young men are implicitly blaming him. He reminds them of the accumulated weight of past structures of inequality. He speaks to the young men of racism and the criminal justice system. He reviews for them contemporary statistics on the disproportionate number of people of color enmeshed in the criminal justice system. When he finishes, another tells him, "You are a waste of humanity." He replies calmly, "I have just gotten through telling you why, historically, logically, even statistically, I am in this situation. What's wrong with my logic?

"I'll tell you what," Daniel continues to the younger prisoner. "I ask you what's wrong with my argument, and if you don't have an answer, then I get to pluck out one of your eyes." (Fieldnotes, 2009)

THIS COULD BE SEEN as so much male posturing, or the banter of people in an extreme situation. I prefer to see the exchange as marking the limits of a certain rationality. One young man marks Daniel as nothing, as a dead subject (see also Ferreira da Silva 2007). Daniel rejoins with a counternarrative that marks the centrality of captive labor and racial subordination in the Americas.

Daniel's response seems to be borne out historically, logically, and statistically. People of color are incarcerated at a much great rate than whites (see introduction; also Carson and Sabol 2012, 8). Michelle Alexander has argued that the prison reinforces and reproduces a racial caste system (2010, 12). In the caste system, law and custom lock people racialized as nonwhite, especially African Americans, into an inferior social position. Daniel's response confronted the young men with this burden, this entanglement of race, caste, and captivity. His line of thinking points to history, and ultimately to the question, Is the institution of prison a descendant of the institution of slavery?

RACE AND THE COLONIAL ENTERPRISE

"About the last of August came in a Dutch man of warre that sold us twenty Negars." The Virginia colonialist Captain John Smith records the purchase as a banal observation in his *Generall Historie of Virginia* (Smith 2003 [1624], 337). Fellow colonialist John Rolfe also mentions this purchase of "20. and some odd Negars" in an otherwise humdrum letter recounting daily events in the colony (Sluiter 1997, 395–396). Yet these words, written in 1619, are some of the most fateful in the history of the United States. "Liken it," Bruce Olds comments, "to reading an eyewitness account of the dawning of creation. Only this—these '20 and some odd Negars'—is the dawning not of creation, but of something very like its opposite" (Olds 1995, 7). Rolfe's letter is the first record of a slave purchase in what was to become the United States. But his narrative does not shake with tension. Neither he nor John Smith records any debate. Neither man remarks on the countenances of those doomed to enslavement. They do not reflect on the moral collapse of a community. Rolfe does not wonder whether the transaction is Mephistophelean. Smith does not offer a rationale, however specious or convoluted. Perhaps they never reflected on these things, or never reflected deeply.

The importance of the year 1619 can be overstated. By that date, Spanish and Portuguese conquerors had already imported some 300,000 Africans to the Americas over the course of the previous century. In fact, racialized slavery in the Americas began as soon as Columbus navigated down the coast of the Caribbean island where he first landed. In his first letters, Columbus reported that he kidnapped a half dozen Caribs to force them to serve as translators as he went island hopping in the Caribbean (Columbus 2011 [1493]). Since Columbus's arrival, explorers and conquistadores had kidnapped indigenous people, enslaved them, or otherwise forced them to work, in some cases on a massive scale, when they did not engage in direct annihilation. Early chroniclers from Álvaro Cabeza de Vaca to Bartolomé de las Casas amply documented the wholesale enslavement and genocide of millions of indigenous people. The Spanish and Portuguese sent some of the early captives back to the home countries as souvenirs. Far more often, however, the captors worked the native peoples to death in the gold and silver mines of Potosí or turned them into peons in the emerging hacienda system.

Most of the European explorers arrived with captives, impressed into service as part of their crew. Explorers who came with enslaved North Africans, convicts, or both include Vasco Núñez de Balboa, Francisco Vásquez de Coronado, Hernando de Soto, Jacques Cartier, and Samuel De Champlain (Christianson 1998, 6). From the beginning, then, captive labor was central to the colonization of the Americas.

As other colonizers before them, the English imprisoned entire groups of indigenous men, women, and children in military brigs, forts, or small cantons, when they did not massacre them outright. More broadly, the British colonial enterprise relied on several kinds of institutionalized labor practices that resembled slavery and that began around the same time the English began to enslave people of African descent. Apprenticeship, indenture, and penal bondage all involved some form of captivity and forced labor. Apprenticeship, for example, legally required the apprentice to stay with his or her master for a set number of years and perform the master's will, for little or no pay.

The formal and informal traffic in women from the British Isles also began around the ill-starred date of 1619. Sir Edwin Sandys of the Virginia Company arranged marriage contracts for Virginia colonialists with English women. Evidence suggests some were shipped against their will and forced to perform sex work, whether through compulsory marriage or through prostitution (Christianson 1998, 11). This would be the fate of thousands of women in the successive decades.

Throughout the seventeenth century, English authorities sent vagrants and "rogues" (to use the contemporaneous term) to the New World. It is estimated that as many as 30,000 Irish and English felons may have been transported to the colonies up to the time of the American Revolution. This relatively large-scale project created a context where unscrupulous traffickers worked with the tacit permission of the authorities to spirit away not only lower-class Irish and English children but also increasingly adults who were not involved in crime. Alongside lawful transport, then, some traffickers operated in a legally gray area, and still others kidnapped and shipped groups of people in ways that were clearly illegal.

Many of the condemned and kidnapped English and Irish subjects were shipped in the same slavers that conveyed the newly enslaved Africans to the New World: a ship might transport Africans to the New World, pick up goods, take them to England, pick up a transport of felons and take them back to America. Felons and indentured servants were often auctioned off at the docks as they arrived, just as the bewildered Africans were (Christianson 1998, 23–37).

At the dawn of their colonial enterprise, then, the British contrived a variety of mechanisms to make penal transport legal, both to rid themselves of the poor, the criminal, and the socially and economically marginal, as well as to populate their new territorial acquisitions, thus killing two birds with one stone.

Nevertheless, during the course of the seventeenth century, the English colonialists began to differentiate the enslavement of Africans (and, significantly, their descendants) from the indentured servitude of the Irish, the Scots, and the English, and, to a lesser extent, the enslavement of indigenous people. By the middle of the seventeenth century, this distinction congealed as a racial distinction. By the end of the seventeenth century slavery had become a life-long and a hereditary condition. Indentured servants were, in principle at least, contracting individuals who did not face perpetual servitude. Slavery, at any rate chattel slavery in the Americas, presupposed dehumanization, since the slave was an object, merchandise, and thus unable to contract. Fully institutionalizing the enslavement of people of African descent and legally reducing them to the status of chattel thus took over fifty years to become codified in law and fixed as custom.

What were the conceptual antecedents for racializing the dehumanization? The conquistadores from the Iberian Peninsula served as a model for the English to emulate. Along with the term "Negro," the English borrowed a conceptual apparatus for understanding people of African descent as subordinate beings, savage, lawless, heathen, dissolute, and subhuman. The entire set of semi- or incoherent justifications, rationales, and popular beliefs that buttressed the racial caste system was formulated over the course of centuries, including fixing hierarchy in terms of skin color.[1]

Bacon's Rebellion (1676) was a crucible in the racial formation in what would become the United States. One of the distinguishing characteristics of the rebellion was that poor whites and African Americans banded together, potentially contesting the power of the white property-holders (A. Davis 2003; Martinot 2007). In response to the threat posed by Bacon's Rebellion, the Virginia colonial council, dominated by wealthy white landowners, adopted a strategy of tainting the concept of rebellion as "African." White fear combined with white violence to shore up racial solidarity among whites against blacks. "The cycle of paranoia and violence unfolded endlessly at the heart of Virginia. Social paranoia toward the slave produced a demand for solidarity among the English, and the demand for English solidarity and allegiance against the slaves made that violence more acceptable" (Martinot 2007, 86). Wealthy whites manipulated poor whites to stand in racial solidarity with them, even though it was not in the economic interest of poor whites. The pattern continued over the centuries and across the breadth of the Americas (see, e.g., C.L.R. James 1989 [1938]). W.E.B. Du Bois wrote later of the importance of just this racial "wage" (also see Roediger 1999). "It must be remembered that the white group of laborers, while they received a low wage, were compensated in part by a sort of public and psychological wage. They were given public deference and titles of courtesy because they were white" (Du Bois 1977 [1935], 700). Even if they were subject to exploitation and economic insecurity, these whites could congratulate themselves by differentiating themselves from someone whose life was even more blighted and benighted than their own.

GENDER, SEXUAL VIOLENCE, AND THE ORIGINS OF NATAL ALIENATION

To debase another, James Baldwin once remarked, is inevitably to debase oneself; so it was with the English colonizers who eagerly adopted practices and beliefs they used to try to differentiate themselves as emphatically as they could from the Indian and especially the "Negro." They codified these beliefs in laws governing sexuality and reproduction. In doing so, the English descended to ever-greater depths of savagery and venality.

The inauspicious colonial English preoccupation with purported African promiscuity dates from the seventeenth century, at about the same time when new legislation first prohibited miscegenation. English attempts to impute uncontrolled sexuality to black people were a bald projection of their own licentiousness. By constructing blacks as oversexed, the English masters sought to justify their own sexual predations on the people they had enslaved. By depicting the slaves as unable to control their passions, the English created a mythic subject whom only the masters could control (Lugones 2007).

The laws and judicial orders that outlawed and heavily sanctioned interracial sexual union cemented the racial separation—or at least kept up the appearance. For example, a judge in a 1630 decision, *Re Davis*, ordered a white man, Hugh Davis, to be "soundly whipt . . . for abusing himself to the dishonor of God and shame of Christianity by defiling his body in lying with a Negro, which fault he is to actk [*sic*]" (cited in Craig 2001). A 1691 law outlawing intermarriage in Virginia communicated disgust with the offense it established. It also fixed the penalty: banishment.

> And for prevention of that abominable mixture and spurious issue which hereafter may encrease in this dominion, as well by negroes, mulattoes, and Indians intermarrying with English, or other white women, as by their unlawfull accompanying with one another, *Be it enacted by the authoritie aforesaid, and it is hereby enacted,* that for the time to come, whatsoever English or other white man or woman being free shall intermarry with a negroe, mulatto, or Indian man or woman bond or free shall within three months after such marriage be banished and removed from this dominion forever. (Hening 1823, 3:87)

If antimiscegenation laws ostensibly kept the races separate, laws of descent guaranteed that white men could enjoy the fruit of their depredations on enslaved women. A key 1662 law established that whether a child was born into servitude would henceforth be determined by the mother's status.

> Act XII: Negro women's children to serve according to the condition of the mother . . . WHEREAS some doubts have arrisen whether children got by any Englishman upon a Negro woman should be slave or free, Be it therefore enacted and declared by this present grand assembly, that all children borne in this country shalbe held bond or free only according to the condition of the mother. (Hening 1810, 2:170)

Slavery thenceforth followed a matrilineal line of descent. As several commentators have pointed out, this law reversed established tradition in English law, where children's status and lineage followed the status of the father, even in cases of illegitimate children (see, e.g., Christianson 1998; Craig 2001; Martinot 2007). Ironically, the very bloodline of connection between a mother and child now became the determining factor in making the child a separate item of chattel who could be sold away from her mother at the whim of an owner.

This set up a legal framework whereby slaveholders could separate even the fetus from the mother. As I argued in chapter 2, slave narratives record the practice throughout the South of overseers and owners placing the belly of pregnant women in a protective hole before whipping the women. The curious perversity of this practice is predicated on the natal alienation of a woman and her issue.

Colonialists thus encoded natal alienation into slave law. This social system of separating mother and child became the means to reproduce natal alienation—to reproduce slavery—over generations. The gendered aspect of the racial division was crucial: fixing inherited, perpetual servitude as based on race depended on gender and on sex.

This law gave white colonizers a legal mechanism to disown offspring from their sexual union with enslaved women. At the same time, it gave them ownership of these offspring—as chattel. This legislation contributed to the conditions for rampant sexual violence against the enslaved.

CRIMINALITY AND CAPTIVITY

In Europe and its colonies, the identification of the slave with the convict and the captured enemy dates from at least the early part of the seventeenth century and possibly much earlier.

"Captivity and criminal justice seemed to mean the same thing," Winthrop Jordan concludes his study of early colonial wars against Indians and the slave trade. "The animating rationale," Jordan continues, "was that captivity in war meant an end to a person's claims to life as a human being; by sparing the captive's life, the captor acquired virtually absolute power over the life of the man who had lost the power to control his own" (Jordan 1968, 55; see also Mbembe 2003).[2]

In the judicial rulings and legislative acts that established it, slavery began to take on the connotation of taking away (or denying) something essential in the humanity and citizenship of the enslaved. The slave was not quite American, not quite citizen; the slave was something of a foreigner, but a foreigner who was not due any regard, nor someone protected by laws the same way a citizen is. In this sense, the enslaved shared qualities with a captive. When the prisoner is perceived as enemy, then domestic social organization contains elements of war within it (see Mbembe 2003).

From the inauguration of the republic, race played a key role in citizenship, with white people establishing themselves as the only candidates for full enfranchisement (Haney-López 2006). Criminality and foreignness became racialized; all those not white came to be besmirched with this suspect status, this hint of foreignness and of potential lawbreaker. The white land-owning elite portrayed people of African descent as licentious, and, after Bacon's Rebellion, menacing as well. They were said to lack self-control, including sexual self-control. These are the chief components of the legal, social, psychological, institutional, and perceptual machinery that set up the rationale for racializing the captivity that is slavery. This chain of associations has persisted over the last 350 years and maintains its potency through the present day.

FROM NORTHERN SLAVERY TO THE NORTHERN PENITENTIARY

After slavery was abolished, the primary mechanism of social death migrated from the institution of chattel slavery to the criminal justice system. The change was not as much of a paradigmatic shift as it first appears. Black people were already suspect. Frederick Douglass noted in 1883 "the general disposition in this country to impute crime to color." The criminality white people had attributed to people of color came to serve as the justification for establishing a new kind of captivity.

Keeping people of color captive also had a clear economic rationale. If the end of slavery made it impossible to hold human beings any longer as private property, the birth of the penitentiary made it possible to hold human beings as public property, that is, as property of the state. The state could then lease those people-as-property to private interests who could exploit them as workers and as captive consumers. As many have pointed out, the Thirteenth Amendment abolished slavery except for those convicted of felonies, and thus provided a useful loophole for the state intent on keeping people of African descent in a state of forced servitude.

New York serves as a good example of how this transition from slavery unfolded. In 1799 the New York legislature passed "An Act for the Gradual Abolition of Slavery" that fully abolished slavery by 1825. As they contemplated abolishing slavery, legislators openly debated the purported dangers of full civil and political emancipation for African Americans. This debate revolved in part around the supposed criminal tendencies of the people they were liberating.

New York devised several tactics to contain not just African Americans but also the rising number of immigrants. The penitentiary and disenfranchisement laws were chief tools in this strategy. The New York legislature established the penitentiary in Auburn, New York, in 1816, and soon after it levied funds for Sing Sing. It would be an oversimplification to reduce the complex social and political pressures that gave rise to the northern penitentiary to white anxiety over black emancipation. The next chapter, for example, describes the role of social and religious movements. Nevertheless, the coincidence is striking and cannot be ignored. By the 1820s, most northern states had abolished slavery gradually or outright and in that same period also established their first penitentiaries. Thus, Pennsylvania approved a law in 1780 for the gradual abolition of slavery and had converted the Walnut Street Jail to a penitentiary by 1790. Connecticut began abolishing slavery in 1773 and established its first prison in December of that same year. Most of the northern states abolished slavery between roughly the Revolutionary War and the 1830s. During this same period, most established their first penitentiaries (see Brooks 2004).

Early visitors to the new prisons noticed the racially disparate patterns of incarceration. In their 1833 study of the American penitentiary, Gustave de Beaumont and Alexis de Tocqueville noted a statistical anomaly, a harbinger of incarceration practices to come. In New York, they pointed out, the prison population was 25 percent African American, even though they were under 10 percent of the population (1979 [1833]). Immigrants also made up a disproportionate number of the incarcerated throughout the nineteenth and early twentieth century.

The penitentiary was only one tool to take away the political freedom of African Americans and other suspect groups such as immigrants. Early New York legislators put in place property requirements (1777) and voter-ID laws (1811) that had the effect of severely restricting the black male vote. A New York constitutional convention in 1821 removed the property requirement for white men but not for black men (women won suffrage only in the twentieth century). Voters ratified this explicitly race-based property requirement in 1846 and in 1869 (Wood, Budnitz, and Malhotra 2009, 6–12).

Other northern states followed this pattern of disenfranchising people of African descent. New York also put into place felony disenfranchisement laws that are still on the books 175 years later (Wood, Budnitz, and Malhotra 2009). In this same period, ten other states disenfranchised felons. Eighteen more had felony disenfranchisement laws by the end of the Civil War (Brooks 2004, 103).

In the North, then, one can see continuities between the institution of slavery and the institution of the penitentiary. The historical continuities in the South between slavery and incarceration are much easier to discern.

RECONSTRUCTION

When did the Civil War end? In his magisterial *Black Reconstruction in America*, W.E.B. Du Bois characterizes the vicious struggle that defeated the emancipatory potential of Reconstruction as a "civil war." African Americans struggled against the oppressive vestiges of slavery in all spheres of life. It was a second civil war, or perhaps a continuation of the first Civil War. This second civil war lasted throughout Reconstruction and contributed to its downfall. "It must be remembered and never forgotten that the civil war in the South which overthrew Reconstruction was a determined effort to reduce black labor as nearly as possible to a condition of unlimited exploitation and build a new class of capitalists on this foundation" (Du Bois 1977 [1935], 670). The Confederate surrender at Appomattox marked the cessation of formal hostilities, and the Union army occupied the South. The Emancipation Proclamation ostensibly brought the end of slavery. Nevertheless, a number of social elements tried to keep a racial caste system in place. Newly formed white militias, including the Ku Klux Klan, struggled to uphold white supremacy. Terror and intimidation, widespread rioting, and massacres throughout the South plunged the region into chaos. Freed men and women sought to reunify their families, assert their political rights, negotiate favorable terms for labor, and establish homes and communities (see generally Foner 2002; Hunter 1998).

Du Bois saw the forces of terror as ultimately successful in undermining the liberatory aims of African Americans and subverting Reconstruction. With Reconstruction defeated, so too closed the brief window of opportunity Reconstruction had promised for a thoroughgoing, authentic democracy, what Du Bois came to call "abolition democracy." "The slave went free; stood a brief moment in the sun; then moved back again toward slavery. The whole weight of America was thrown to color caste" (Du Bois 1977 [1935], 30).

The continuity between slavery and manumission was felt most acutely by those formerly enslaved persons who were not allowed to taste freedom in any robust sense. George Rawick, editor of the nineteen-volume oral history project, *The American Slave, a Composite Autobiography*, comments: "As one reads through the slave narratives, one is constantly impressed by the fact that many ex-slaves did not see any crucial difference between their pre- and post-slavery way of life. They often lived in the same slave cabin, on the same plantation, with the heirs of the old master, and worked the land on shares. Patrols to keep them in line and paternalistic relationships with certain whites existed as before" (Rawick 1972, 141). Terrifying practices such as the lynching bee operated outside the law, though often with tacit permission from white authorities, including the police. These extrajudicial practices were an element of the struggle to maintain continuity with the past. However, the tactics whites used to reduce African Americans to their former state of subordination were not only illegal and extrajudicial.

A prominent marker of the decline of Reconstruction was the infamous Black Codes. State legislatures throughout the South established these explicitly racial laws. These laws notoriously outlawed vagrancy, often in explicitly racial terms, making it punishable with jail time. They also authorized sheriffs and law enforcement to hire out prisoners. The Black Codes outlawed miscegenation. The Mississippi Black Codes, for example, made intermarriage a felony punishable by life in prison. Some Black Codes authorized special taxes on "Freedmen, free Negros, and mulattos," purportedly to pay for a special "Freedman's Pauper Fund." As I mentioned in chapter 2, states passed apprenticeship laws, which empowered civil officers to place African American orphans (or even children whose parents were poor) under the age of eighteen in compulsory apprenticeships until the age of twenty-one, with a preference given to placing them with former owners. These Codes also required African Americans to have work contracts. Southern states criminalized "enticement"; that is, it became a crime to try to tempt an African American away from his or her place of employment.

These Codes were not new in the American experience. They recuperated older measures, such as forced apprenticeship and vagrancy laws, that the British had used to get rid of its undesirables and populate its colonies. The Black Codes recast these older measures in racial terms. Other Black Codes merely transposed laws previously directed at slaves to the newly freed African Americans. They accompanied other institutions such as sharecropping and paying the workers in scrip that worked to subordinate the freedmen in legal and economic terms.

The emerging partnership of law enforcement with the agricultural and industrial sectors was invested in maintaining a class of people who could be exploited for the needs of capital. Fredrick Douglass foresaw how the society would be distorted by allowing capital investment in a racial caste system. In a post–Civil War speech, "The Color Line in America" (1883), Douglass pointed out:

The holders of twenty hundred million dollars' worth of property in human chattels procured the means of influencing press, pulpit, and politician, and through these instrumentalities they belittled our virtues and magnified our vices, and have made us odious in the eyes of the world. Slavery had the power at one time to make and unmake Presidents, to construe the law, dictate the policy, set the fashion in national manners and customs, interpret the Bible, and control the church; and, naturally enough, the old masters set themselves up as much too high as they set the manhood of the negro too low. (Douglass 2008 [1883])

The immense amount of capital that had backed slavery exercised undue control over politics and civil society and thus deformed the culture in deep ways. The resulting dynamic rooted racism deeply within many social institutions. Long before such terms as the "prison industrial complex," Douglass saw with perspicacity how the entwining of race, money, and the criminalization of people of color disfigured the republic. He was unrelenting in his poor opinion of the nation's halfhearted attempts to incorporate fully African Americans and other people of color.

Out of the depths of slavery has come this prejudice and this color line. It is broad enough and black enough to explain all the malign influences which assail the newly emancipated millions today. . . . Slavery is indeed gone, but its shadow still lingers over the country and poisons more or less the moral atmosphere of all sections of the republic. The money motive for assailing the negro which slavery represented is indeed absent, but love of power and dominion, strengthened by two centuries of irresponsible power, still remains. (Douglass 2008 [1883])

Both Du Bois and Douglass argued that the social and economic system that undergirded slavery and subordinated African Americans could not be transformed merely by changing the law. "The difficulty with this legalistic formula was that it did not cling to facts" (Du Bois 1977 [1935], 188). They argued that white people used the criminal justice system to reassert a racial caste system and to nip in the bud the democratic possibilities implicit in Reconstruction.

In the 1870s, in a context of enormous violence, white politicians pandered to white fears by using racially loaded populist language to appeal to the basest and most reactionary impulses of the white electorate. They were successful in ousting African American officials elected during the Reconstruction era, despite the efforts of African Americans in both the North and the South. A burgeoning class of southern industrialists in agriculture, mining, and other sectors capitalized on these victories. By ensnaring recently freed men and women through the criminal justice system, they were able to secure the inexpensive services of a large class of African Americans. This was the logic of the convict lease system.

CONVICT LEASE SYSTEM

The convict lease system refers to a criminal justice practice that began in the South after the Civil War and continued in some states as late as the 1940s (although one could argue compellingly that elements still exist today). Under convict lease legislation, the state could lease people convicted of felonies to private companies for their labor. Industries as varied as turpentine production, mining, railroad construction, and farming leased not only convicted felons, but in some cases even misdemeanants. This allowed states to recuperate much of the cost of incarcerating people.

Northern prisons such as Auburn and Sing Sing had leased the labor of inmates to private industry since the early nineteenth century (see next chapter). Earlier penal practices also attempted to exploit prisoners as a captive workforce. However, the convict lease system was unique in how it introduced the profit motive into a system that aimed to return the newly freed African Americans to as near a condition of slavery as possible. Given the newly minted Black Codes that criminalized African Americans, the convict lease system became an effective mechanism to try to reinstitute racial subordination. In some states, more than 90 percent of the convicts leased by the state were African American (Foner 2002, 205). Their labor power was crucial in a region struggling to industrialize after the devastation brought by the war.

If slave owners arguably had an economic interest in preserving the health of their slaves for their laboring power (much in the way a farmer would have an interest in maintaining his or her horses or team of oxen), the industrialist who leased convicts to work in a mine or to cut lumber had no such incentive. This led to widespread abuse. Lessees often housed convict labor in filthy conditions and made them work intolerably long hours under horrific conditions. Bosses were allowed to discipline labor, which led to its own forms of excess and abuse. The mortality rate under the convict lease system was horrendous.

Through the corrupting influence of the convict-lease system, the state not only colluded with private interest, it benefited directly from the new "crimes" it created to control the freed people. In his essay, "The Spawn of Slavery: The Convict-Lease System in the South" (1904), Du Bois went further in arguing that the state, in using the criminal courts to "reduce the freedmen to serfdom," finally became "a dealer in crime, profited by it so as to derive a net annual income from her prisoners" (4–5).

The convict lease system mimicked practices instituted under slavery. "To control prisoners southern states copied methods of labor control perfected under slavery, including torture, whipping, patrols, and cash rewards for run-aways," writes the historian Mary Ellen Curtin (2000, 19). The criminal justice system that spawned it was successful, in this sense, at re-creating a social institution that produced and reproduced social death now that slavery had been abolished. Since slavery was, and is, such a potent symbol in our society, slavery lived on as a memory, and as an organizing concept for the workings of the convict-lease system.

The whip was an important holdover. The "convicts were to be punished, and the slave theory of punishment was pain and intimidation" (Du Bois 1904 [1901], 5). Historian of the period Matthew J. Mancini sees the whip as a sort of pain that was particularly degrading: "Whipping is a punishment not just of insupportable pain but of deep humiliation as well. Few men or women can bear it in silence. The vulnerability of the recipient and the power of the boss who metes it out are underscored by the ritual nature of the chastisement" (1996, 76). Du Bois cites a nameless critic: "Of all the degrading positions, to our mind, that of the whipping boss in the Georgia penitentiary system is the worst" (Du Bois, 1977 [1935], 699). Citing George Orwell's *1984*, "the object of torture is torture," Mancini continues: "The dismal history of the brutal and ingenious punishments that leased convicts were forced to undergo provides powerful confirmation of such a view. Many punishments often bear no discernible connection to production or even security, but in the end seem mere expressions of hatred, self-disgust, and a will to power" (1996, 75). The lessees generally operated in an atmosphere of impunity. Often, no legal instrument or institutional authority monitored the treatment of leased convicts. A neighbor of a landholder who had leased prisoners to work on his plantation commented: "The reports are that [the landholder] often [rears] his horse over and against them, that he clubs them with sticks and clubs and clods of dirt and that he allows the guards to do the same . . . that he whips them unmercifully often giving them from 75 to 100 lashes, that he works them in the rain, that he gives little or no attention to the sick; that often their rations are insufficient and badly cooked" (Curtin 2000, 19). Curtin concludes that "[t]he need to control labor cannot explain such sadistic cruelty; it sprang from a deeper source." The labor conditions themselves approached unceasing torture. "Convict labor worked in Alabama mines, often running three miles at three o'clock in the morning to begin the work day, shoveling thousands of pounds to make each quota or risk the whip, only to end the workday at eight P.M. to sleep in a poorly ventilated, windowless chamber chained to other prisoners" (Curtin 2000, 20). Du Bois quotes at length an unnamed southern white woman:

> In some states where convict labor is sold to the highest bidder the cruel treatment of the helpless human chattel in the hands of guards is such as

no tongue can tell nor pen picture. Prison inspectors find convicts herded together, irrespective of age; confined at night in shackles; housed sometimes, as has been found, in old box cars; packed almost as closely as sardines in a box. During the day all are worked under armed guards, who stand ready to shoot down any who may attempt to escape from this hell upon earth—the modern American bastille. Should one escape, the bloodhounds, trained for the purpose, are put upon his track, and the chances are that he will be brought back, severely flogged and put in double shackles, or worse. (1977 [1935], 698)

Du Bois concludes that, through the convict lease system, "[t]he innocent were made bad, the bad worse; women were outraged and children tainted; whipping and torture were in vogue, and the death-rate from cruelty, exposure, and overwork rose to large percentages" (1904, 4).

On examination, the distinction between slavery and convict labor seems to break down a bit, certainly as it was often experienced. Mancini cites David Brion Davis: "If one has been working on a plantation or in a penal camp for most of one's life, it probably makes little difference whether one got there by the legal fiction of sale as a piece of property or as the result of some alleged civil or political crime that has almost faded from memory" (Mancini 1996, 21).

During slavery, disciplining and punishing the enslaved fell mostly to masters. They had a variety of means at their disposal to imprison, torture, maim, brand, or even kill the bondsmen. Punishment, in short, was meted out within the institution of slavery. Consequently, in the antebellum South, most state prisoners were white. Soon after hostilities ceased, as a result of the racially motivated transformations in the criminal justice system, larger numbers of African Americans found themselves in the maws of the criminal justice system. Within a short time, the vast majority of the prison population throughout the South was of African descent (Curtin 2000).

This was no southern aberration. As I pointed out above, northern states began imprisoning a disproportionate number of African Americans as they phased out slavery, as well as a bloated number of immigrants (Beaumont and de Tocqueville 1979 [1833]; Rothman 2005 [1971]). Southern historian Edward Ayers confirms, "The rate of growth in the prison population of the North reveals a contour virtually identical with that of the black prison population in the South throughout the second half of the nineteenth century—including the years of Reconstruction" (Ayers 1984, 170–171). Imputing crime to color knew no geographic bounds within the United States. The southern states were simply more brazen in their use of the judiciary to convict the freed men and women and to hire them out. But the North was hardly innocent in using the criminal justice system once slavery was abolished.

CONCLUSION

Fields of green. A single-file row of men, mostly African American, with felt hats or kerchiefs on their heads, wearing blue denim outfits. They walk with heads bowed. They carry hoes or shovels on their shoulders, holding them the way an infantry division would carry their rifles. A guard in a cowboy hat and duster monitors on horseback nearby.

The scene could be 1950, or 1850, 1750, or even, perhaps, 1650. Hoes and rough cotton indigo pants and shirts. Black people forced to work in rows. In fact, it is the opening shot of *The Farm*, a documentary made in the 1998 about the Louisiana State Penitentiary (also known as Angola), which I described in the introduction. "The survival of agricultural operations within the penal system into the 1960s," commented Mark Carleton in his book of the early '70s, *Politics and Punishment: The History of the Louisiana State Penal System*, "suggests the terms 'convict,' 'slave,' 'Negro,' and 'farm work' have remained unconsciously interchangeable in the mind of institutional Louisiana" (Carleton 1971, 7). William Faulkner was pithier: "The past is never dead. It's not even past."

The legacies of slavery are alive in structures and strategies of racist and sexist repression in the contemporary penitentiary, even if the form they take has evolved. Early slave legislation put in place the legal framework that created a radical division between a parent and his or her issue. Slavery has bequeathed a structure that facilitates sexual violence against captive people, group humiliation, and the rending of kin. The legal infrastructure has continued to be essential in dehumanizing and debasing practices.

From the first years of the colony to the present day, astute politicians and speculators have always tried to wring a financial reward from the bodies of the captives, whether as raw material, forced labor, commodities to be bought and sold, or as captive consumers. But the history of the penitentiary cannot be reduced to labor history or legal history, or to tracing the profit motive, though a proper history must include all these elements. On a more intimate but no less powerful level, we have inherited what are sometimes centuries-old sets of meanings related to criminality, sex, citizenship, race, reproduction, punishment, property, and their interrelation. The history of the penitentiary cannot be told without reference to these practices, perceptions, desires, and structures.

A recent article from the *New York Times* profiles a program that operates as a latter-day convict-lease agreement between private industry and a state penitentiary system.

> In a pilot program run by the [Colorado] Corrections Department, supervised teams of low-risk inmates beginning this month will be available

to harvest the swaths of sweet corn, peppers, and melons that sweep the southeastern portion of the state.

Under the program, which has drawn criticism from groups concerned about immigrants' rights and from others seeking changes in the criminal justice system, farmers will pay a fee to the state, and the inmates, who volunteer for the work, will be paid about 60 cents a day, corrections officials said.

"This feels like the re-invention of the plantation," said Christie Donner [of the Colorado Criminal Justice Reform Coalition]. "You have a captive labor force essentially working for their room and board in order to benefit the employer. This isn't a job-training program. It's an exploitative program." (Frosch 2007)

One of the foundational paradoxes of the United States is that the constitutional guarantee of individual liberty was coextensive with, and even contained within itself, the social death of the captive. Framed in this way, this chapter has provided a narrative history of a contradiction still with us: institutionalized debasement amid a social preoccupation with freedom, democracy, and individual rights. The constitutional guarantee of liberty, indeed, the Enlightenment quest for liberty, coexists with premodern ideas and practices of separation, flogging, and denying humanity. Contemporary social death, in its modern avatar of the prison, emerges from several tributaries, especially the history of slavery and the subsequent subversion of democracy during Reconstruction, the imposition of the convict-lease system, and the imputation of crime to color, which we have not, even now, surmounted.

CHAPTER 6

The Birth of the Penitentiary

June 2012. Only ninety days shy of his release date, prison authorities found THC in Todd's urine consistent with marijuana use. He is punished twice for the same offense: the parole board refuses to grant him parole, citing the failed drug test, so he has to wait a minimum of two more years before he can petition for parole again. On top of that, the Department of Corrections punishes him with ninety days in the special housing unit, also known as solitary confinement. Each punishment seems harsh to me—two years for smoking a joint! Ninety days in solitary! But neither penalty is easy to appeal. Normal due process does not apply: he is punished after an administrative hearing where he has no legal representation.

He is at a prison only about an hour from home so I go to visit after I get the news. I make my way through the several sets of security gates and sally ports. Since the person I'm visiting is in the special housing unit this time, the corrections officer presiding over the enormous visiting room motions me to the other end of the room, past the dozens of families sitting at card tables enjoying their visits. Once back there, I stand ill at ease beside a series of thick doors that open to little cubby-like rooms I had never noticed before.

After about ten minutes, Todd, a small, slight man with a stoop, enters the room escorted by six guards. His hands are handcuffed behind him. No other incarcerated people enter the visiting room with handcuffs. This must be the procedure for visits with men in the special housing unit, I think to myself. Two officers—one on either side, leading him by his elbows—guide him over to the row of cubbies and uncuff him into the one nearest me. The sight of the phalanx of officers handling a prisoner makes many of the visitors uneasy. Most of the fifty or sixty people pause in their visits to watch and so the din dies down to a murmur. Suddenly I feel self-conscious. Corrections officers motion me into the cubby. Once I enter, they close and lock the door behind me. And there we are, in this

tiny visiting room, perhaps ten feet by five feet. We take each other in.
Usually Todd is carefully groomed and clean-shaven, with his prison issue
clothes creased and pressed. Today I notice that he wears a four-day beard
and looks haggard, unwashed, his hair clumped, his clothes rumpled. He's
a bit bent as he hunches over the table and looks at me, his eyes slightly
bloodshot.

"How you doin', big guy?" His voice is a little hoarse.

"I'm all right. How are you?"

"It's been crazy. You know I got ninety days in solitary and the parole
board hit me with two more years?"

Todd tells me that another prisoner offered him half a joint. Without
thinking, he smoked the joint. I commiserate with him, or try to. It's
a little hard for me to take stock of his situation. Truth be told, I am also a
little mad at him for screwing up so close to his release date. Am I blaming him unfairly? Inwardly, I try to inventory my emotions while trying
to be supportive.

We chat for a bit, catching up, and then he says, "Am I speaking too
loud?" No, why? "I haven't spoken to anyone in weeks, and it's hard to tell
how loud I'm speaking or whether I'm acting normal." His eyes grow big.
"You know, where they have me they also have a lot of the chronics . . .
they scream all day long. Can you hear the screams from here?" He listens
intently for a minute. "No, I guess not. They scream all day long. It's insane.
It's hell." (Fieldnotes, June 2010)

TO ENTER SOLITARY CONFINEMENT in the contemporary
prison is to enter into a remnant of early nineteenth-century practices of
incarceration. Absolute solitude, as French visitors Alexis de Tocqueville and
Gustave de Beaumont characterized it in the 1830s, was the United States'
first great contribution to the history of the modern penitentiary. Conditions
have changed since the beginning of the nineteenth century, of course. The
condemned in the first cells were shrouded in silence, whereas today, as Todd
commented, the noise is infernal: it is not uncommon for enraged or even
unhinged people confined in special housing to "stand at their cell gates ful-
minating . . . for hours on end" (Blake 2012).

As the use of extreme isolation has proliferated in the modern penitentiary, the language used to describe it and the stated aims of employing it have
also changed. Solitary was originally intended to redeem the soul through
quiet contemplation. Now solitary is usually a form of punishment within
the punishment that is prison, when it is not used simply to isolate problem
prisoners and hold them incommunicado.

Yet most incarcerated people in the United States live in congregate housing and work in a group setting. The intertwined stories of congregate and solitary housing in the modern prison are due not entirely to the decline of slavery, since slavery, like the convict lease system, was aimed primarily at labor exploitation and arguably sexual exploitation. Racism and sexism nevertheless played an important role in the rise of the penitentiary. So did the good intentions of religious reformers early in the republic. The contemporary prison thus offers a palimpsest of failed visions, many religious, of how to respond to the wrongdoer. They shaped state punishment in ways that have lasted until today.

EARLY PUNISHMENT AND QUAKER REFORM

Until the end of the eighteenth century, state punishment in England and its colonies often amounted to the stocks, the pillory, the ducking or cucking stool, public flogging, and transport, with frequent recourse to hanging and other forms of public execution.

Throughout their history, the Society of Friends perceived these forms of punishment to be cruel and degrading. They argued particularly against public forms of humiliation, and sought some device to substitute. They were no armchair reformers. As an oppressed religious minority, many English Quakers had suffered these punishments when they had been convicted of heresy.

In the wake of the Revolutionary War, Pennsylvania Quakers achieved sufficient political hegemony to put some of their reforms in place. They proposed an experiment: putting the condemned individual in seclusion. The designers envisioned quiet, private separation without the violence and humiliation they saw in public whippings or in the pillories. The very name of "penitentiary" marks the influence of religious reform. Since the eighteenth century, and perhaps earlier, the concept of crime had been infused with the concept of sin in the public imagination. It followed, then, that the felon should pay for crime through penitence.[1]

The Quakers founded Eastern State Penitentiary in the late 1820s. Eastern State was not the first penitentiary in the United States. New York Quakers had founded Newgate in Manhattan in 1794 and named it for the more famous prison in England. Other reformers in Philadelphia had converted Walnut Street Gaol in 1789–90 into a state prison with a separate wing to house prisoners in isolation cells.

But Eastern State was the most radical in its design and execution. The architecture embodied the religious ideal. Each person sentenced to Eastern State lived in an isolated cell designed for solitary contemplation of past misdeeds, and was subject to a spartan diet and a regime of total silence. Architect John Havilland described the cells as a "forced monastery." No newspapers were allowed in, and the prisoners were to receive no visits. To protect their identity from public disgrace, the administration assigned each person a number by which they were identified. Prisoners were conducted to and from their cells in hoods (Rothman 2005 [1971], 94–95). The conditions led the young visitor Alexis de Tocqueville and his travel companion Gustave de Beaumont to describe the Pennsylvania experiment as one of "perfect isolation" (1979 [1833]).

The organization of Eastern State signaled a sea change in penology. The key element was physical separation. Authorities took the individual out of his or her community, away from family, and placed him or her in an institution that strictly patrolled contact with the outside world. After a period of time, he or she (and both men and women were confined at Eastern State) rejoined the community with the expectation that this process has taught the individual a lesson.

Reformers framed their experiment as an enactment of symbolic death, followed by rebirth and redemption upon release. Reformer Benjamin Rush struck a romantic tone as he foresaw friends and families "running to meet [the condemned] on the day of his deliverance.—His friends and family bathe his cheeks with tears of joy; and the universal shout of the neighborhood is, our brother was lost, and is found—was dead and is alive" (cited in C. Smith 2009). Rush saw a similarity between the redemptive possibility of the penitentiary and the parable of the prodigal son (Luke 15:24 and 15:32).

Rush was not alone in likening the penitentiary to death. Other written accounts of the time from both champions and critics of the new system, including penitentiary administrators, legislative review committees, and journalists, were similarly replete with references to symbolic death, even if not in the full sense for which I am arguing in this book.

In the 1830s, Charles Dickens, an early observer (and critic), had occasion to interview women and men imprisoned at Eastern. In his *Notes on America*, a travelogue of his trip, Dickens described the prisoner of Eastern State as "a man buried alive" (2001 [1842], 241). In an oft-quoted passage, Dickens acknowledged the good intentions of the founders, but predicted the dreadful consequences.

> In its intention, I am well convinced that it is kind, humane, and meant for reformation; but I am persuaded that those who devised this system of Prison Discipline, and those benevolent gentlemen who carry it into execution, do not know what it is that they are doing. I believe that very few men are capable of estimating the immense amount of torture and agony which this dreadful punishment, prolonged for years, inflicts upon the sufferers; and in guessing at it myself, and in reasoning from what I have seen written upon their faces, and what to my certain knowledge

they feel within, I am only the more convinced that there is a depth of terrible endurance in it which none but the sufferers themselves can fathom, and which no man has a right to inflict upon his fellow-creature.

I hold this slow and daily tampering with the mysteries of the brain, to be immeasurably worse than any torture of the body: and because its ghastly signs and tokens are not so palpable to the eye and sense of touch as scars upon the flesh; because its wounds are not upon the surface, and it extorts few cries that human ears can hear; therefore I the more denounce it, as a secret punishment which slumbering humanity is not roused up to stay. (2001 [1842], 238–239)

As Dickens surmised, many people subjected to isolation soon became deranged. Tocqueville and Beaumont wrote, "This absolute solitude, if nothing interrupts it, is beyond the strength of man; it destroys the criminal without intermission and without pity; it does not reform, it kills" (1979 [1833], 41). Other prisons abandoned such extreme isolation for precisely this reason. Of one such prison, Beaumont and Tocqueville reported, "five of the [prisoners] had already succumbed during a single year; their moral state was not less alarming; one of them had become insane; another, in a fit of despair, had embraced the opportunity when the keeper brought him something, to pre-cipitate himself from his cell, running the almost certain chance of a mortal fall" (1979 [1833], 42).

Throughout the nineteenth and twentieth centuries, as the practice spread, observers continued to comment on how solitary confinement inflicts psy-chological damage (Gawande 2009; Grassian 2006; Haney 2008; Heidenreich 2011; Lewis 1965; Rhodes 2005). As early as 1890, the United States Supreme Court noted the indefensible psychic harm of solitary: "A considerable num-ber of prisoners fell after even a short confinement into a semi-fatuous con-dition from which it was next to impossible to arouse them. Others became violently insane, others still committed suicide" (*In Re Medley,* 134 U.S. 160 [1890]).

Despite the weight of over a century of criticism and the evidence this criticism has marshaled, the use of isolation has expanded. "It is both tragic and highly disturbing," writes the psychiatrist Stuart Grassian, "that the lessons of the nineteenth century experience with solitary confinement are today being so completely ignored by those responsible for addressing the housing and the mental health needs in the prison setting. For, indeed, the psychiatric harm caused by solitary confinement had become exceedingly apparent well over one hundred years ago" (2006, 329; also see Haney 2003, 2008).

The persistence of the practice, especially in the face of so much evi-dence and so much criticism, could itself serve for a fascinating portrait of the United States, its history, its people, and our collective psychology. "We as

Americans," observed Anthony Graves, "are driving other American citizens out of their minds and we act like it's okay" (2012). Little historical evidence suggests that exposing the abuses or the psychic harm will stop the practice. No advocacy, no lawsuits, nor even federal decisions seem to dent the expansion of solitary confinement.

To the contrary, the contemporary prison has multiplied exponentially the failed experiments of the Philadelphia Quakers. The contemporary United States now leads the world in the number of people it places in solitary confinement. The estimates of how many people are held daily in some form of restricted or special housing vary between 25,000 and 81,000 (Casella and Ridgeway 2012; Gibbons and Katzenbach 2006; Browne, Cambier, and Agha 2011, 2). These estimates include "special housing units" (SHU), control units, and administrative segregation. But even the larger figure may be an undercount, since it may not include people serving shorter terms in solitary, such as my friend Todd. The figure also does not take into consideration untold numbers of people held in special housing units or solitary-like conditions in local jails and detention centers, or people held in the nether space of Guantánamo and other special military installations (see Gibbons and Katzenbach 2006, 461).

In a strange throwback to the early days of Eastern State Penitentiary, these days entire penitentiaries are built on the same principles of isolation, if not the Quaker moral vision of reform (Mears 2009; J. Ross 2013). These facilities are often referred to as supermaximum prisons or "supermaxes." As of 2004, forty-four states have supermax prisons, up from thirty-four states a decade before and just one in the mid-1980s (Mears 2005, 2009).

The use of extreme isolation has proliferated, but the goal of moral and spiritual redemption has been abandoned long ago. Because of its harsh, punitive character, solitary is sometimes called "going to jail" in prison parlance. Administrators usually justify solitary as incapacitating those who pose a risk to others or to staff, as well as segregating people who are accused of being involved in gangs. Correctional authorities occasionally claim administrative segregation is a way to protect people who are at risk of harm, such as transgender people and women who have filed charges of sexual harassment against staff. Yet transgender people and women dispute this justification for solitary confinement and often regard it as in effect punishment and retaliation against prisoners who report abuse (*Cruel and Unusual* 2006; Levi and Waldman 2011; Reid 2013, 2093).

Nowadays, people in isolation are held alone in a small cell, usually for twenty-three hours a day. For exercise, they are conventionally let out one by one into what has been called a "dog run," a concrete patio three times the length of their cell with no opening to earth or vegetation. Exercise and meals are also taken in isolation, leading in many cases to an existence entirely without human contact. In extreme cases, people are held this way for as much as several decades or even for the rest of their natural life.

The effects are still as dire as they were nearly two hundred years ago. I can see the deterioration even in incarcerated people who did not suffer from mental illness before they went in. When I visited him after only a few weeks in solitary, Todd was already beginning to show signs of neurosis. William Blake, who has served over thirty years in solitary, perceives psychological decline all around him: "I've read of the studies done regarding the effects of long-term isolation in solitary confinement on inmates, seen how researchers say it can ruin a man's mind, and I've watched with my own eyes the slow descent of sane men into madness—sometimes not so slow" (Blake 2012). Though only a small percentage of the incarcerated population are held in solitary conditions at any given time, the harm is extraordinary. Yet because of prison reform in the early nineteenth century, the vast majority of people in prison today sleep, eat, work, and recreate with others.

THE AUBURN MODEL, CORPORAL PUNISHMENT, AND THE GROWTH OF THE CONGREGATE PRISON

If the Pennsylvania reformers who designed isolation cells were hopeful Quakers, it was dour and flinty New England Calvinists who designed the model of prison life that was ultimately to take hold as the norm in the United States (Duguid 2000; Stanko, Gillespie, and Crews 2004). Unlike the Quakers, who held out for a change in the soul through repentance, the New Englanders tended to believe that adult felons were incorrigible reprobates who needed to be whipped (quite literally) into compliance. They believed in discipline and hard work.

New York's Auburn Prison was founded in 1816 and is still open today. The last chapter placed its founding in the context of the racial panic spurred by the gradual abolition of slavery. Religious reformers also played an important role. Auburn's founders believed as the Quakers did that separating the condemned from the society was key. Administrators at first imitated the Philadelphia system's total isolation. They prohibited almost all visits from family or friends, and banned even the exchange of letters and other correspondence. Reading material was confined to the Bible. And just like the Quakers, they imposed a rigid regimen of silence at all times, leading many observers to liken Auburn to a living tomb.

But this proved disastrous. Some of those placed in solitary attempted suicide in the most violent ways imaginable. Impressed by the dramatically unsuccessful results, prison officials tried varying the regime. They put prisoners to work together in a factory-like setting. Tocqueville and Beaumont described the transformation in penology at Auburn: "The problem was to find the means by which the evil effect of total solitude could be avoided without giving up its advantages. It was believed that this end could be attained by leaving the convicts in their cells during night, and by making them work during the day, in the common workshops, obliging them at the same time to observe absolute silence" (Beaumont and Tocqueville 1979 [1833], 41–42). Henceforth at Auburn, men slept in separate cells at night and worked together during the day. Having inmates work together was also a more efficient and profitable way to organize labor production. Congregate labor in prison mirrored changes in labor practices taking root in the rest of the society as the United States went through the industrial revolution. The Auburn system spread throughout the country and the world after the 1840s.

Another obvious way the founders of Auburn differed from the Quakers was that they were strong advocates of flogging for any infraction. Thus the Auburn model reintroduced the physical brutality, fear, and mortification into punishment that Quakers had found so repellant. Elam Lynds, often credited with designing the Auburn system, resolutely defended his harsh policies with his pessimistic views of the possibility of rehabilitating lawbreakers: "I don't believe in reformation of an adult criminal. He's a coward, a willful lawbreaker whose spirit must be broken by the lash" (cited in Macintyre 2011, 22). Indeed, for many critics as well as advocates, the lash or cat-o'-nine-tails came to epitomize the Auburn system. Frequent use of the whip led one former inmate at Sing Sing (also founded by Lynds in the mid-1820s) to refer to the regime as a "cat-ocracy" (cited in Christiansen 1998, 125). Critics found its prevalence appalling. The Prison Association of New York reviewed the practice in the 1840s: "There is no degradation like the lash. . . . We confess that if we believed it to be indispensable, we should be prepared to abandon the whole system . . . The other improvements in our prison discipline are overshadowed, and sink into comparative insignificance, before this towering atrocity" (Prison Association of New York 1846, 138). After flogging was outlawed in the 1840s, guards still had various means of imposing corporal punishment. One technique was to place weights on the limbs of prisoners and then guards would stand on those weights. Guards also tied prisoners to wooden posts so that they could be turned upside down. One of the most infamous innovations was to fix a bowl around the head of a person and then douse him with gallons and gallons of cold water, which gathered around his head and then slowly drained out, a nineteenth-century precursor to modern waterboarding. Many who were critics of the whip had no problem with the water treatment.

In an irony not lost to all, the penitentiary, intended by the Quakers as an alternative to physical punishment, ended up multiplying geometrically the opportunity to flog the convicted. Before the founding of the penitentiary, the condemned was whipped (or placed in the stocks, the pillory, and so forth) for a discrete, relatively brief moment in time, and then he or she was released. With the Auburn model, staff had the opportunity to visit physical punishment on the convict's body repeatedly over the course of months or years. This practice was also a means of imposing labor discipline, whether in Sing Sing's stone quarries or in Auburn's factory. The violence impressed on the person his or her status as prisoner, but it was also a mechanism to maximize the captive worker's productivity.

Other practices the Quaker reform sought to abolish crept back into use in the Auburn Penitentiary. For example, Auburn prisoners were displayed to paying tourists. This kind of public humiliation was anathema to the Quakers, who sought to protect people's anonymity and privacy. The pedagogy of prison was thus both implicit and explicit: they were removed from the society, cast out, and forced to endure a cruel combination of boredom, isolation, corporal punishment, occasional public display, and forced labor.

One similarity between the Philadelphia and Auburn models, however, was that the administration saw incarceration as a temporary death. In a metaphor that has become commonplace, Gershom Powers, a former warden, recalled that he addressed reprovingly each new prisoner, "You are to be literally buried from the world" (Powers 1829, 14). "Instead of forfeiting your life on an ignominious gallows, as would have been the case under most other governments, you are only restrained for a time" (Powers 1829, 13; also cited in Lewis 1965, 114–115). Through industry, right action, and good works, the dead could be redeemed and brought back to life. The warden rehearsed some of the same language and biblical imagery as Benjamin Rush: "If you will but faithfully improve the opportunities with which you will be thus favored your case is far from being hopeless; friends and society will receive you again with open arms and, like the compassionate father to his prodigal son, will say to you, 'he was dead, and is alive again; and was lost, and is found'" (Powers 1829, 14).

The parable of the prodigal son encapsulates the essential similarity between the Pennsylvania and the Auburn paradigms. Founders of each prison had reason to evoke the idea of separation and repentant return as an allegory to describe their respective models of correction and redemption. Though the relative benefits and harms of each approach were debated for decades (indeed, until the present), they differed surprisingly little in practice, as David Rothman has pointed out (2005 [1971], 109).

The importance of religious movements also should not be exaggerated. Significant changes to the prison, though accompanied by moral argument, were often due more to requirements of capital, to racial animus, and sexist thinking (as we shall see). As I suggested above, the ascension of the brutal Auburn congregate system over the Pennsylvania system of isolation can be attributed in large part to the need for labor practices that resembled the factory floor more than the cottage-style production that emerged from the individual cells in Philadelphia.

As the Auburn model took over from North to South, the goal, the irreducible condition, the constant, was to force incarcerated people to labor and to try and extract a profit out of them. The northern penitentiary had this in common with the later privatization of convict labor in the convict lease system in the American South (see Lichtenstein 1996; Rothman 2005 [1971]). Under the convict lease system in the South, as we saw in the previous chapter, states leased bodies wholesale, allowing lessees to set many of the conditions, including work discipline, food, living quarters, and so on. Prison administrators and state legislatures in northern states tried a range of more regulated means, allowing piecework in prison, for example. On occasion, entrepreneurs were allowed inside the prison shop, but under strict conditions not to speak with prisoners. Already in the first years of Sing Sing, one man imprisoned there complained that the institution was "a monstrous individual speculating, money-making prison, where these very contractors are pocketing the hard earnings of the convicts" (cited in Christiansen 1998).

WOMEN IN PRISONS BUILT FOR MEN

Early Quakers were also responsible for the binary system of gender that structures the penitentiary system. In 1827, Elizabeth Fry, an English Quaker, set off debate on both sides of the Atlantic when she published a scathing report denouncing the conditions she found in London's Newgate Prison. Her *Observations on the Visiting, Superintendence, and Government of Female Prisoners* ignited a campaign that led to significant prison transformation for both men and women. Fry's campaign for better conditions for incarcerated women included a demand for separate facilities for women. Influenced in part by Fry's campaign, the Philadelphia reformers designed a prison where women were placed in cells separate from but identical to men's.

Under the Auburn model, women generally faced a fate different from, and perhaps more terrible, than the men. Early on in New York's Auburn Prison, prison administrators placed women in a large common garret. Women were rarely let out and were forced to endure boredom and idleness, often for years at a time. Screams, cries, and shouts wafted down to the rest of the prison. Incarcerated women suffered malign neglect.

The contact among the women clearly went against Auburn's overall philosophy. In the words of one historian, women were given "little separation [from each other], no supervision, and few opportunities to labor," precisely the opposite of the characteristics that identify the Auburn model in its peno-logical approach to men (Rafter 1985, 234). They were treated as a residuum: Auburn was designed for men. "To be a male convict," the Auburn prison chaplain observed, "would be quite tolerable; but to be a female convict, for any protracted period, would be worse than death" (cited in Lewis 1965, 164).

Generally speaking, guards appeared only to bring food and take away refuse; evidence also emerged with time that staff abused their access by sexu-ally assaulting the women. One of the first scandals at Auburn involved an incarcerated woman. In January 1826, a prison guard severely flogged Rachel Welch, an Irish immigrant, while she was pregnant. She had become pregnant while incarcerated, probably by a jailer, possibly by the warden, Elam Lynds. Although she was able to bring her pregnancy to term, she died shortly after giving birth. One of the attending physicians attributed her death in part to the earlier flogging (Lewis 1965, 94). The ensuing public outcry brought wider attention to physical and sexual abuse in prison and supported the sus-picion that women were subjected to widespread mistreatment.

Due in part to the uproar in the wake of Rachel Welch's death and a gen-eral public dissatisfaction with the conditions at Auburn, reformers once again strove to come up with a better solution. Through their efforts, the oddly named Mount Pleasant Prison Annex for women was founded in 1839. It was a custodial facility separate from, though adjacent and administratively linked to, the new prison at Sing Sing. As part of the reform, women were hired as matrons. Administrators initially applied the same principles of discipline, work, and silence, enforced by the lash at any hint of insubordination. The reform was from leaving women to languish in isolated quarters to treating the women the same as the men.

But this model was forced to contend with new waves of reform-minded, largely middle-class white women who eschewed the idea that prisons should emphasize corporal punishment to enforce silence and submission to author-ity. These women championed instead an ideology of redemption. Their cru-sades only had spotty success at first; it was only after the 1870s that the movement resulted in a proliferation of reformatories throughout the country as many states began to incarcerate women on a relatively large scale (Dodge 2002; Freedman 1984).

These new reformatories were dedicated more to "saving" putatively "fallen" women rather than whipping them into total capitulation. They were based on the model of a domestic setting. The structures were often called "cottages." Where men might be paddled or beaten at a reformatory, prison matrons could send women to their room without supper. The infantilization was deliberate (Flynn 1963, 44–45; Freedman 1984; Rafter 1985, 237). Implic-itly or explicitly, the goal was to train women in feminine domestic enterprise (sewing, cooking, cleaning, and so forth) and to socialize them into docility (Dodge 2002).

The 1870s thus saw the emergence of a dual, stratified system for incarcerating women. Women sentenced to the reformatories were disproportionately white. This is because the white reformers tended to see women of color as beyond saving. Women convicted of more serious felonies and women of color were still sent to special sections of larger penitentiaries that were predominantly male. Then as now, the criminal justice system tended to view women of color as both less feminine and more incorrigible than white women (Rafter 1985, 241–242; Richie 1996).

Under slavery, owners disciplined the enslaved, although the constabulary and the night patrols also provided policing and enforcement functions, and could be called upon to whip or detain slaves. In the American South, after manumission and the subsequent defeat of Reconstruction, African American women were often put on gangs with men under the convict lease system (see previous chapter; Curtin 2000). This forced them into situations of vulnerability to sexual assault and other kinds of mistreatment, not to mention public humiliation and separation from networks of support (I discussed this at greater length in the previous chapter).

CONCLUSION

Embodied in the contemporary prison is a set of contradictions that have plagued the institution since its beginnings. From an institution intended for moral and spiritual uplift, based on a monastic ideal, the prison became a site of degradation and debasement. From a reform intended as an alternative to physical abuse, it became the site of mental and bodily torture. From an institution that intended to preserve the dignity of its charges, it became an institution used to break people. Though the Quakers intended to preserve prisoners' privacy by designating each with a number, the penitentiary has become a modern symbol par excellence of dehumanization precisely through reducing human beings to numbers.

These contradictions can be accounted for by seeing in the contemporary penitentiary "a graveyard of abandoned fads" (Martinson 1976). Not all fads have been buried. Quaker doctrine taught that the penitent should look within herself or himself. The corresponding penological theory held that the criminal must contemplate his or her past actions for the good of the soul. The Calvinist philosophy of predetermination tended to see criminals as irredeemable. Both paradigms, essentially religious conceptions of the soul and whether a sinner can be reformed, are still with us. Some contemporary criminal justice approaches see the criminal as capable of rehabilitation. Neoconservative theories see the criminal as predator, even superpredator, and incapable of rehabilitation (e.g., Bennett, DiIulio, and Walters 1996).

As the history of the Pennsylvania system and the Auburn system demonstrates, psychic and physical violence has been intrinsic to the environment of the prison from its beginnings through the present day. Once prisons began experimenting with solitary confinement and corporal punishment to enforce discipline, a veritable Pandora's box was opened. The effects are still felt. If the Pennsylvania mode of organization bequeathed the special housing unit, administrative segregation, and the supermax, then arguably the Auburn model has given us the prison factory, prison discipline enforced by guards armed with nightsticks, as well as more modern devices of subduing prisoners, such as pepper spray and the Taser. The idea that the criminally minded are incapable of reform is used to justify "three strikes" laws and sentencing people to life without parole, as well as other punitive sentences predicated on incapacitating people for long periods rather than rehabilitating them.

In his famous account of the history of the penitentiary, Michel Foucault saw the movement from public torture to the Panopticon as the consolidation of power (1995 [1975]). While not contradicting Foucault's account, I have emphasized instead that still with us are many of the premodern practices the penitentiary was intended to displace, including physical brutality, torture, humiliation, execution, and displays of the overwhelming power of the state on the body of the condemned.

Foucault, moreover, paid no attention to race and gender. We are missing something fundamental in our understanding and analysis of the modern prison if we do not analyze the specific historical conditions in the United States, including gender oppression and racial stigma, as well as the role of religious reform movements and industrialization.

Successive waves of feminist and women of color historians have contributed to integrated histories of race and gender in the prison system. Feminists, especially feminists of color, have argued that women have been incarcerated in smaller numbers because insubordinate women were historically either disciplined in the home or put in insane asylums (see A. Davis 2003; Freedman 1984, 10). In this view, the prison has been for women a public punishment to supplement the private punishment of the home (Bhavnani and Davis 2000; also see A. Davis 2003).

As the beating and subsequent death in 1826 of the pregnant Rachel Welch demonstrates, the link between physical and psychological abuse of prisoners, sexual abuse, and reproductive justice has also been there since the beginning (see Freedman 1984; B. Smith 2003, B. Smith 2005). Threats to women's reproductive freedom have continued through the present, as the examples in chapter 2 demonstrate. The recent revelations of improper permission procedures in the sterilization of incarcerated women in California I mentioned in that chapter (Howle 2014; McGreevy and Willon 2013) are just a glaring contemporary example of these attempts to control the reproductive freedom of poor women and women of color. The dehumanization and the sexualization are tied.

The violence these practices embody is not hidden (Galtung 1969; Scheper-Hughes and Bourgois 2004). Critics and reformers have exposed conditions and argued against them over and over since the early nineteenth century. Taking stock of that history, one is led to conclude that denouncing prison practices has little practical consequence.

PART III

Abolition Democracy

CHAPTER 7

"Doesn't Everyone Know
Someone in Prison or on Parole?"

"DOESN'T EVERYONE KNOW SOMEONE in prison or on parole?" We are at a community meeting in the NAACP offices in Binghamton, New York. It's 2006. Four of us had organized these meetings, sensing rising community outrage over the conduct of the local parole officers. We have been meeting for months.

People speak up around the room, angrily protesting that the parole officers are overstepping boundaries. They share stories of parole officers following and stopping them arbitrarily. One says her parole officer tries to trip her up intentionally, misleads her, and bullies her. Many feel driven to desperation or despair. They feel harassed. They are all on edge.

Their worry is borne out by statistics. According to the Bureau of Justice Statistics, most people released from prison are released on parole. Of these, 68 percent are rearrested within three years (Langan and Levin 2002).[1] Distant statistics, however, do not capture the experience of being subject to the arbitrary tyrannies and caprices of parole agents unaccountable to the public or to the courts. Parole officers can send people back to prison for even minor violations of their conditions of parole, violations that do not in every case even amount to illegal activity.

As far as I know, this is the first organizing effort aimed at defending the rights of people on parole and their families against a parole office. While organizations exist to advocate for parole release, rarely do community organizing efforts focus on the abuses and excesses of parole officers who monitor people back at home in their communities. Parents and partners are the most outspoken. Things seem to be getting worse. They are definitely heating up.

After meeting for a few weeks, we had decided to organize a petition drive to express community frustration with our parole office's practices. We believed they were trying gratuitously to ensnare and torment people on parole and their families. Our petition, gathered over several weeks, netted over five hundred signatures, which in this small town was enough to land a write-up in the local newspaper. Local politicians started returning our phone calls and setting up meetings. More people started attending our meetings or contacting us with their stories of harassment. In the following months, we interviewed about two dozen people on parole and their families. Now we are writing up a list of demands. (See appendix to this chapter.)

At these weekly meetings, people tell their stories. "Parole officers act like cowboys," says one woman. "Sometimes they go around in groups of four, five, six, and they lie in wait for people." The attitude of the parole officers suggests they view their job as a blood sport (Simon 2001): they ride around and try to catch a person on parole having a drink, or leaving a bar, or in the company of another convicted felon. They make surprise night visits to people's homes, sometimes at two or three in the morning, rousing whole families who must wait in their own home while the parole officers conduct their searches and question family members. Parole officers stop and frisk people in the street, force them to take off outer garments, and oblige them to undergo spontaneous sobriety tests wherever they are. This humiliates them in front of friends and family members, as well as any stranger passing by.

At the meeting, an older interracial couple whose son is on parole complains that parole officers searched through their belongings during a home visit, even though it is their son who is on parole. The parole officer made lewd comments and asked them several times, "Are you really married?" Pawing through a shelf of the woman's undergarments, he taunted them by asking, "Do you do anything kinky?" The wife wonders aloud whether the officer was bothered because they are a mixed-race couple.

A blonde white woman in her early twenties backs up the older couple. Her husband is African American, and he is on parole, but she is not. She tells us that her husband's parole officer nevertheless trailed after her in his car—she used the verb "stalked"—and showed up unannounced at her place of work, seized her cell phone, and rifled through its numbers. His monitoring of her movements as an officer seems to meld together with the creepiness of a male stalker. She is terrified, but she is also terrified of speaking up. She is worried the parole officer will mistreat her husband, since he has already sent her husband back to prison once before. Is this racist sexism? Or just sexism? Sometimes the confluence of different oppressive structures functions through ambiguity.

"Of course, this has nothing to do with racism." The speaker is a huge, older white man, and he looks like a Hell's Angels biker, with a bald head, a bushy beard, tattoos on broad, folded forearms, and a black leather vest. He occupies a lot of space at the table. He hadn't said a word until this point and his voice resonates throughout the room. People fall silent. An African

American woman sitting near me, bouncing a baby on her lap, shoots the man a sharp glance. Then she notices he is speaking ironically and she chortles. The man is acknowledging that racism is self-evidently operating, even while he is sardonically remarking on the usual tendency to deny racism. The man tells a chilling story.

A few years earlier, the man's son, petrified when his parole officer repeatedly threatened to reimprison him, went into hiding. A massive manhunt ensued for the young man, now a fugitive since he absconded. When they found him, police killed him in a violent confrontation when he resisted arrest. At the meeting, the father blamed the death on the parole office. The parole office needled his son constantly until the boy broke. The son couldn't take the prospect of going back to prison. A short silence follows his account.

Then others speak up, people similarly pushed to the edge. An older man says his daughter died recently in jail while he, the father, was in the penitentiary. Now that he is out on parole, he finds his parole officer constantly jibes and taunts him about his daughter's death, which he finds intolerable. "All I want is a fair shake for my son," says a man whose son suffers mental illness. A woman pipes up, "He's been violated for drinking. I mean, he was drinking, and he's not supposed to drink. But hell, he's an alcoholic. How do you punish somebody for having a disease? So it's just a total blank thing that nobody on parole drinks. Now, you're not even dealing with the illness that he has." Another woman says her parole officer told people in her building she is on parole, needlessly trying to embarrass her in front of all her neighbors. Her neighbors do not need to know she is on parole, she protests to us. Others nod sympathetically.

As I listen, I recall all the messages I have received at work. After the newspaper article, I got a ton of mail. People continue to call or send me letters, sometimes anonymously. A man left a long message on my phone to tell me that his parole officer shows up at his job, tells other employees and the boss he is on parole, and tries to get him fired. People say they are sick of living in a state of apprehension. Since they do not want to come forward or come to our meetings, I am reminded of the necessity of reckoning with an atmosphere of fear while we are doing our organizing.

As our meeting continues, a middle-aged woman, transplanted from the South, tells us how not just she but her children as well are afraid because her parole officer constantly tells her that he is going to send her back to the penitentiary. "My children get nervous the night before I go in for a meeting with my parole officer. They can't eat. They are always worried I'll go in through that door and not come out again."

(As she feared, her parole officer sends her back to prison a few months later for failing a drug test. She gets word to me through other people that she's incarcerated and I go up and visit her. She's surprisingly upbeat and conversational, though once we begin to talk I see how frustrated she is. She tells me of other women in lockup that I know, most of them imprisoned for dirty urine or minor possession. In one case, she expresses concern for a woman we both know, an older woman in particularly poor health. "We have to tell her that she has to get out of bed in the morning or else she won't make it. She signed up for boot camp," which will mean early release if she gets through it successfully, "but Josh, she doesn't have what it takes. I know, I've been through it, and she's not going to make it.")

A List of Demands for the Office of Parole

At the meeting, we now move on to writing up our demands. As we figure out how to formulate the list, a lot of our discussion revolves around how the parole officers force family members to separate from one another, and more generally the mistreatment family members suffer when a loved one is on parole. For example, our final list of demands includes:

- No mistreatment of the family. The family is not on parole.
- No racist or sexual comments to people on parole or their families.
- Family members who are on parole or who have been convicted of crimes should be allowed to associate and live together.[2]

This last demand alludes to the general "no-fraternization" rule that forbids people on parole from associating with other convicted felons. Parole officers often interpret this to include family members. Consequently, the parole office sometimes separates spouses, as well as parents and children, even if their crimes are not linked or are decades old. These rules force a wedge in families.

The no-fraternization rule also poses a fundamental problem for our organizing efforts. Although we are merely exercising our First Amendment right to assemble, people on parole could theoretically be charged with fraternizing by coming to one of our meetings since they are coming into contact with other people convicted of crimes. We are constantly worried that the parole office will get wind of a meeting time. They could station officers outside the NAACP offices and arrest people as they exit. Reasonable fear or preposterous overreaction? People are taking tremendous risks in coming to our meetings, particularly because some parole officers have shown themselves to be vindictive.

At some point in the meeting, I hear Tina call out in her booming voice. "Doesn't everyone know someone in prison or on parole?" The tone suggests the question is rhetorical. I know where she is coming from. For Tina, the parole office is a fixture of daily life. For legions of people like her, it has been that way for generations. Their kin, running buddies, childhood friends, and offspring share the entanglements with police, local judges, fines, court dates, prison visits, parole, custody, county jail lockup. For them, prisons and parole may seem inescapable. The criminal justice system encroaches on all spheres of life. Prison and parole touches everyone they know.

Yet I don't know if she means to exaggerate or if she's carried away with the moment. Does she really think that everyone knows someone in prison? Kara, a student of mine sitting across from me, steals a look at me and titters. I know what she is thinking. She does not know anyone in prison or on parole, and probably most of her friends and family don't either. Kara is a young white woman from Long Island who wants to go to law school. This is the second semester she has interned for me. From her point of view, she sees Tina's world as circumscribed, as provincial, and perhaps she sees Tina as a bit crude. Kara still feels a bit out of place here. Hence the snigger, the nervous reaction.

Tina, for her part, is no fool; she usually has a pretty good handle on the students. Because of her experience and acuity, I've asked her to help me oversee the research and act as field supervisor for some of these students. She screens the questions they ask, and helps ensure their safety, as well as the safety and anonymity of the families and the people on parole.

Generally speaking, she sees these students, as I sometimes do, as hopelessly naïve, well-meaning but lost, green, and provincial in their own way. She could be excused for having this impression of the students. After a couple of students accompany her on visits to conduct interviews, she comments, much to my surprise, that she is somewhat scandalized by how poor their writing is. I had thought they would help with recording the interviews. But because most of them are so inexperienced, they are often not sure what to record or write down. Smart, capable, and emotionally present, she is a woman who has lived her entire life in poverty and has known hunger. She is also acutely sensitive to any hint of condescension.

For Kara, as with many of the students, working with me is an excursion into a different America. For these students, the prison had been a marginal thing, on the outskirts of their imagination. The specter of the prison, the prospect of coming into contact with bars and actual prisoners, is bracing. Kara is beginning to reckon with her preconceptions about crime and danger.

Other students have lived their lives in this reality, or in a similar one, and so the predations of the prison are familiar. A handful of students over the years have told me, usually in private, that they have been incarcerated. Far more have told me, also in confidence, that they have had siblings incarcerated, or a parent who has been to prison or is in prison still. As they study incarceration with me as students, the criminal justice system takes on a new significance. They contemplate new frameworks for understanding their own experiences and that of their families. They are sometimes forced to reckon with their previous ideas of blame, responsibility, and life possibilities.

The gap between Kara and Tina could be said to structure their relationship. How could it not? One is a working-class white woman whose social network, and social horizon, involves people bouncing in and out of incarceration; the other, a young white student from Long Island, may not even be able to imagine such a thing. How could it not fail to color their experiences as they go up to the jail? Their differential life experiences must affect what each finds to be plausible or implausible, what is outrageous or normal.

CONCLUSION

During her internship, my student Kara met weekly for months with an incarcerated man who was desperate for a prosthetic limb that jail administrators had confiscated at the time of his admission, since it contained metal rods. She diligently filed fax after fax to different agencies, businesses, and organizations to track down his prescription and then arranged for a charitable donation so the man could get a new one. The man wrote me later and commended Kara for her persistence.

A lot of prison activists focus on dismantling the prison, reducing the population in prison, or reforming prison conditions. This work is important, urgent, and necessary. Yet the split between Tina and Kara exemplifies a massive divide in the society that goes beyond the prison (Santos 2014). This crucial fracture in our society must also be addressed.

The prison is embedded within a range of other institutions such as the parole office and child protective services, and social structures like racism and poverty. In order to overcome the significant split between Tina and Kara, one must put the prison in the context of these other institutions and structures in an unequal, deeply divided society. Otherwise, one cannot see fully the breach between people who live in terror, instability, and crisis, and those who live out some version of the freedom promised by American liberalism.

One way to highlight this divide is by focusing on the strange social death people suffer even after they are released. The formerly incarcerated do not generally gain or regain their civil and social status as full citizens. Rather, they are relegated, often permanently, to the status of despised and excluded subordinate, contemplated by the rest of the society with suspicion and hostility, and forced to live a life grounded in an uncertain, unstable future. This seals rather than undoes their marginalization.

In bringing people together who would otherwise never meet—or meet only in a situation of mutual suspicion—the coalition work shows that the abyssal divide is not inevitable. The divide can be bridged, despite institutions and organizations such as the local parole office, whose rules, policies, and practices pose obstacles to organizing. Fatalism, fear, isolation, and a sense of hopelessness well up as additional barriers.

In this chapter I have touched briefly on some of the harm that prison and parole visits on families and what at least one community has tried to do to address that harm. In the next chapter, "Spirit Murder," I zero in on the precarious position of the formerly incarcerated themselves.

APPENDIX: LIST OF DEMANDS
FOR PAROLE OFFICE

Dear [State] Assemblywoman [Donna] Lupardo,
The Broome Working Group on Parole Violations is an ad hoc committee of concerned community members.

We have been meeting weekly since February 2006. We first organized a petition drive to express community outrage with the treatment of people on parole. In the following months, we interviewed many people on parole and family members of people on parole.

Based on our discussions, we have prepared the following list of recommendations regarding policies and procedures for the Broome County Parole Office. We would like a written response from the Office of Parole and from your office. We would also need a mechanism to insure continued compliance.

We appreciate your continued interest and involvement in this matter.

1. People on parole should have the right to bring a witness or to tape record their meetings with their parole officer.

2. People on parole should be treated with respect by parole officers.

3. No mistreatment of the family. The family is not on parole.

4. No threats.

5. Mutual respect.

6. Parole officers should follow official procedure for pulling over motor vehicles.

7. We would like parole officers to facilitate successful transition in all spheres. In particular, there should be real assistance with housing, education, mental and medical health care, and employment.

8. No illegal searches. Search limited to the personal living area of the person on parole.

9. Parole officers should be required to get approval in writing from the bureau chief prior to their intruding into the home, work, or school of someone on parole. A record of that approval should be kept and be available to the person on parole.

10. Parole officers should not be permitted to interview or visit with family members of people on parole in public places such as work, school, etc.

11. Neighbors should not be notified without cause that a person is on parole.

12. Home visits should not be done in such a way to bring public attention or humiliate the families.

13. No racist or sexual comments to people on parole or their families.

14. People on parole should be provided with reasonable opportunities to comply with parole requirements, e.g., substance abuse treatment, appointments for housing, jobs, etc.

15. Every time a parole officer has to come into a home, visit work or school, he or she should write a report, just as police officers have to do. That report should be available to the person on parole.

16. Home visits should be at reasonable hours (i.e., not in the early morning hours when families and children are asleep).

17. Curfews should be non-punitive, non-arbitrary, and need to be signed off on by the bureau chief. The curfew hours should accommodate employment, family, and educational circumstances and needs.

18. Family members who are on parole or who have been convicted of crimes should be allowed to associate and live together.

19. If contraband is found in a home that has been approved, this should not automatically be attributed to the person on parole, especially if the person is living with others and/or if the contraband is not in the area controlled by the person on parole.

Based on our interviews, we believe that all these points above are breached, violated, or disregarded by the parole office.

We would like an independent review of parolee violations over the past two years to determine whether they indeed meet the test that the people were in violation "in an important respect" as per regulation.

We are still interested in obtaining a copy of the parole officers' manual through your office.

We look forward to your response.

Thank you for your attention.

Sincerely,

The Broome County Working Group on Parole Violations

CHAPTER 8

Spirit Murder

REENTRY, DISPOSSESSION,
AND ENDURING STIGMA

Q: If you go to the social worker and say I'm about to be
released in *x* amount of days, and I don't have a place to go,
no money to get food or clothing . . . ?

A: They tell you to go to the Y[WCA] and to the VOA [Vol-
unteers of America]. And if them are crowded, you fucked.
And if you go to the Welfare, you know you got to be waiting
forty-five days. That's just like telling them to go back out
there and do what they got to do. Steal, sell drugs, or whatever. (Interview with a formerly incarcerated woman, 2011)

Never think or believe once you've paid your debt to society. There's no such thing. You're not a part of society no
more. Never think you're part of society. You're an outcast.
(Interview with a formerly incarcerated man, 2013)

And I can understand them wanting a criminal check, but,
OK, after they do the criminal check, what's the problem
with getting an apartment? . . . And they don't understand.
It's hard. People of color and disabled people go through a
lot of stuff. Yes, they do. (Interview with a formerly incarcerated woman, 2010)

FORMERLY INCARCERATED PEOPLE are banned beings. They
live as the resident excluded, second-class citizens in a society that denies it
has a hierarchy in citizenship (also see Agamben 1998, 18; Espiritu 2003). The
condition is permanent, or nearly permanent. In the worst cases, the sum of
a person's life, her trustworthiness, her worth as a human being, and, alas, her
future prospects are reducible to the criminal act for which she was originally

convicted. "You are what you have done," says one man. Time is oddly col-
lapsed; the original criminal conviction still defines the person, years, even
decades afterward. "I did my crime thirty years ago, but it might as well have
been yesterday," a man convicted of a capital crime tells me.

The society treats a person who has been to prison as a failure, a security
risk, a thief, and a liar (Barrios and Brotherton 2009). "They don't believe you.
Automatically they don't believe you. . . . Then they going to prejudge you.
So, yes, there's discrimination and you're an outcast" (Fieldnotes, 2011). She
(or he) is distrusted, regarded as unpredictable, lacking self-control, a potential
menace, and so on. He (or she) is called dehumanizing names that reduces
him to his crime—felon, con or ex-con, offender or ex-offender (Ellis 2013).
A person with a felony conviction provokes uneasiness in others when he or
she does not provoke outright fear, contempt, anger, repulsion, and vengeance.

These qualities are not really attributes of a person like hair or eye color. They
are stigmas that operate more as gerunds rather than as actual traits: the dominant
group is stigmatizing the subordinate group. What may appear as a characteristic of
the stigmatized person in fact signals social relationships of distrust.

The distrust, rationalized by ascribing these antisocial qualities or characteristics to the formerly incarcerated, provides a rationale for treating them
poorly. The attributes and the strong reactions they prompt are used to justify
legal exclusion from benefits and privileges enjoyed by full citizens. At the
same time, the legal disenfranchisement engenders, legitimizes, and promotes
social exclusion, discrimination, and dehumanization. Thus, the psychological,
cultural, and sociological dimensions reinforce the institutional, bureaucratic,
and legal dimensions, and vice-versa. The circular loop is at times self-fulfilling,
since when they are treated as if they had these ominous qualities, the chances
they will succeed are reduced (see Goffman 1963). Other times, I suspect that
the stigma of incarceration serves as a useful cover or alibi to discriminate
against people on other grounds, such as on the basis of race.

To undergo this degree of social exclusion is to experience spirit murder.
Spirit murder is "the disregard for others whose lives qualitatively depend on
our regard," as Patricia Williams puts it (1991, 73). If prison is an induction
into violence, humiliation, and natal alienation, then spirit murder is an ongoing social ban (Martha Fineman, personal communication).

Although many who have been made socially dead receive significant
support from loved ones and others, this is by no means true for all. Social
death involves rupturing precisely those ties to people who might otherwise
accompany and support the formerly incarcerated. To make matters worse,
the stigma of incarceration attaches itself not only to the formerly incarcerated person but also to his or her family, albeit in a more limited, residual
form. Beyond the institutional barriers to maintaining family relationships, the

shame of having a family member incarcerated leads many families to distance themselves from their incarcerated relative. Social science literature and well-meaning (and even otherwise effective) community organizations sometimes reinforce the stigma suffered by family members when, for example, they refer to children of the incarcerated as at-risk, since that label can itself can be stigmatizing.

Exclusion and discrimination in housing, employment, and education contradict the commonsense notion that people are given a second chance. The discrimination also belies the image of the government as offering shelter to vulnerable people, at least to this class of people. Indeed, not only does the law abandon the formerly incarcerated, in significant respects it brings about spirit murder, gives it form and legitimacy, creates the shadowy status of social death as an unequivocal social fact.

RESTRICTED FREEDOM

Freedom for the formerly incarcerated is appallingly limited. Plainly, a person who is released has regained some elements of personal freedom. She is no longer caged; she does not have to follow the schedule of movement, sleep, interaction, and solitude prescribed by prison administration. Still, she is dispossessed of an enormous number of liberties and rights basic to any robust account of autonomy. She has lost, or not regained, or perhaps never been given basic sovereign and civic freedoms.

Voting rights is still the most potent symbol of citizenship and full civic participation in the United States. In eleven states, people convicted of a felony may be barred for life. In twenty-four additional states, people cannot vote until they are discharged from parole. In some states, this has meant that one of every eight African American men is disenfranchised. Since the number of disenfranchised voters is much denser in some zip codes (in poor neighborhoods in urban centers, for example), the disenfranchisement rule in effect makes these areas less powerful in electoral politics, a condition King and Mauer (2004) call "voter dilution." Beyond its direct consequence in abridging civic participation, voter disenfranchisement has a profound symbolic influence on a person's sense of place in the society. "Without a vote, a voice, I am a ghost inhabiting a citizen's space . . . I want to walk calmly into a polling place with other citizens, to carry my placid ballot into the booth, check off my choices, then drop my conscience in the common box" (Joe Loya, cited in Fellner and Mauer 1998). The United States leads the world in disenfranchising people convicted of felonies (Fellner and Mauer 1998). Some countries simply do not disenfranchise people in prison or on parole.

But voter restriction and disenfranchisement is just the tip of the iceberg. Most of the other restrictions on civic freedom are imposed as conditions of parole. About 80 percent of people who are released each year are subject to parole conditions (Hughes and Wilson 2014). In some cases, they will be on parole for life.

People on parole must submit to a curfew, sometimes as early as seven P.M. Some are obligated to wear a GPS monitor. They must keep the parole office informed of their address and place of work. Their freedom of movement is restricted: they are not allowed to go outside of the county to which they are paroled without written permission from the parole office. In many cases, people on parole are not allowed to drink or to enter a bar or pub. They must not be in the presence of drug paraphernalia. They are subject to frequent drug testing. They are not allowed to own or have weapons, including knives. Individual parole officers set additional conditions, with the consequence that rules may be arbitrary, unevenly applied, and subject to sudden change. Officers may require a person to attend substance abuse treatment, anger management classes, or psychiatric therapy, often every day.

These conditions do not just exist in theory—they are restrictions that are fully enforced, as we saw in the last chapter. A parole officer revoked the parole of a pregnant woman I know for arriving late to a meeting with housing officers. Officers revoked the parole of a man I know when they accosted him and his wife in Syracuse, an hour north of Binghamton. He was outside the county to which he had been paroled. He and his wife were made to alight from the car at gunpoint and he was taken off to jail. In these cases, they are not accorded due process. Parole officers can be capricious.

> One time they violated him for dirty urine. But it wasn't, because I know. Because it wasn't his urine. It wasn't. I'm not going to tell you how it wasn't, but it wasn't even his urine. And the person it belonged to doesn't even do an aspirin. He was violated for a dirty urine, and it came back "alcohol." You tell me. So, twice he's been violated and had to go in [to prison] and we cheated. (Fieldnotes, 2008)

As this woman indicates, people on parole and their families are hardly passive in this process. They resist individually and collectively, sometimes by organizing (as in our local effort I discussed in the last chapter) and sometimes through individual acts of dissemblance or sabotage (Kelley 1994; Scott 1992). But, as this woman points out, cheating is a two-way street: How did the urine test come back dirty if the couple cheated by submitting clean urine?

Parole restrictions are so numerous, and the discretion of the officer so great, that a parole officer, if he or she is eager, has no end of opportunities to send a person back to prison. "Parole is a system set up to find failure," commented Michael Jacobson, former president of the Vera Institute of Justice in New York and former chief of corrections and probation for the city. "If what you're interested in is finding failure and putting people back in prison, it's like shooting fish in a barrel" (cited in Eckholm 2008). Criminologist Beth Richie interviewed a woman who echoes Jacobson in her textured sense of what she also terms a set-up for failure:

> I start my day running to drop my urine [drug testing]. Then I go to see my children, show up for my training program, look for a job, go to a meeting [Alcoholics Anonymous] and show up at my part-time job. I have to take the bus everywhere, sometimes eight buses for four hours a day. I don't have the proper outer clothes, I don't have money to buy lunch along the way, and everyone who works with me keeps me waiting so that I am late to my next appointment. If I fail any one of these things and my PO [parole officer] finds out, I am revoked. I am so tired that I sometimes fall asleep on my way home from work at 2 A.M. and that's dangerous where I live. And then the next day I have to start all over again. I don't mind being busy and working hard . . . that's part of my recovery. But this is a situation that is setting me up to fail. I just can't keep up and I don't know where to start. I want my kids, I need place to stay, I have to have a job, meetings keep me clean, and I am required to be in job training. (cited in Richie 2001, 380–381)

INSTITUTIONAL AND STRUCTURAL VIOLENCE AGAINST WOMEN

People with drug convictions face a lifetime bar on food stamps, denial of federal financial aid for higher education, and exclusion from public housing. In legislation that has been upheld by the courts, these housing restrictions result in rendering literally millions of people ineligible for public housing (Allard 2006, 158). As I mentioned in chapter 2, the Federal Adoption and Safe Families Act of 1997 makes it easier for incarcerated parents to lose parental rights and prevents people convicted of drug crimes from becoming adoptive or foster parents (Lee, Genty, and Laver 2010).

Patricia Allard (2006) has demonstrated that the food stamp ban disparately affects women, especially women of color. The bar on federal housing for women convicted of drug crimes makes their housing choices tightly restricted. People we interviewed confirm this.

A: My niece, when she was up here, she had to deal with the [name of a local homeless shelter]. Now, how is she going to go up there with a brand-new baby? Would you take your brand-new baby up there? The only reason she got early release is because she had that brand-new baby in [the county jail], early, for real. She went to my cousin's house. They wouldn't let her come and live in here [public housing].

Q: Because of her criminal record?
A: That's right.
Q: How come they let you live here?
A: Because I had a . . .
A: A misdemeanor?
A: A misdemeanor. I had to fight to get back in here. I've been up here three, going on four years.
Q: And it was hard to get here because you'd been to jail?
A: Yes. (Fieldnotes, 2009)

Inadequate housing options renders battered women vulnerable to further abuse (Price 2012b). If they are in an abusive or otherwise dangerous situation, they may find it more difficult than other women to find resources, safety, refuge, and support.

> May 2012. When she called and told me someone was trying to kill her, I had assumed it was her husband. She didn't know where she should go, just anywhere, anywhere out of town. I tried to take stock of the situation and gauge her fear.
>
> I assumed it was her husband because he had beaten her up so many times before. I knew, for instance, that once the police jailed him for the weekend after he had punched her in the face in her hospital bed—that is, when she was already in the hospital! On several occasions she had shown me the bruises he'd inflicted. In fact, he'd beaten her as recently as the week before. She had driven by with her mother as I was getting out of my car in front of my apartment. She pulled up, rolled down her window and shouted out a greeting with typical warmth and good cheer, "Hey, Josh!" I went over to her car window. I was glad to see her and asked how things were going. "Not so good." It was her husband again. She showed me a black eye and, in a gesture I found a bit forward, she tugged down on her collar a little and showed me where he had bitten her, high on her breast. Her mother, seated beside her in the car, said nothing and looked straight ahead until her daughter said in despair, "I don't know what I'm going to do." Her mother said, like clockwork, "Trust in the Lord. Pray to Jesus." I wanted to ask, "What will that do?" but of course I said nothing.
>
> And so I was ready to believe that he would threaten her life. On the phone the night before, she sounded desperate and terrified. She asked me for the number of a local civil rights worker we both knew. What's up? I asked her. "I have to leave town before I'm killed." Hesitatingly, I volunteered to help out, knowing I was putting myself in a risky situation. We arranged that I would pick her up the next day.

The following morning, I pulled up to her house and called her from my cell to tell her I was outside. Only then did she come to the door of the house, lean her head out of her front doorway and look up and down the street. Seeing that the street was empty in both directions, she came down the stairs quickly, and then glanced up and down the street again once she got to the sidewalk before approaching the car. She moved quickly over to the car, tossed two garbage bags full of clothing in my trunk, and set up her baby seat in the backseat before hustling her five-year-old into the car. She slid into the front and told me to drive on. By then, we were all a little intimidated. Statistically speaking, I knew, abusers are the most violent when a woman is separating or severing a relationship (Brownridge 2006; Mahoney 1991; Price 2012b). Though I knew the statistics, I had never been in a situation quite like this. I've never had to drive this scared before, so I tried to control my breathing.

Pulling out into the street, I asked her where she wanted to go. "We have to get my birth certificate from my mom's." We drove over and turned into a parking lot beside her mother's apartment. Once I pulled into a spot, she left the car but then returned immediately after she had walked only a dozen yards, telling me to leave the parking lot at once by a separate exit. She will deal with getting her documents later. She thought she'd seen someone. She kept looking around us with the quick, nervous glances of a small bird. I realized I wasn't sure what was going on. Weren't we running from her husband? She crouched down in her seat as I navigated out of the parking exit to the street.

Later, once we were safely on the interstate and she'd calmed down a bit, she filled me in: it wasn't her batterer she was running from. It was a local gang. She had her first run-in with them after her first arrest at seventeen. One of her co-defendants blamed her for the arrests. He was an active gang member. A few weeks after she got out of prison, just two days before our flight from town, she was in a grocery store and someone she didn't recognize came up to her and called her by her name. He drew in close and began threatening her. "We will cut out your asshole," he told her, "and then cut the rest of you to pieces and throw you in the river." She took this as a viable threat.

I was confused. Why didn't she call a women's shelter? "I tried. But they told me that because it was a gang who was after me, and not my husband, they couldn't take me. It's against their policy. They told me to call the police." (Months later, at a policy meeting of local organizations, I asked a representative of this shelter if this was in fact their policy, and she said it was.)

I didn't even have to ask her if she called the police for help. The police had never done anything except mistreat her. On more than one occasion, moreover, the police had worked with the parole office and with social services to take her children away from her. She felt she could not expect protection from them, especially given her criminal record.

She had to uproot, leave town, and go into hiding in the face of the credible threats to her life. We drove a couple hours north on the interstate to another town where she will take a bus to stay with relatives out of state. (Fieldnotes, 2012)

Women who are in violent situations after they are incarcerated may be more vulnerable than other women to further abuse. At the same time, currently and formerly incarcerated women are off the conventional map of abused women. Their situation is complicated, Beth Richie comments, "because 'victims' are not supposed to also be 'offenders'" (Richie 2001, 376; also see Koyami 2006). Shelters for battered women may bar women with criminal records. This makes them more vulnerable to homelessness. Such policies implicitly raise the price of leaving a batterer. Support for the formerly incarcerated thus must include support both for women facing violence and for their children. The support must take into account how formerly incarcerated women may have been separated from their children in the past.

Formerly incarcerated women have good reason to fear police, the department of social services, the courts, and even personnel at their children's schools. It is not only law enforcement, parole, and judges who monitor and control them and have the power to take away their liberty. Agencies that are supposed to offer support and refuge for women and their children in situations of risk or potential harm are at times responsible for putting those ties at risk. Services, community organizations, and even individual citizens, such as neighbors, wield enormous power over formerly incarcerated people. Social workers, school nurses, and other mandated reporters in their children's school, at the hospital, at battered women's shelters, and at homeless shelters also have the power to watch them and police their parenting skills, as one of my students, Noelle Paley, pointed out. They form a net of institutions of gendered control and surveillance. Noelle writes:

> One of JF's children had breathing problems as a small child. Childcare workers question the way he was nursed, how much drainage was on his bandages, and whether this was an indication of neglect. Her neighbors call child protective services. The investigations to which she was subject would show the charges to be unfounded, but she has to defend the way she mothers her children. These forces keep her off-balance, in a state of stress, economically out-of-balance. She and her children are ripped out of the social structure each time she is sent to jail or prison. (Fieldnotes, 2008)

The state engenders this vulnerability in significant respects since it authorizes so many institutions and deputizes so many proxies to monitor formerly incarcerated women and empowers them to wield control over them.

EMPLOYMENT AND SPIRIT MURDER

"There is discrimination, yes. From A to Z," one formerly incarcerated man tells me. One of the most frequent complaints of formerly incarcerated people is how difficult it is to find a job. Regardless of the nature of their crime, many states bar them from public-sector jobs, or from working in a hospital or with children, or from professional licenses, such as permits to work as a plumber or a barber. Parole officers may refuse to allow a person to apply for a driver's license, making certain kinds of employment impossible, including work that requires a car to commute.

Beyond the formal restrictions, other barriers impede employment. When they get out of prison, they may have had little practice in developing a résumé or presenting themselves for a job interview, and may even lack proper clothes. They may lack the social connections so many use to get employment.

Yet the biggest stumbling block may be the stigma of having served a prison sentence for a felony. The state confers a negative credential when it sends a person to prison argues sociologist Devah Pager. A negative credential restricts rather than enables access and opportunity (2007, 32). With the negative credential of a criminal record, Pager argues, "a wide range of social, economic, and political privileges becomes off-limits." What is peculiar about the negative credential of a criminal record is that it "represents a unique mechanism of stratification, in that it is the state that certifies particular individuals in ways that qualify them for discrimination or social exclusion. It is this official status of the negative credential that differentiates it from other sources of social stigma, offering greater legitimacy to its use as the basis for differentiation" (Pager 2007, 135). Pager has measured statistically the effects of a criminal record on employment for men. Unsurprisingly, she has found widespread discrimination in employment based on a criminal record. White men without a criminal record were twice as likely to get called back for a job as white men with a criminal conviction. For black men, the difference was even more notable: those without a criminal record were almost three times as likely to get called back compared to black men with a criminal record (Pager 2003). (Though her study was not focused on racial animus per se, it is worth pointing out that she discovered an additional disturbing trend: whites *with* criminal records received more callbacks than blacks without criminal records.)

People's firsthand experiences confirm Pager's statistical evidence that it is hard to get a job with a felony conviction. One man who had served multiple stints in prison remarked to me: "Like I said, we have discrimination in the workforce. And they say, 'Oh, he been in prison? He was a drug dealer? Four times? OK, I can understand and forgive him one time. But four times?!? And he's working with me?' And I'm out of there. I went through that. I went through that" (Fieldnotes, 2009). This man suggests he was fired for the unforgivably habitual nature of his criminality ("I can understand and forgive one time. But four times?"), the perceived danger he posed ("And he's working with me?"), and the discomfort that might engender in coworkers and employers.

> June 2010. I am sitting on my back porch with Richard. We are discussing challenges people face after they get back into town after having been in prison. Richard, who served fifteen years, comments that the psychological challenges are poorly understood. "When you are in prison, you have lots of fantasies about what it's going to be like when you get out. You picture yourself and what your life could be like. And then when you get out, the cold water hits. You can't get a job, you don't like where you live, maybe a halfway house or whatever. You don't have money for meals. Now, you could go to a soup kitchen, or wait in line at a church." But that is to admit to a deep failure, he continues. You have imagined things will be different, that you will be able to get by, to live well. After imagining—daydreaming about—life after prison for so long, a person has acquired a psychic investment in achieving a certain independence and well-being. It is that moment of failing to achieve those goals, and facing that failure, Richard continues, at which they are susceptible to return to old ways of getting by, of making a living. (Fieldnotes, 2010)

Without a better sense of the internal life of formerly incarcerated people, and their experiences surviving on the outside, social programs and social services will only have limited utility. Pantries, soup kitchens, and homeless shelters seem to offer temporary or emergency assistance for people who have a pressing need for shelter or food. But given the internal and external obstacles to seeking help, many of the solutions, even the best intentioned, may miss the mark. This is why it is necessary to put the voices, insights, and perspectives of the currently and formerly incarcerated at the center of policy decisions.

> December 2008. I am talking to a group in protective housing at the jail about pursuing their education. We are trying to put together a pilot program at the jail since we are only minutes from a state university. Many of them tell me they would like to go back to school after they get out. Two men sitting off from the main circle call out that they would like to understand opera better. A young man says a bit shyly that he would like to learn ancient Greek and a few people chuckle. Another man says he draws and would like to learn how

to put together a graphic novel. After the session breaks up, he brings over a few of his drawings to show me. (Fieldnotes, 2008)

It is very common for formerly incarcerated people to desire to return to school, either for their GED or for an advanced degree. However, universities often pose obstacles to them. My university, for example, requires people convicted of a felony to submit to a long bureaucratic review by a special committee. This committee frequently turns people down. Even when a candidate is successful, the committee process delays students from enrolling for at least a semester.

Congress has rolled back funding for the incarcerated and formerly incarcerated to pursue their education. It has restricted Pell grants and banned federal aid for people convicted of drug convictions. These restrictions are shortsighted on a number of counts. Access to education is important in any society and qualifies as a human right. Apart from that, study after study has shown how effective education is for larger policy goals in reducing recidivism, improving employment, and saving taxpayer money (Chappell 2004; Davis et al. 2013).

IMMIGRANTS AS FORMERLY INCARCERATED

Immigrants to the United States face severe consequences after they are incarcerated. Immigration and Customs Enforcement often hold them past their term, sometimes for years. Immigrants who were previously legally documented face deportation after they have served a sentence; it goes without saying that undocumented immigrants are also often deported after they are incarcerated. This can be especially cruel. Some legal as well as undocumented immigrants have spent ten, fifteen, or twenty-five years in the United States and may have few resources or support in the country of their birth, and may not even speak the language of the country to which they are deported (see Barrios and Brotherton 2009). The children of the deported, if they do not have a relative to take them, face foster care (Wessler 2011). It is beyond the scope of this chapter to explore this topic in depth. However, new interagency collaboration has meant that people detained in jails, and sometimes even when police accost them, routinely have their immigration status checked with federal authorities. This has been one of the contributing causes to the unprecedented rates of deportation, bringing no end of misery, fear, and instability to immigrants, their families, and communities.

CONCLUSION

Spring 2012. Sitting with Gordon by the river behind my house, he tells me of his life before and after prison. He has spent over thirty years in prison. When he was much younger, he worked with one of his brothers, selling drugs and robbing people. His job was to intimidate, to frighten people. He was accustomed to fighting and enjoyed it. And now?

"I'm a retired gangster living on a pension," he says with a laugh.

He wants to live quietly with his two daughters. To get by, he repackages and sells things he finds in dumpsters. Gordon tells me that when he goes through garbage, sometimes people scream at him, treat him badly, call him names, a dirty old bum, and so on. "Like I was less than human." He remarks, with bitter irony, that in a previous life he had been a tough guy, armed and dangerous, and it was precisely when he decided to stop, when he had had enough, that others began to take advantage of him. He tells me of a particular time recently when he was going through garbage that was sitting on the curb and a man came out and started yelling at him, telling him to get away from his garbage, and insulting him. "What that man did not realize," Gordon tells me reflectively, over a cigarette, "is that I could put the fear in him very quickly. The fear of fire." Gordon casually puffs and then knocks the ash off his cigarette. He is astute and experienced in making people feel afraid, making them feel as if they've walked into a living nightmare. (Fieldnotes, 2012)

Gordon's story could serve as a morality tale. I don't mean to propose using reactive violence to settle scores or to scare people. Instead, I take it that the hidden cost of spirit murder may be in missing the rich human realities among us, replacing the curiosity one might have in the interior life of contemporaries and compatriots with phantasms that inspire hostility and loathing. Another man comments:

It's up to the individual—what he want to do. I'm ok with that. Guess what? I got a car. I pay my bills, whatever. . . . But certain guys, it takes the life out of them. Just like the guy coming and he's writing all of these pretty letters to his wife and it's a lot of guys that fall victim when they come with these expectations, when they come home and his wife say, "I want to stay with you because of the kids but we don't have a life. You ain't been here." . . . and that's when this guy, he went, he educating himself, he strongly believes that he is going to do the right thing. And when he comes with these expectations he gets slam dunked. Society slams him, family slams him, kids slam him. (Fieldnotes, 2012)

The demand by formerly incarcerated people for an end to the social ban is sometimes put in terms of civil rights or human rights. This is the approach favored by All of Us or None, an organization of formerly incarcerated people. They aim to "eliminate the lifelong punishment resulting from past convictions or imprisonment"; "To achieve full restoration of the rights of formerly-incarcerated/convicted people"; "To advocate for the human rights of currently and formerly incarcerated people." Since spirit murder is a fundamental social and cultural rejection, to my understanding the restitution of civil rights alone does not speak to the depth of the problem. In the United States, however, claims for redress to injury are often framed in legal terms. In this case, the legal demands are against the (very real) outward, institutionalized manifestations of deeper forms of social, even ontological rejection, intimidation, and humiliation. Contemporary campaigns on behalf of the formerly incarcerated that focus on civil liberties thus need to be understood literally as demands for civil liberties. But they are also projects to reclaim a disenfranchised self, a murdered spirit, an attempt to heal the damage of the prison system and to end the social ban on the formerly incarcerated. In that spirit, All of Us or None also demands, as part of its self-determination pledge, "the right to speak in our own voices." They also aim "to overcome the fear and heal the shame associated with being a convicted felon or former prisoner"; "to accept responsibility for any acts that may have caused harm to our families, our communities, or ourselves"; and "to develop a national movement of formerly-incarcerated people and people with past convictions so we can build political power for our communities" (All of Us or None 2010).

In liberal theory, an individual is free if he or she is unencumbered by socially imposed obstacles. This is liberty understood in negative terms: freedom from interference (see Berlin 1969). The conceit is that we are independent of one another and we do not rely on one another.

But how free can someone really be if she lives freedom in this purely negative sense? The vulnerability of the social dead belies the viability of this concept of freedom. The outcast lives at the mercy of the society and its members; abandoned, he or she lives not within a social order but rather in a state of socially constructed disorder, of chaos (cf. Agamben 1998, 19). Living a purely negative version of freedom is to live a nightmare that approaches not a hypothetical unreality, not an imagined dystopia, but rather the state of social death lived as a concrete reality. Spirit murder captures this psychosocial, material, and legal complex of paternalism, disregard, resentment, and pitiless derision.

People subject to spirit murder are not helpless, and there is little evidence that they have internalized the scant regard in which they are held. A man commented defiantly:

> You can look around, a lot of fallen soldiers out there. You can't force yourself. You got to re-integrate. The only way you can re-integrate back in society is stay in society. You got to deal with me. The same way I got to deal with you, you got to deal with me. Be steadfast in your belief. Keep a steady course. 'Cause you'll never be accepted. Not even by your

family. It's always a stigma. So that's something you gotta live with. But you got to keep your head up. When I come out of prison, I come out of prison no matter what. It took me a long time to do this. This eleven years taught me a helluva lot to know who I am. But I made it out. I'm confident in myself. I don't mind talking about my past. I used to didn't talk about my past. I'm confident in speaking. I can speak to one, I can speak to a thousand. This is me. You don't have to accept me. I don't have to be around you. But guess what? The same piece of pie that's out for all of us, I'm going to get my slice. You know, if I can't help you, I'm not going to harm you. And please if you can't help me, don't harm me. But I'm going to be here. And like I said, you have to be steadfast. You got to be a rock. You got to be a rock, you know? And that's what I mean by change. (Fieldnotes, 2012)

CHAPTER 9

States of Grace

SOCIAL LIFE AGAINST SOCIAL DEATH

IN A SHORT ESSAY entitled "The Prisoner's Perspective," Larry White urges other incarcerated people not to reduce themselves to their condition. "You are living your life," he reminds them. "A prisoner's perspective begins with the realization that the situation that you find yourself in is not merely one concerning a prison sentence. That you are not just serving time, but more importantly that you are living your life and your sentence is merely an aspect of that life" (White 2009). White emphasizes consciousness, recognition, and expression. "Once you realize that serving time is all about living your life, rather than serving a sentence, then your perspective changes. You begin to understand that how you perceive and respond to your imprisonment has value and needs to be shared and articulated." Gaining perspective and sharing your perceptions can be a way not only to serve time but also to overcome the social fragmentation and isolation engendered by prison.

Many scholarly and journalistic articles and books have treated the causes and consequences of the high rate of incarceration. My concern here is different. If prisons are a form of institutionalized material, public, and spiritual negation that amounts to social death, then this chapter focuses on what Avery Gordon has called "social life" (2004). People sustain themselves and struggle to live lives of dignity and purpose when assaulted by the state. They, their friends, allies, and communities, engage in humanizing activity when they otherwise face social death.

My analysis is based chiefly on three examples. First, I take the activist work of the late Martina Correia, sister of Georgia death row inmate Troy Davis, who was executed in late 2011. I attended a street protest in Atlanta that illustrates how she struggled with others for her brother's life. The other examples emerge from our participatory action research in Binghamton. In each case, people understand and work to overcome the imposition of the prison on them and their loved ones, and they take up and resist the consequent social destruction wrought on their lives. For example, Correia resisted breast cancer even as she campaigned tirelessly for her brother. She connected chemotherapy—the "poison" she injects into her veins, as she put it—to the lethal injection her brother faced.

AMY GOODMAN: Martina Correia, How do you fight for your own life and for your brother's?

MARTINA CORREIA: Well, it's amazing, because when I go into my oncologist's office, I always seem to get in the same exam room, and there's a saying on the wall by Robert Schuller that says, "Don't think about all the things you have lost, but the things you have left to do." And I have dedicated my life to saving the life of my brother, because there's times when I couldn't get up and take care of myself, and my mother took care of me. And my brother has been on death row professing his innocence all these years, and he's only been concerned about me and my family and our health. And if he can be on death row and be the same type of person that he's always been, then I can fight for him on the outside, and I will continue to do that with every breath that I have. (Goodman 2007)

In an atmosphere of death, cruelty, and humiliation, Correia and the others in this chapter resist the abridgement of their humanity, to borrow a phrase from Chinua Achebe (2009, 23). They strive toward a state of grace.

Grace is a state of contemplative equanimity amid the onslaughts of social death. It is not a passive state. Rather, one asserts, in a hopeful and unexpected way, a certain conviction in one's own worth and the worth of others (see Butler 2001, 621). A state of grace is a form of critically affirming social life.

Grace in the context of grassroots politics implies reflective striving rather than piety. Shorn of its theological connotation, grace refers to people who take up the conditions of their lives and come to celebrate life and defy forces that try to trivialize their suffering and foreclose their possibilities.

I AM TROY DAVIS

"I Am Troy Davis." This is the slogan of the protest. It is September 2009 and the State of Georgia has just scheduled an execution date for Troy Davis. I am living in Atlanta for the year. I arrive just before six P.M. at the Georgia state capitol building. The NAACP and Amnesty International have had a long-standing campaign to free Davis. Seven of nine nonpolice informants who testified to witnessing Davis murder an off-duty police officer in 1989 have recanted, citing initial police coercion. No material evidence linked Davis, who had no criminal record, to the crime. Davis looks youthful in the prison photos, even a bit nerdish with his wire-framed glasses. He has spent almost twenty years in prison, most of them on death row. He is exactly my age.

It is a small group by my reckoning—a few hundred people—and I already recognize a few from the last gathering I'd gone to. I'd expected crowds in the thousands, since the case is getting a lot of publicity, and political and religious leaders as diverse as the pope, the president of the European Union, and Archbishop Desmond Tutu have pronounced their reservations about his guilt. People are holding simultaneous rallies throughout the United States and the rest of the world.

The crowd is composed of anti–death penalty activists, civil rights advocates, a range of progressives, and students. Since this is Georgia, many of the speakers are ministers and other religious leaders. The crowd is about 60 or 70 percent African American—of all ages and perhaps social classes.

At first I am a little depressed by it—not just depressed by their killing Davis ("Troy"), although that is the biggest part of it, but also by the small turnout and the implicit social acquiescence to his killing, and by what feels to be a routinization of protest. Here we are, playing our part. We, the demonstrators, politely stay off the street and wait until the cops close it off for our benefit. A police officer eventually comes over and tells one of the protest organizers we can move into the street and the organizer thanks him. It is only then that the organizers announce we could go into the street. I think ruefully of social protests in Latin America. In the Latin American protests I have participated in, protestors do not ask police to close off streets. They do not seek government approval or permission to protest publicly. They decide as organizers when the streets will be shut off, and then they link arms and simply shut off the street traffic. I wonder how far the people around me are willing to take a protest. But then I remember that we are in Georgia, and that I am a visitor here. I also realize that many of the people—at least the older people–have faced down fear and death, and any number of police, in order to protest in the past, and I chide myself for my self-importance.

It is a cold evening for Georgia. I stand around helplessly for a while, and then I offer to pass out signs that read "Justice Matters." People are wearing T-shirts and carrying posters that say "I Am Troy Davis." For those of us who don't have the T-shirts, the organizers distributed little "Hello, My Name Is . . ." stickers, the kind you wear to a meeting or a party. Except these said "Hello, My Name Is . . . Troy Davis," so I put on a sticker that said "Hello, My Name Is Troy Davis."

The speeches are inspired, with the exception of a few that tread the predictable cant. When the executive director of Amnesty International USA speaks, he remarks that this execution was one of the most unjust things happening around the world at that moment. He tells us his colleagues have criticized him for focusing too much on it. Time was, I think, when Amnesty International did not focus sufficiently on the United States. I wonder at the renewed use of "human rights" to refer to political injustice within the United States. The head of the Georgia NAACP gives a rousing talk. He appears to be central in this organizing effort. Then the rapper Killer Mike speaks with the solicitous, reverberant baritone of a church preacher. He says that he is the son of a police officer, and he always prayed his father would get home safely. He understands that the blood of a dead officer cries out for justice. But what happens, he asks, when there are two men in the ground whose blood cries for justice?

Then Martina Correia takes the stage. One could feel her strength of character and of spirit. Correia admits she has had her strength sapped because she is on chemo for breast cancer. She takes the slogan of the day "I Am Troy Davis" and asks everyone to repeat it. She asks us to think about what it means to say that. To say "I Am Troy Davis." To utter it.

"It is not a corrections system," Correia continues. "It is a system of vengeance, violence, and destruction. I do not know what God they pray to." She names people—prosecutors, people appointed to the parole board—and accuses them of misconduct, misrepresentation, and mishandling witnesses. She blames the machinations of the government of the State of Georgia. She, like many who had spoken earlier, criticizes the parole board for meeting in private. She will keep fighting for her brother, but she reminds us the struggle is about "every black and brown and poor white's face" that she has encountered from going to visit her brother in prison over the last twenty years. This struggle, she concludes, cannot stop with Troy Davis.

A local radio announcer comes up after her and gives a short talk in the tones of a Sunday minister. His imagery is replete with invocations of Jesus. He says he is ready to put himself on the line. He works the crowd up.

Some speakers argue that, in killing Davis, the state is contributing to the end of the death penalty. When it becomes clear how unjust it was to execute Davis, so the logic runs, then the society will abandon the death penalty. "When I'm finally released from this Death Camp," Troy Davis has written, "my path will remain Righteous as I help bring an END to the DEATH PENALTY."

I am Troy Davis, we chant. "There is still lynching in Georgia," one speaker says.

I am Troy Davis. "It is ironic," another speaker offers, "that we may have a black man as president while they are executing another in the state of Georgia." This, the speaker proposes, "is the barometer of whether the United States is fulfilling its ideals."

I am Troy Davis. "You owe it to civilized society to say the death penalty is wrong."

I am Troy Davis. "You don't have to be H. Rap Brown to acknowledge that violence is as American as apple pie."

I am Troy Davis. A man came from North Carolina who had been imprisoned for nineteen years until a DNA test exonerated him. "I know how Troy Davis is feeling."

I am Troy Davis. "If they decide to kill him, if they have evidence, then let it be public and transparent. If they want to kill him, let them show the hate and blood-lust they have in their heart."

I am Troy Davis. Martina Correia takes the stage again to comment that the authorities had threatened her brother with cutting off visits with family members if he spoke to the press.

"With God, everything is possible." A woman from Georgians Against the Death Penalty reads a statement Troy Davis had written for the occasion. I am unaccustomed to this prophetic mixture of God, Jesus, and justice. It's at the core, not something external. Davis has written:

> I die a little each day, behind these walls, mentally, emotionally and physi-cally. It is like I have a deadly disease and the government refuses to approve the cure, that my doctors (lawyers) have discovered. Sometimes I don't feel like a "Dead Man Walking," I feel like "The Walking Dead." I refuse to be bitter or angry because I have faith in God, that he will soften the hearts of my oppressors, to do what is right.
>
> I am in a place where execution can only destroy your physical form but because of my faith in God, my family and all of you I have been spiri-tually free for some time and no matter what happens in the days, weeks to come, this Movement to end the death penalty, to seek true justice, to expose a system that fails to protect the innocent must be accelerated. There are so many more Troy Davises. This fight to end the death penalty is not won or lost through me but through our strength to move forward and save every innocent person in captivity around the globe. We need to dismantle this unjust system city by city, state by state and country by country. (Davis 2008)

Afterward: following several stays of execution, the State of Georgia finally executed Troy Davis on September 21, 2011. Martina Correia died within three months of her brother. Together, they faced down death in its most concrete and jarring forms: as cancer, as chemotherapy, as state-administered execution. They openly confronted their identity as condemned. Beyond or through literal death, and a criminal justice system predicated on "vengeance, violence, and destruction," they found another justice, in which they put their faith and for which they fought with unceasing dedication.

Organizing in a Small Upstate Community

I met Jenny and Shaun James in 2004, soon after I had begun a collab-orative investigation into health care conditions at the county jail. One of the civil rights leaders at the NAACP arranged for me to interview Shaun James.

I met Shaun at the NAACP offices. One of my students taped the conversation and hazarded an occasional question. Shaun began by telling me of close relatives who had also been incarcerated and suffered because of medical neglect. As he continued to talk, describing conditions in the county jail and in the various state penitentiaries where he had served time, he seemed to me brilliant, with a gift for a turn of phrase. But he was also deeply troubled. He told me that he has been diagnosed with post-traumatic stress disorder. "I have nightmares that would make Freddy Kreuger blush." Months later, his wife Jenny confided in me that he drank himself to sleep every night to avoid the nightmares.

In that first interview, Shaun echoed what I had heard others tell me, that it was important to have someone on the outside.

SHAUN: Say you're my friend and you come and visit me. Then I have an outlet to, I can call Josh up (that's your name, right? Josh?) "Josh, listen, man, could you call the head sheriff or something like that and make them give me my medication or something like that." If you don't have nobody out there to connect with and the same thing in prison, you're finished, man. You're finished. That's about the gist of that. And you really don't get the medical attention. You just don't.

JOSH: What if you got somebody, though?

SHAUN: If you got somebody then you got a shot; you got a shot of surviving.

JOSH: So, at the county jail at least, this last time they were good with you.

SHAUN: Yeah, that's because my girl is in my corner and she ain't going to let anything happen to me, too tough, you know what I'm saying. I was one of the lucky ones, you know. If you don't have nobody, you might not get out of there. (Fieldnotes, 2004)

After the first interview, Shaun and I speak frequently. He gives me advice on how to handle myself, whom to trust, whom not to. Personally, he is a bit wary of participating too openly because he is still on parole and he is petrified of being put back in prison. He is content to stay at home with Jenny and their little lap dog and give me advice from the confines of his apartment.

The irony, if it is irony, is that he was sent back to jail anyway. What had his silence bought him? Surely not safety or protection. Why did parole want to put him in prison again? He was already cowed. He was already beaten.

The traumas of readjustment are not borne alone. Loved ones, friends, and relatives often bear the brunt of the difficulties. Since Shaun is back in jail, Jenny has been spending most of her time alone. She is angry all the time. I sympathize, but I can also see that it is wearing on her nerves. She's worried about her health, her failing kidneys. She is having enormous difficulty walking. Jenny is stricken, lonely, terrified, flummoxed. She seems to spend most of her time by herself, though I try to stop by from time to time.

I decide to invite her to come to speak to a class I'm teaching on prisons. It would definitely be good for the students. I also think it would be good for her, too, to break her isolation and speak publicly of what she perceives as an injustice.

She asks me what she should say to the students. I ask her to tell them how she is affected by Shaun's incarceration. I tell her she should tell them what it's like to have someone on whom you depend sentenced to prison.

To bring her up to speed with the class, I brief her on our class discussions of the "prison-industrial complex." I tell her the expression was adapted from President Dwight Eisenhower's warning long ago of the increasingly interdependent relationship between the military industry and government interests.[1] Angela Davis and Eric Schlosser helped popularize the expression. Schlosser, writing in the *Atlantic*, underscores how the emerging prison–industrial complex kidnaps public safety concerns in the interest of profit.

> A set of bureaucratic, political, and economic interests . . . encourage increased spending on imprisonment, regardless of the actual need. The prison-industrial complex is not a conspiracy, guiding the nation's criminal justice policy behind closed doors. It is a confluence of special interests that has given prison construction in the United States a seemingly unstoppable momentum. It is composed of politicians, both liberal and conservative, who have used the fear of crime to gain votes; impoverished rural areas where prisons have become a cornerstone of economic development; private companies that regard the roughly $35 billion spent each year on corrections not as a burden on American taxpayers but as a lucrative market; and government officials whose fiefdoms have expanded along with the inmate population. (1998, 3)

Schlosser charts how since Nelson Rockefeller proposed tough sentencing laws in New York in the early 1970s, politicians of both parties have made a lot of political hay in promoting legislative and fiscal reform that promotes incarceration. Jenny and I both know people who have served decades in prison because of the Rockefeller Drug Laws. Angela Davis's account of the prison-industrial complex coincides with Schlosser when she defines it as "an array of relationships linking corporations, government, correctional communities, media, and the exploitation of prison labor. . . . Thus the prison-industrial complex is much more than the sum of all jails and prisons in this country. It is a set of symbiotic relationships among correctional communities, transnational corporations, media conglomerates, guards' unions, legislative and court agendas" (2003, 107). She sees the prison-industrial complex not so much as an analogue to the military-industrial complex but as linked to it. They mutually support and promote each other and share technologies. In meshing large federal agencies with private corporations, they share important structural features. Both reap profits from social destruction. The raw material of the massive prison industry, Eric Schlosser holds, "is its inmates: the poor, the homeless, and the mentally ill; drug dealers, drug addicts, alcoholics" (1998, 4).

Later that week in class, I introduce Jenny as the guest speaker. She walks to the front of the room on a homemade cane. She explains to the students that her husband has severe heart problems. A private company, contracted at enormous cost to the State of New York, provides his medical care. He doesn't trust the prison medical care, so he's putting off having a stent put in his heart. She details many of the other ways in which private industries make money from her and her husband. The prison places a monthly quota of how much canned and packaged food she can send. After that, he must purchase goods in the prison commissary at highly inflated prices. Jenny raises money any way she can to buy packaged food to send him. (I have been frustrated, too, because I have tried to send him books, but this is not allowed. He must purchase them himself directly from licensed booksellers with his commissary money.)

She also tells us how, six months after her husband was incarcerated, her oldest son had his legs blown off in Iraq. She gives a detailed explanation of the failures of the military medical care in Texas, where he is recovering from his wounds. For his injury, her nineteen-year-old son was presented with a $100,000 check by the U.S. government: "50,000 dollars for each leg," Jenny comments ruefully. Jenny thinks the government acted irresponsibly in giving cash under these conditions. The boy, a poor kid from a small town in upstate New York who has never seen so much money before, a boy who has recently experienced a life-altering event, promptly spent all the money on sundries including a series of expensive iPods, a Harley motorcycle, and an SUV, which he crashed soon after. He now has no money and no savings to show for the experience. "Now how are you going to give a young man in that circumstance $100,000 in cash, and not even supply a financial counselor?" Jenny concludes to my class, "my family is hit on both sides by the military and the prison system."

The students seem a little stunned and caught off balance by her presentation. They are not sure what to ask. They seem respectful and ask their questions gingerly. I know that not all of them will agree with her analysis, but even the most skeptical students speak with restraint, for which I am grateful, because Jenny is already a bit on the edge.

Since I know Jenny, I can see she is in a state of constant crisis management and emotional overload. She is always nervous, spread thin, without resources, isolated, and forced to confront her trauma with little care or recognition.

She joins our efforts to fight for those on parole with vigor, despite her poor health.

WEEKEND IN JAIL

Dorothy is in her late fifties. I meet her for the first time when Emily brings her along to a meeting at a local coffee shop. A judge had ordered Dorothy to spend the weekend in jail, and she is due there in a few hours. At our meeting, we were planning to discuss the interviews Emily and Ibrahim have been conducting with formerly incarcerated people. Emily is a white woman in her fifties who is in recovery from drug addiction. She has served several short stints in the county jail. Ibrahim, an African American Muslim, served ten years in prison. It was their idea to start a local drop-in center for people getting out of prison. Binghamton has few resources, opportunities, or organizations to assist people in adjusting to life after prison. I was Emily and Ibrahim's professor but we have continued working together since they graduated. In order to proceed, I had suggested that they interview formerly incarcerated people on the challenges they face and what they perceive as their needs once they get back into town. I ask them about the interviews they've recently conducted. What are they hearing?

Ibrahim summarizes an interview he just conducted. The man he interviewed had been released recently after a conviction for a sex offense. There was no room for him at Volunteers of America, so he went down to the police department and they advised him, in violation of the law, to stay at the YMCA where he's been for several months (people on the sex offender registry cannot stay there because there are children in the building). Emily tells us that the parole office usually sends sex offenders to a downtown hotel. They send not only older people but also young people who have touched their siblings in inappropriate ways. This strikes all of us as a bad idea.

"The guys I'm interviewing are pedophiles," Ibrahim adds. I am struck that he had gone and done the interviews, because he had remarked at an earlier meeting on his moral disgust with pedophiles. But I am glad he had taken the initiative to find out the resources available to them, because it is important not to exclude anyone. I ask to see the transcripts, as much to review Ibrahim's questions as the answers they give. Ibrahim pushes an audio recorder across to Emily and asks her to make a transcript for him from his interview. Emily tells me she will give me a transcript once she has it done. I object to their division of labor—why should Emily do transcripts for Ibrahim?—but I decide to hold my tongue. I don't want to break the rhythm of the work since we are just starting, but I'll say something if this persists.

I glance over at Dorothy. Her skin is drawn and leathery. She nervously peers at the menu. She was having trouble deciding. Emily helps her select a dessert. She seems to guide her friend a bit. Then Emily looks over at me and explains that Dorothy has been sentenced to spend the next few weekends in jail because she arrived late at a mandatory meeting with "drug court," an alternative-to-incarceration program that monitors her. "Half an hour late, can you believe it?" Dorothy remarks, "And there was nothing in the urine test. Now, I could understand if my urine was dirty . . ."

I try to think what it must be like, to prepare psychologically to enter jail. She frets about her medication. "Should I take it with me? Will they administer it on time?" The people at the table agree she shouldn't take it with her. I know, we all know, that she is going to have a lot of trouble getting staff to administer it in a timely fashion. Dorothy seems stuck. Later, Emily tells me Dorothy has been an addict for decades. Even though she was supposed to be in "drug court" for two years, they have prolonged it, so she has been forced to attend it for over three years.

It is the Friday before New Year's, and she will spend New Year's incarcerated. When she had arrived at the diner she had commented with enthusiasm how hungry she was. Now, as she peruses the menu, she observes that this is the first time she has ever gone into jail without handcuffs. In the past, she had always been high when they brought her in. Now she is sober, and has been sober for over a year and a half. "Boy, has it been hard! And I've stayed sober."

The waitress swings by the table again. "I'll just have coffee," Dorothy says after a moment, pursing her lips. We encourage her to eat. "We came here for you!" I say, trying to lighten the mood. "Well, maybe I should eat, at that." "The food is terrible in the jail," Emily reminds her. Finally, she settles on a slice of cheesecake. She gets up and goes to the bathroom. Emily gazes after her. "When you are high, you don't care if you're brought to jail because you're out of your mind. But now, today, going in like this . . ."

"Just half an hour late," Dorothy repeats, returning to her seat. "My nephew just got sentenced to ninety years in prison. And he's only twenty-one. Ninety years. And he didn't even enter the bank. He was outside." So many people in Dorothy's family are in prison. Here they surround us, along with these stories about them, memories, and perceived injustices. All these families smothered, torn apart. Dorothy seems nervous, damaged, distracted. She seems a bit broken.

"Are you close to your nephew?" I ask.

"Well, sure, he's my nephew. But he's down in West Virginia." I try to communicate sympathy. To be honest, I am a bit torn, because we have a meeting to hold, with an agenda. Yet part of me sees this as momentous in its own way. It would be strange, strange to the point of diminishing her, not to attend to her at this time. She is preparing to go into jail. She tries to quell her nerves. I watch her as she inhales and exhales slowly. She tries to focus on the menu so she can order something to eat before she enters the jail, but I can tell she is distracted, this woman I've never met before, brought unannounced by a team member to meet me.

What about our work? I wonder what the others think. Ibrahim stares absently out the window. Emily is marking something down in her book. They have all served time. I often don't know how they are reading a situation or reacting to it.

"You know, and it's really crazy, because the judge ordered me not to talk to my son. My own son. If he came in here right now, I wouldn't be allowed to talk to him. What do you think of that? And just because they say he's a user. But they had no evidence! They didn't have any evidence against him."

Ibrahim breaks in and says we need to work to change the social services rule that requires a forty-five-day wait period to get social service benefits after one applies, because that's a hardship for people who come back from incarceration. "What are they supposed to do during those forty-five days?" I respond that we need to move slowly in planning solutions, I don't want to go for band-aid solutions. He says, "But we need to do something or else this is all just talk." "Fine. Talk to Stan, he's worked on this forty-five-day rule for people in jail. It's good to think about solutions, but let's also keep doing the interviews." "I'm not saying we stop doing interviews," Ibrahim affirms. I see our relationship is improving.

I tell them about a woman I know who had her parole revoked and was remanded to jail because she was staying with her daughter, who was also on parole (people on parole are not allowed to associate with others on parole). They ask me her name but out of discretion I pretend not to hear. It is not my place to reveal confidences.

The meeting draws to a close. We signal for the bill, pay, linger a bit, and finally head out to our cars.

"Hang in there," I say to Dorothy, as we part.

"I can handle this," she tells me. "I can handle this."

"I'm sure you can, but it's a big bummer."

"I was trying so hard," she says, as she gets into the car with Emily.

I have forgotten my hat and go back for it. I bump into Debbie at the entrance to the diner. Debbie served ten years in Albion. She is waiting in line with her boyfriend and grandchildren for a table. We embrace, and she wishes me a happy New Year. I ask after her brother. "He's pulling himself together. He even has a car and a cell phone. Call me and I'll give his number to you." "I'm going out of town for a couple weeks," I tell her, "but when I get back and we get started again I'll give him a call." "Great," she says, and I pat her grandchildren on their heads and make a funny face, shake her boyfriend's hand, find my hat, and walk out into the brisk night air.

CONCLUSION

Nothing particularly extraordinary distinguishes the cases above. With the exception of Troy Davis, who has received considerable national and international attention, the stories above are admittedly minor in the scope of corrections and the behemoth that is the prison system. I have included them in part because they are so ordinary. In their everydayness, they show striving in an unequal war, as people try to gain footing in the chaos around them.

Our age, observes Flannery O'Connor, "not only does not have a very sharp eye for the most imperceptible intrusions of grace, it no longer has much feeling for the nature of the violences which precede and follow them" (O'Connor 1961, 112). Violence, she writes, is "strangely capable of returning my characters to reality and preparing them to accept their moment of grace." This idea, that "reality is something to which we must be returned at considerable cost, is one which is seldom understood by the casual reader, but it is one which is implicit in the Christian view of the world" (112). I acknowledge that violence plays a complex role in the intrusions of grace in our lives. Nevertheless, violence is neither necessary nor desirable to achieve grace. People can reflect on their lives, and they can attain grace without the shock of incarceration or its attendant humiliations and degradations. We can live considered lives through other means. After discussing all the insight he gained in prison, Lige Dailey Jr. cautions:

> In no way, however, am I attempting to endorse, glorify, or recommend prison. I would never want to repeat the horror, the violence, and the degradation of the prison experience. I was able to accomplish my major reentry goal "in spite of" and not "because of" any constructive assistance from the criminal justice system. . . . I sincerely believe that prison rehabilitation will never become more than empty rhetoric in the United States. The U.S. penal system is clearly not designed to rehabilitate; it is designed to punish . . . I believe that society's thirst for revenge has blinded it to our escalating cycle of recidivism. (Dailey 2001, 262–263)

In the preceding cases, social engagement with others was crucial to stave off social death. The threat of social death, moreover, was intimately tied to the risk of literal bodily death. To be accompanied, then, is crucial for survival in every sense.

As they affirm social life, they expose their vulnerability. Each person made his or her need for others palpable and immediate as they strived for survival. James Baldwin calls this love: "Love takes off the masks that we fear we cannot live without and know we cannot live within. I use the word 'love' here not merely in the personal sense but as a state of being, or a state of grace—not in the infantile American sense of being made happy but in the tough and universal sense of quest and daring and growth" (1985, 373). Baldwin complements Larry White's proposal to "live your life." "It seems to me that one ought to rejoice in the *fact* of death—ought to decide, indeed, to *earn* one's death by confronting with passion the conundrum of life. One is responsible to life: it is the small beacon in that terrifying darkness from which we come and to which we shall return. One must negotiate this passage as nobly as possible, for the sake of those who are coming after us" (Baldwin 1985, 375). In trying to achieve a state of grace, the people above gather themselves, more or less ably, more or less smoothly, to confront this gap, this incommensurability, between the social negation they experience and their attempts to safeguard their humanity, bound up, as that humanity is, with other people. They labor in tandem with loved ones against the profiteering of the prison-industrial complex in its many guises. In the face of the mighty powers summoned by capital and by punishment, it is through their spoken insistence on that humanness that they perform their worth, that they speak their worth, that they confront the conundrum of life, through which they perdure, almost broken and on the edge of defeat (see Butler 2004, 73–74, in a different context). This is the incommensurability between the social death meted out to them and the people they are and aspire to be.

CHAPTER 10

Conclusion

FAILURE AND ABOLITION DEMOCRACY

June 2010. Last night at a meeting Cheryl said, "Well, we won't end injustice, but we must keep working." Larry replied impatiently, "We can't say that, we must be able to say we will end injustice." Dana, an older African American student who was also at the meeting, remarked, looking at me, "They said they would never end slavery, that we would be slaves for centuries." She had a sense awake within her that she could have been still in bondage, had it not been for the deliberate actions of people who came before. The exchange brought me back to a day when I was interviewing a man at the jail. Through the thick glass, he told us of the poor health care at the jail. I explained to him that there was little we could do, meaning little to aid and support him. He responded, "Do not say that. That is giving up too easily. You have too little hope. We can do things." I was struck by the resurgent hope. Sustained work against prison must contain an alchemy of pragmatism and enduring hopefulness, pessimism of the intellect and optimism of the will. (Fieldnotes, 2010)

AS I LOOK BACK at my journal, from where I've taken the preceding text, I see a contrast between Larry's commitment to a better future and the failure I now feel all our best efforts amounted to. The narrative arc of this book, in other words, ends in disappointment. We didn't make any lasting changes at the Broome County Jail. In 2007, the sheriff imposed new administrative restrictions on NAACP visits, effectively ending our access to people at the jail (see chapter 1). Though I continued to go up to the jail to visit with people in the general visiting room, I was no longer allowed private visits, nor was I permitted to take notes. I slowly eliminated the jail visits as an option for students and we suspended our biweekly meetings at the NAACP office.

At about the same time, two of my students who had served time urged me to focus more on the difficulties people had integrating into society after being released from prison, especially in finding employment, adequate housing, and proper health care, and in reuniting with children and dealing with parole officers. Through subsequent discussions, several other formerly incarcerated people joined us in forming an organization to support and advocate for formerly incarcerated people and their families. But we have not been able to sustain the organization. The obstacles and disappointments were demoralizing. For now, it seems, the best we can do as members of the Southern Tier Social Justice Project, the organization we formed, is offer assistance on an individual, informal, and case-by-case basis.

Glancing back over the history of attempts at prison reform in the United States, I can see now that our failure to change anything is not surprising. For as long as there have been penitentiaries, people have decried the sexual abuse of women, the terrible psychic price of solitary, and the general inability of prison and jails to rehabilitate. But with only a few significant exceptions (such as the Attica uprising of the early 1970s), criticism and protest have rarely resulted in any significant change.

When conditions do change, it may be due more to state interest than to moral argument. For example, between 2009 and 2012 the prison population ebbed slightly for the first time in thirty years before increasing again in 2013. This is probably attributable more to the fiscal crisis of 2008 and the resulting state budget crises than to a principled decision on the ethics or utility of incarceration, or because of the efforts of activists.

It is difficult to say how large the role of advocates, lobbyists, and activists has been in other transformations in the criminal justice system. For instance, beginning in 2012, voters and legislators in Washington, Colorado, New York, and elsewhere began to modify drug laws to make them less punitive. In 2014, California voters passed Proposition 47, which reduced nonviolent crimes such as simple drug possession and petty theft from felonies to misdemeanors, keeping people out of jail and redirecting money to prevent crime and help victims. There are even rumblings of sentencing reform at the federal level. But these are small steps, and it is not clear yet whether they indicate a significant redirection in criminal justice policy. They do suggest we are in the midst of a cultural change in attitudes toward drug use. But is the society becoming less cruel? Are we rethinking the utility of penal solutions to a range of social problems?

And are grassroots activists playing a part in some of the potentially large-scale shifts in criminal justice policy? One can find evidence to support the conclusion that activists' role has been crucial, but one can also find data to maintain that their contribution was minimal.

If the latter position is correct, that is if advocacy has done little historically to change conditions in prison, then what is the use, if any, of engaging
in community-based advocacy against incarceration? Were our attempts worth
the effort?

Conducting this research has transformed my conception of my
community—and my country, for that matter. It has transformed many of
my personal relationships. I have met people whom I would otherwise never
have met, or, if I had, it would have been in a context of fear, hostility, or exploitation. Instead, I met them in a project of solidarity, geared toward a participatory democracy and horizontal (as opposed to hierarchical) decision making. A
handful of students and a few people from the town also went through profound
changes.

> February 2005. Two of my interns, young white women, say in class that
> the women they interviewed at the jail as part of our monitoring project
> for the NAACP are "just like us." At first I have an impulse to correct
> them: I want to tell them that they need to reflect on differences among
> women, that there is a price to be paid for identifying too quickly, with-
> out taking stock of social difference—for example around race and class.
> But then I think more about it. One of the things I like about the project
> is that so many of the people involved are not politicized yet. The proj-
> ect itself politicizes them. A month ago these women had never crossed
> the portal of a jail, never talked to a person in jail about jail conditions
> and the horror they face, and probably had never reflected on women in
> prison much at all. One significant moment in their psychic and political
> development is to sustain a sense of identification. Identifying in a real
> way with the women inside, a "this could have been me" moment, seeing
> the women's exposure, frustration, anxiety, and fear of the uncertain as
> their own, taking that in, dwelling in that, even at the risk of diminishing
> social difference—this dwelling could augur real changes in the women's
> consciousness. They are making a connection, and they may complicate
> that connection later, but in making a connection they can come to
> see things about themselves and about other women, and that could also
> be the precondition to connections they allow themselves in the future.
> It's better than Othering them, says an activist friend. (Fieldnotes, 2005)

Participating is a way of developing an investment if they did not have
one before, a concrete, immediate investment in liberation, not just an abstract
conviction to social justice. This is a way of crossing a divide to others.

But these changes are on an individual level, which is not the same as
transforming institutions. The personal is surely political, but the political
cannot be only personal.

By way of conclusion, I will inventory briefly the lessons I learned from the community research, including presenting some contradictions we encountered that we were unable to resolve. In taking inventory, I noticed that the local, the state or regional, the national, and the global overlap and inter-penetrate (also see helpful, practical suggestions in Chen, Dulani, and Piepzna-Samarasinha 2011; Heidenreich 2011; INCITE 2007; Levi and Waldman 2011; Richie 2001; Spade 2011).

Since our goals never came to any fruitful conclusion, I submit these recommendations with no small sense of irony. Some of the proposals seem quixotic—at least they do to me—especially given our experience. Neverthe-less, failures can yield insight. We'll see.

NAVIGATING CONTRADICTIONS
Abolitionist Reform

Pushing for incremental changes in agencies and institutions that act with impunity, such as the parole office or the county jail, put us in significant contradiction with a deeper belief that the structure of these institutions was rife with abuse and racism that no measure of reform could possibly remedy without dismantling the institution entirely. Though we met with the sheriff, he always dismissed our concerns out of hand and continued to act with cal-lous disregard for the health and well-being of people held at the county jail. We tried to cooperate with the parole office so that they would not revoke people's parole so often, and instead support successful reentry a bit more, but the parole office treated us with a mixture of bureaucratic indifference and disdain. Both they and the sheriff usually, though not always, framed our rela-tionship in adversarial terms.

In pushing for change, we used a rule of thumb that we learned from a group that advocates for transgender people in prison in California. We did not adopt or advocate for any policy or position that would lead to increased expenditure or reliance on the corrections system, including jail health care or parole. We also resisted solutions predicated on expanding surveillance. Avery Gordon has called this "abolitionist reform," or prison reform that aims ulti-mately toward the eventual abolition of prison, rather than reform that serves as an apologia for the prison system (A. Gordon 2004).

Yet unintended consequences can undermine efforts at abolitionist reform. At what point does one (did we) tacitly support jail expansion by advocating for better health care? I am haunted by the thought that we did exactly this. In early 2013, after a series of suspicious inmate deaths around the state, the New York State Attorney General's Office announced an investiga-tion into the health care at fourteen county jails around New York. The inves-tigation may have been prompted in part by activists, especially in Buffalo and perhaps in Binghamton as well. As a result of the investigation, the attorney general ordered several county jails to make changes to their mental health and medical units. Astutely, several sheriffs around the state used this mandate to propose capital-intensive expansions to their respective jails. Our sheriff, for example, requested a multimillion-dollar expansion of the county jail.

In February 2014, the Broome County Legislature voted to provide several million dollars to build more bunk space at the jail and enlarge its medical unit. Other New York counties that have recently expanded their jails include Erie, Tomkins, Tioga, and Cortland in the face of small but vocal opposition. In vain we entered the county legislators' chambers, leafleting and carrying banners protesting the expansion. But I knew—we all knew—we were going to lose. I saw the sheriff and several of his upper-echelon staff across the room, standing by the podium, receiving public kudos from the county executive. They could not avoid seeing us with all our noisy posters and hand-painted T-shirts. Their lips were pursed in quiet disapproval. I could see how furious they were with us, but I thought—they've won! They've won. They've triumphed. This is their moment, not ours.

Several years of documenting and fighting against deficient prenatal care, the abominable rates of miscarriage, a lack of sympathy or psychological support for the mentally ill, and the lackadaisical diagnostic protocols in our county jail that have been responsible for at least one death (New York State Correction of Commission 2012) has gotten us little, except that the jail budget will now be greater.

This mirrors the expansion of prison medical care at the state level, as the New York State Department of Corrections copes with large numbers of mental health patients and an aging prison population.

> Rozann Greco, a friend who works with me on the advocacy, visits a new medical unit at Fishkill Correctional Facility in New York. She is part of a delegation on aging in prison. They tour the facility, one of five popping up throughout New York State. It specializes in geriatric care. It provides colonoscopies and prostate surgery. It also treats many of the "cognitive deficiencies," as they term it, of incarcerated people. She tells me that at first she was impressed with the level of care and the attention provided by these clinics. The doctors and staff seem serious, competent, and committed. It is well-staffed and the medical facilities seem up-to-date. But then, as she gets back in her car she thinks, with horror, "What happened to compassionate release?"

We discuss the experience at length. Is this the future of prisons? Some right wing pundits argue that people receive better medical care in prison than they do on the outside, as a way to show how comfy prisons are. Is this what we have decided to do as a society, invest more in prison health care instead of health care for the poor and the formerly incarcerated? Is this our vision for better health care and responsible investment?

Rozann tells me of a man they told her about during her visit. He routinely banged his head against the bars. The medical facility detected he has mental health problems and diagnosed him based on videos made of his behavior. They issued the man a helmet and prescribed a combination of occupational therapy and antipsychosis medication. His behavior, she was told, has improved remarkably.

By all accounts, the incarceration of the mentally ill is a significant social challenge, with some estimates as high as one third of inmates evincing some problem of mental illness. Is this our response to the problem of the incarceration of the mentally ill? Issuing them a helmet and a Prozac? My discussion with her depresses me profoundly. (Fieldnotes, 2009)

Advocating for reform thus must aim for more, or something other, than better health care; it must promote alternatives to incarceration.

But simply advocating for decarceration or alternatives to incarceration is not enough. Chapter 7, which details our skirmishes with the local parole office, underscores that the criminal justice system polices and controls people through other institutions.

In an era of mass supervision, a web of governmental and nongovernmental organizations jousts to impose themselves on the lives of the formerly incarcerated and their families (Robinson, McNeill, and Maruna 2013; McNeill and Beyens 2014; Miller 2014). The nonprofit and the service sector, in other words, begin where parole, probation, and the prison system leave off.

Aiming for abolition, even if couched as "abolition reform," proved of limited utility to me in negotiating this reentry industry. I can be more specific. Our organization, the Southern Tier Social Justice Project, tried to push for concrete changes in policy that emerged from the perspectives of the incarcerated, the formerly incarcerated, and their families, and that would be of direct benefit to them. In 2008, we formed a reentry task force with area service organizations, including residential treatment centers for drugs and alcohol and the parole office. The goal was a "one-stop shop," to use the jargon of those in the field—a comprehensive reentry center that would encompass all of a person's needs when he or she came back into town. I went along reluctantly, because I was worried that in forming a task force we were abandoning our work with community people and focusing too much attention on working with middle-class service providers and state agents such as the Office of Parole and the Department of Social Services (DSS). Our efforts were successful insofar as we formed a task force for reentry.

As it turned out, the victory was pyrrhic. Once state funds became available, the Department of Social Services quickly moved in and took over the task force. DSS drummed out nearly all of the formerly incarcerated people who had formed the task force. Although we had always strived for democratic and nonhierarchical decision making, the task force became hierarchical and dominated by a white middle-class service sector as well as the Department of Social Services and the Office of Parole.

This linked to a deeper problem inside our organizing efforts. The most committed formerly incarcerated people wanted to form a nonprofit, and, they hoped, get jobs as full-time advocates and peer counselors for the formerly incarcerated. This goal was in tension with our organizing for a political movement, since a nonprofit structure tends to impose hierarchy on an organization. The tension, quite frankly, boiled down to a question of time and focus. Becoming a nonprofit meant focusing a lot more on grant writing, which meant attending to the funding agendas of foundations and government agencies (see generally INCITE! 2007). Nonprofits have received a lot of criticism by progressives alert to the possibility of reproducing the logic of capitalism and of oppressive structures of service provision that sap the strength of political projects (see Rodriguez 2006; Spade 2011).

As an all-volunteer effort that was unfunded we had several advantages. We were not beholden to anyone except each other and to the incarcerated. No one had a financial stake. On the other hand, had we applied for nonprofit status (501[c]3), we might have had more stability as an organization. Funding and jobs would have allowed committed community members to dedicate themselves full-time to our efforts to support the formerly incarcerated and their families.

Political Organizing as Consciousness Raising

Addressing concrete problems directly, usually in a situation of crisis, did not always leave sufficient space for overall reflection on the direction we were taking. Our own impatience (mine included) with too much analysis (too much talk) at the expense of action made it difficult to speak enough about what we were doing, why, and how our efforts combated larger institutions of oppression that affected all of us. We made too little space to interrogate our own and others' ideological and political commitments. As a result, we found ourselves often reacting to external circumstances. Eventually, we found ourselves at odds with one another about overall goals and, perhaps, individual ambitions.

The participatory research we carried on throughout was a means to raise the consciousness of students, the currently and formerly incarcerated, and community members (like me) of the implications of the conjunction of capitalism, the state, racism, and sexism for the treatment of people in jail or prison, almost all of them poor people. I could start to see changes in the relations people struck with one another. I could see it dawn on students that research skills can be used to open the world around them to rethink the conditions of the society they live in. The research opened up avenues for critical exploration for students who had been forced to reckon with the imprisonment of a family member.

We organized with two relatively transient groups of people, students and people who had been to jail or prison. Students would come and go. For most, their involvement was just a stage of their lives. All told, over the years about seventy students became quite involved for a window of time—six months, say. But then they would vanish, their participation ending with the school semester. Only a few remained involved for more than a year. Incarcerated and formerly incarcerated people were also in transition, but of a different sort. Many were subject to state-induced crises, but also personal crises, extreme economic hardship, and, occasionally, violent interpersonal situations. In the case of those participants who were still incarcerated, they could be spontaneously transferred and then we usually never heard from them again. Some would come find us when they got out of jail and others disappeared from our lives. I was also out of town a lot. This also made it difficult to organize. It made our progress punctuated. The lack of continuity made it more difficult to protect whistleblowers and other people who took risks, such as those who spoke out publicly while their loved ones were still on parole. On the other hand, students and people in prison also sustained the project and made it exciting, inspiring, and hopeful.

I have written elsewhere of how I tried to make the antiprison work attentive to immigrant detention and deportation and our successes and failures in this regard (Price 2012a). Linking antiprison work with the immigrant rights movement was an attempt to link our organizing work to other political movements. But our endeavors in this area were only intermittent and inconsistent.

Coalition

I described in the first chapter how the project involved people from a range of cultural backgrounds, political orientations, and life experiences. Some saw the project as legal and pragmatic, trying to force the jail to provide adequate health care, framed within the terms of the modern liberal state, its legislative procedures, and its institutions of punishment. Others were prison abolitionists and embraced a socialist or anarchist politics. Some saw change only on the level of institutions; others looked for it interactively and incrementally, in the transformed social relationships themselves. And some people were just beginning to have a political understanding of the world. Many of the students came to this as a mildly intriguing assignment for class. Those who were incarcerated also approached our work in a range of ways. Some seemed to see this project as a way to help them out of a bad situation, while others took this as an opportunity to teach outsiders about what incarceration was really like. The most politicized framed this as a potential means to promote institutional change. Here the institutional link with the NAACP helped, since everyone recognized the project as part of a civil rights struggle.

In order to encompass all of these goals within a coalitional politics, I could call this a politics of towardness (Denise Ferreira da Silva, personal communication; Guha 2001). "Tendencies can be dissimilar and unequal in important respects and yet share an orientation toward some horizon each can recognize as its own. What is significant here is the dynamics of 'towardness' with its characteristic movements of inkling, approaching, and approximating" (Guha 2001, 37). This coalition encompassed several distinct horizons of understanding of political action, strategy, tools, and concepts.

The legal means favored by many members of the coalition were, I think, an attempt to force a public recognition of the actual lives of incarcerated people: the abuse they suffer through an admixture of neglect, malfeasance, and the operations of punishment. The impulse to appeal to legal institutions was a way to counter their dehumanization. In the United States, legal action is often on the level and in the idiom of lawsuits or legislative reform (lobbying efforts). These tactics are a way to protest state abuse in the terms set by a liberal state.

I can take an example from California. All of Us or None is a civil rights organization that pushes for better treatment of the formerly incarcerated (I described this organization in greater detail in chapter 8). It is a political organization whose contours are different from traditional civil rights organizations. They have a Janus-faced relationship to the law (and I mean that in a good sense): they appeal to the law while acknowledging that the law plays an important role in upholding racial hierarchies, gender violence, and class oppression. Mari Matsuda has termed this ability multiple consciousness (Matsuda 1989).

This ability is reflected in their view of voting rights. All of Us or None campaigns to restore the voting rights of people convicted of felonies. This campaign should be taken at face value—as promoting all the rights and privileges of citizenship. But a deeper drive for full personhood lies beneath the formal, explicit campaign, a drive for the affirmation of their humanity and their identity against the mechanisms of social death.

Human Rights

Calling prison or jail abuse a human rights issue provides a name that most people recognize immediately. It is a way to say that a state-sponsored activity is wrong. Human rights also provide a legal framework. Several human rights conventions afford tools to name and fight abuse. The Standard Minimum Rules for the Treatment of Prisoners, adopted by the United Nations in the 1950s, and the Universal Declaration of Human Rights contain provisions that apply to people in U.S. prisons and jails. The International Convention on the Elimination of All Forms of Racial Discrimination and the Convention on the Elimination of All Forms of Discrimination against Women recognize the barriers and exclusion faced by women of color (Cynthia Chandler of Justice Now!, personal communication). But human rights conventions are difficult to enforce or to litigate.

The language of human rights can be used to link social and political movements, such that the movement to stop violence in prisons and jails can be linked to organized attempts to close Guantánamo, and to other struggles around the globe. Critics have charged that some human rights organizations have engaged in Western moral imperialism or have been too closely aligned with U.S. government policies (Bhatt 2014; also see Hernández-Truyol 2002). While skeptical of universalist projects "from above," Boaventura de Sousa Santos sees promise in campaigns for human rights that come from the grassroots and form "cross-border solidarity among groups that are exploited, oppressed, or excluded by hegemonic globalization" (Santos 2002, 43; also see Schulman 2004).

Denouncing human rights abuses in the United States is a good way to try to deflate or at least sidestep American exceptionalism and its tendency to see human rights abuses only elsewhere. Of course, such a strategy risks falling victim itself to American exceptionalism when American authorities dismiss out of hand reports of human rights abuse.

Do human rights denunciations of prisons and jails open the possibility for alternatives to incarceration? Or are they geared more to regulate existing conditions of incarceration? If a human rights campaign is undertaken only to demand codification of standards of treatment in prison, or in order to combat abuses, then it falls short of addressing problems basic to the organization of prisons and jails. Natal alienation, for example, is intrinsic to modern incarceration in the United States.

Let me put the political challenge another way. In the chapter "Natal Alienation," I discussed briefly the story of Danielle Ferreira, a breast-feeding new mother and immigrant detained pending deportation in Charlotte, North Carolina (Manware 2007). Her story encapsulates the dilemma of jail reform. According to her jailers, inmates are not allowed to express milk without a court order. We are assured by jail spokespeople, however, that the jail is equipped to deal with the symptoms when the mothers abruptly stop nursing. From the standpoint of substantive reproductive justice, the irony of championing women's reproductive rights while they are incarcerated is captured in the image of jails preparing to treat women's symptoms when they abruptly stop nursing; the inhumanity is in the circumstance that forces women to stop nursing suddenly, and only secondarily in the poor health care they get once they are incarcerated. Pushing for thorough reproductive justice implies an antiprison, or prison abolitionist, position.

Building Safe Communities

Perhaps the most important element of our work was trying to build healthy communities. A healthy community with healthy relationships is in itself a way of supplanting prisons. Marc Mauer has observed that a safe neighborhood does not have to rely on the criminal justice system: "When we think of a 'safe' community, we don't think of a community with lots of police or with the death penalty. Rather, it is one with clean, well lit streets, open businesses and little fear. Poor communities that lack this should be given more resources" (Mauer 2006, 6). A safe community means adequate health care, housing, education, and employment. If our communities were healthy in this sense, the perceived need for prisons might dissipate on its own.

The push for more accessible housing, educational opportunities, and employment must be discerning. Increased funding is not enough. For example, through placing low-income students and disproportionately students of color in special education, entrenching de facto school segregation, instituting punitive suspension policies, police substations located inside schools, and through other policies and practices, many schools in low-income neighborhoods and communities of color have constructed what has been termed a school-to-prison pipeline. The elements of this pipeline must be removed as part of any effort to dismantle a consolidated prison-industrial complex. Opportunities for education must involve educational reform. An education must equip a person with critical faculties to be an informed citizen. It must, in short, be something more than a way to reproduce class and caste differences.

In chapter 8, "Spirit Murder," I discuss the barriers incarcerated people face in attempting to continue their education during or after incarceration. Formerly incarcerated people often identify access to higher education as the most important area for improvement. One of the most impressive experiences I have ever had as a teacher was guest lecturing for a colleague in his class at Elmira State Penitentiary. The focus and intellectual engagement of the students was striking.

Finding employment or going back to school is usually a condition of parole. But in our city and throughout the country, people with a criminal record face discrimination in both of these spheres. People tell me of all the job-readiness training programs, so popular with reentry organizations, that they have been through. But these programs are only marginally helpful if not accompanied by a campaign to hire people with a criminal record.

A national movement to "Ban the Box" in employment applications has been meeting with some success. Banning the box means not asking whether a job applicant has ever been convicted of a felony, since a criminal record is often taken as the basis for not hiring a person. Many municipalities and even some states no longer ask about a criminal history in job applications, nor do they allow employers who receive city or state contracts to do so.

But Ban the Box and job-readiness programs are not useful if there are no jobs. (And one should be able to hope for more than minimum wage jobs in the service sector.) Economic recessions affect almost everyone. But for people with a criminal record, the difficulty of finding a job when there are few jobs to begin with makes life bleak indeed.

Finding housing after incarceration is a frequent problem in Binghamton, especially if people would like to reunite as a family. Advocating for housing for the formerly incarcerated must involve reforming HUD policies that ban people convicted of drug felonies from federal housing. Generally, a housing campaign must involve identifying or developing attractive, secure, bright, encouraging places to live.

"Justice" is a social concept and it relies on communities-in-action. Justice cannot be achieved in the absence of robust social ties; individuals cannot live healthy lives without a vibrant community. In this way, justice is socially guaranteed or socially deprived. "Reproductive justice" in particular implies a multigenerational understanding. Interruptions of kinship ties are clear interruptions of the possibility of healthy reproduction and health more generally. Housing and reproductive rights are linked.

Building a Decent Society

Building a safe community is part of building a decent society. A decent society is one whose institutions do not give its members reason to feel that their dignity has been hurt (Margalit 1998). In chapter 3, I described several examples of institutional humiliation.

As of this writing (June 2014), hunger strikers in California have called off their latest hunger strike. It was a protest of monumental proportions, with 30,000 incarcerated people participating in the beginning. They were protesting the arbitrary process of sending people to isolation units, often for years and even decades. This process requires them to debrief, or inform, on others in order to be released from that slow torture. Solitary confinement, or the special housing unit, is an institutionalized process of wreaking psychic havoc. In earlier chapters, I reviewed the demands of the California hunger strikers. I described debriefing as a form of humiliation that implies the rending of social ties through engendering suspicion, hostility, and disloyalty. Coordinated efforts against solitary confinement are beginning in New York and around the country, inspired, perhaps, by the California protests. But I find that most of my colleagues and students who are involved in antiprison campaigns are more hopeful than I am for their success. History eats my hope.

Stopping Violence against Women and Transgender People

Most, though not all, of the women I know who have survived prison have also survived intimate abuse, which has usually included sexual abuse. Statistics bear this out: a majority of women in prison are survivors of violence. In prison, they face horrendous forms of violence. I have also detailed how transgender people also face enormous amounts of violence.

Many still face abuse when they get out, but with fewer options to end the violence than most other women, who, generally speaking, also face scant options. The movement to stop violence against women must encompass women in prison and formerly incarcerated women. Stopping gender violence, in other words, must include stopping violence against women and transgender people who have committed felonies, including violent felonies. Many women have several generations involved in the criminal justice system, often with a consequent set of challenges. This requires stopping violence and humiliation that is institutionalized (as in prison) or structural (as in poverty). Seeing violence against women in this expanded way links the fight for reproductive rights, the movement to end rape and domestic violence, the movement for immigrant rights, antipoverty activists, and people organizing against police brutality, to advocates for the rights of children and the LGBT community. These directions will result in new alliances and new strategies (see Price 2012b, 139–149).

Many laws are gender neutral on their face but have disastrous consequences for women and transgender people. For example, drug laws and immigration laws that seem neutral often have disparate effects on women (Lindsley 2002; K. Smith 2005). Other laws are overly punitive or criminalize activities that in many countries would not result in a prison sentence and may not even be considered a crime, such as prostitution, drug abuse, or writing bad checks. The legal system is still not sufficiently cognizant of how some "crimes" are tied to intimate abuse. Sending women to prison for injuring or killing a batterer in self-defense is itself abusive and represents state collusion with the abuse of women. Sometimes, women are forced into criminal activity by their batterer, including theft or drug crimes, a pattern that criminologist Beth Richie has termed "gender entrapment" (Richie 1996).

My commitment to the struggle to end violence against women in all its forms sometimes tests my principles to fight against incarcerating people for wrongdoing.

January 2013. I am at the jail interviewing a man in the visiting room. It's a crowded day, so the room is filled with the noise of chatter and activity, most of it warm and excited, as people greet each other, catch up with each other, and babies are handed over the long divider that separates us from the side where the incarcerated sit.

The man I am visiting was just sentenced to twenty years for raping his wife's daughter, who is ten years old. He is about sixty. "I am retiring you," the judge told him at sentencing. I am the first person he has spoken to since he was sentenced. "I don't have anyone to talk to," he tells me. He is distraught. He is having so much trouble comprehending the sentence and adjusting to it emotionally that he cannot remain still. He clutches his head and interrupts himself. "I didn't do it," he tells me over and over. He claims that the prosecutor offered to drop the charge if he pled guilty to another charge, of assaulting a fellow prisoner, and when he refused to plead guilty to that charge he faced the full charge of child-rape. I listen without comment, cutting him off only when he begins to tell me how his ex-wife contrived the story as revenge.

I am in no position to evaluate whether he raped the little girl. I know that it is perfectly possible he did, of course. If so, he is responsible for bringing a violent fracture into a young girl's life and is unwilling to accept responsibility. The horror of that prospect notwithstanding, I find I am troubled by his physical and emotional reaction to the sentence. It is as if his body is having trouble accepting the sentence, the sudden shift in his life that will now force him into a cage for as much as two decades. Afterward, I will spend hours analyzing this moment, running it over and over in my mind. Do I find myself moved? I'm not sure. Perhaps a bit. I definitely experience an ethical and emotional dissonance.

At the end of the interview, as we get up, he leans forward across the barrier with his arms open, inviting me for a farewell embrace. I do not want to embrace him. I do not want to hug him. I am also conscious that people are observing us. Though I lean forward, I thrust my hand forward for a handshake and to forestall an embrace. I leave, shaken by the encounter.

The next week, I am driving home with Suzanne after a meeting. "Why do you think there are so many sex offenders who come to our meetings?" I ask her. We have met many by now, as well as their parents and girlfriends. It's challenging for me, especially when they, or their parents, minimize or deny their original offense. "Do you think it's because no one else defends them?" "It could be," she answers; after a moment, "No one stands up for them." She looks at me a bit wryly. She is a survivor of intimate abuse. Some time ago, she told me how a relative raped her when she was a child. At the meeting we just left, a father had come with his nineteen-year-old son, who was just released from prison. We can see that the son has obvious cognitive difficulties when he tries to speak for himself at the meeting. The father and son tell us that the young man had been convicted of having sex with a fourteen-year-old "who looked sixteen." The father came to the meeting because he is outraged that the parole office would not let his son live at home with them when he was released from prison. The parole office required instead that he live in a downtown rooming house, a notorious slum-dwelling where sex offenders are often required to live. In our discussion, it came out that the young man has several younger sisters at home. This left me feeling torn. I can see why they required him to live outside the home. His younger sisters need to be protected, and the father, keen on defending his son, dismisses out of hand any possible rationale parole had for intervening in the living arrangement. He did not seem inclined to worry as much about his daughters' well-being; at least he did not raise that concern with us. Did his son pose a risk to them? I do not know. On the other hand, the downtown fleabag, populated with older, seasoned men convicted of sex crimes, seemed like a terrible place to send this young man. The parole office is singularly unprepared to facilitate safe, healthy arrangements in complicated family situations. In my experience, they approach most problems with coercion, baiting and intimidating people on parole, and exercising their power with caprice and arrogance, often dividing up families without cause ("If the only tool you have is a hammer . . . ," I think to myself).

I reflect with Suzanne that when we try and advocate for people convicted of sex crimes, we must demand a reciprocal agreement that they will honor the integrity and dignity of women, girls, and other vulnerable people. We cannot abide the chaos and violence they bring into others' lives. But there is little infrastructure or context in our organizing to make these demands, or to make sure people who have committed outrages comply. (Fieldnotes, 2013; also see Chen, Dulani, and Piepzna-Samarasinha 2011)

Individual and Social Responsibility

April 2010. I am at a small daylong symposium at my university I helped organize. Kathy Boudin is the keynote speaker. She discusses the tendency of prison reformers to focus on the injustice of incarcerating nonviolent felons such as drug dealers and addicts. Who advocates for violent offenders? she asks. (Fieldnotes, 2010)

Critics of the drug war often argue that people who commit nonviolent crimes could be usefully tracked into alternatives to incarceration. This seems to imply that people convicted of violent crimes should be incarcerated.

In reducing the number of people who are incarcerated, or otherwise supporting a politics of decarceration, we need to rethink our collective response to violent crime as well. To start with, we must disaggregate what counts as violent crime instead of lumping all violent crime together: a woman killing her abuser should not be dealt with the same way as a person who chronically abuses children. Separating offenses implies a range of responses. Secondly, the character of response could fruitfully follow the logic of restitution rather than of retribution. In one of my classes, a guest speaker, a man who spent twenty-four years in prison for armed robbery, concluded his talk by remarking how senseless it was that his punishment did not involve a moral, emotional, psychological, or financial reckoning with his criminal act. "You know, to this day I have not been asked to return one cent to my victims. I was not asked to consider the terror I forced them to experience. Does that make sense?" Even the victims (especially the victims) of violence might find restitution more satisfying if they were consulted at every stage of the criminal justice process and their needs attended to. Victims' rights supporters argue that the criminal justice system is inattentive to their needs and perspectives. Angela Davis proposes redescribing criminal violence as tort, so that if a person hurts another, he or she is liable for damages rather than simply for punishment, since most forms of punishment do not assist a victim at all (2003). Her suggestion opens up possibilities for other kinds of responses, other ways of understanding and responding to behavior or comportment that is harmful or that the society wishes to prevent.

Kathy Boudin ends her talk at my university by discussing her current work: helping prepare long termers for their parole board hearings. She points out that, from the standpoint of the convicted, one of the qualities of the criminal justice system is that up to the point of the parole board hearing the logic of criminal justice leads defendants and the accused to minimize their role in a crime. The defendant argues for her innocence, or makes a case for leniency by trying to excuse illegal behavior or otherwise mitigate her responsibility.

But at the parole board, the opposite is required. One must take responsibility and show remorse for one's actions. Pleading innocence or diminishing one's role is not a winning strategy. Boudin is helping people prepare for the board by exploring their culpability, so that they arrive at genuine remorse.

I'm asked to moderate the Question and Answer period. Hands go up immediately. "Doesn't this approach ignore structural reasons for high rates of incarceration, such as poverty and racism?" asks a graduate student. Boudin acknowledges the workings of oppressive structures, but says that people need to look inside themselves and explore what they have done. The session becomes contentious as many of my colleagues and students, most of them sociologists, raise their hands to be called on. "Aren't you taking the criminal justice system too much on its own terms by emphasizing guilt and innocence?" Each response by Boudin aggravates and emboldens the audience more. At some point, taking stock of the onslaught and the ever-growing field of hands vying for recognition, I close the Q&A, trying not to sound flippant. "OK, this may be the best time to stop, while the crowd is still hungry for more." I thank Kathy publicly and we adjourn, while some still linger in their seats, clearly frustrated. The department chair and I take Boudin and a few graduate students and local advocates out to dinner at a Chinese restaurant. (Fieldnotes, 2010)

I can understand the sociologists' response. I share with my colleagues in sociology an aversion to discussion of crime that remains fixed on questions of individual guilt and innocence and does not take into account racism in the criminal justice system, as well as its wholesale attack on poor people, while letting wealthy and well-connected wrongdoers largely off the hook for the harm they've caused. (Why are those who authorize torture or drone attacks on civilians never held to account? Why aren't corporate criminals prosecuted? . . . and so on). From the sociologists' perspective, Boudin seemed to be presupposing that the convicted carry, or should carry, guilt and responsibility.

However, are the sociologists letting people off the hook for wrongdoing? Feeling shame upon contemplating one's moral shortcomings is healthy. Introspection, accountability to others, and critical reflection on one's ethical responsibility are important for a strong civil society.

Ultimately, these positions are not incompatible, even though people seemed to be so much at odds in our discussion. Discussion of oppressive structures that send historic numbers of people to prison need not evacuate individuals of responsibility. But we have an impoverished vocabulary to discuss ethical responsibility, with the result that responsibility becomes so frequently, and so quickly, enmeshed with liberal concepts of individual agency and moral blame, often with echoes of religious concepts of sin. And the criminal justice system is better at humiliating people than at creating a context for ethical reflection.

This speaks to a certain spiritual malaise and an inability, as Flannery O'Connor argued, to perceive the intrusion of grace in our lives. I have tried to take up her concept of grace to contribute to a language of individual and collective responsibility and solidarity.

In what may have been one of the more elegiac moments of his presidency, Dwight Eisenhower alluded to the "even spiritual" influence on the culture of an untrammeled military establishment conjoined to a large arms industry in his famous speech on the military-industrial complex. "The very structure of our society," he remarked, hangs in the balance. Eisenhower did not elaborate on what he might have meant. Eric Schlosser perhaps gives us a clue when he provocatively points out another sense of the term "complex": its psychological use as "an overreaction to a perceived threat" (1998).

The spiritual or psychological sense of complex-as-overreaction brings us into a world of fear, racism, and obsession. A complex in this technical sense implies a loss of perspective. Delving into the psychic realm of the prison-industrial complex helps explain irrational economic behavior (such as investing in prisons rather than schools), disproportionate reaction, and perhaps other, darker pathways of human sensibility, such as sadism and voyeurism.

To read the explosion of the prison complex and the swelling ranks of incarcerated people in purely economic terms would be to miss the role of this dangerous side of the human psyche as it expresses itself through, for example, racism. One need only glance at the plethora of documentary-style television shows that masquerade as exposés to offer viewers frisson at seeing "real footage" of prisoners, as well as the legion of other made-for-television dramas that involve crime and corrections. Stoked by the omnipresence of media representations, people's imaginations often seem to me to be both attracted and repulsed by the specter of the penitentiary. As a faculty member, I see increasing numbers of students come to my class motivated by an interest in forensics and other aspects of solving crime that focus on the visual and on excitement.

The stubborn persistence of the death penalty when most other countries abandoned it decades ago is another manifestation of a society invested in unmistakably brutal and vicious practices. The continued popularity of the death penalty betrays an attachment to justice as vengeance and to seeing punishment as the proper form of compensating the victim. The thirst for violent and humiliating punishment is widespread:

> A couple has invited me to a café. I order a croissant. They ask me about the book I'm writing. A bit self-conscious, I try to explain what I am doing while I munch. I present the idea of social death to them and say that I argue that prisons humiliate and natally alienate the incarcerated. I give several examples of punishment practices that humiliate. "I think that's a good thing!" says the woman. "They should be humiliated." In my worst moments, I fear the dominant culture is moved by cruelty,

vendetta, and retribution, often for the most minute of offenses. (Field-notes, 2014)

Chipping away at the prison-industrial complex is not just a question of legal reform. It requires retraining the senses, our concepts of justice, the desire to humiliate, and the industries that have been generated to satisfy those desires. Change includes rethinking the solutions to social problems currently constructed as criminal questions, such as drug addiction.

An abolition project, in other words, is not a Luddite scheme of taking a hammer to the granite walls of jails and prisons. To do that would be to attack only the outward manifestations of a larger social process, including designating certain acts as "crime," where selective indictment, prosecution, and discriminatory sentencing maintain inequity and a racial caste system. Instead, an abolition project would require restructuring not just the concrete institutions but the financial incentives, the pleasure in cruelty, the attachment to punishment, to white supremacy, and to a binary system of gender.

> April 2013. My teaching assistants and I are reading midterm student evaluations for my class, "The Prison-Industrial Complex." I bemoan aloud the indifference or resistance most students seem to evince to the readings on the depredations of the prison on people's lives. Xhercis, one of the teaching assistants, says to me that many undergraduates don't buy painting incarcerated people as victims. (Fieldnotes, 2013)

Since Xhercis made this observation, I have been haunted by the thought that I have misconceived my entire pedagogical strategy in how I argue against prisons. I wonder if I have been implicitly attempting a moral education, to use an old-fashioned expression. I have been trying to reeducate the students' desires away from justice as revenge, trying to get them to reflect on their idea of justice. I think back to a moment a few years ago, when I had an epiphany about my students, an insight that brought on a low point in my morale when it came to teaching. It started in the wake of a horrific earthquake in Pakistan.

> On October 8, 2005, an earthquake that measured between 7.6 and 7.8 on the Richter Scale killed more than 80,000 people and left more than 3.5 million homeless. Within a week of the disaster, two Pakistani students contact me and ask to show a short video they made on the earthquake. I'm surprised by how professional and slick it seems for a student film. Over eighty thousand dead, and many more times that to die in the cold winter if no help comes. The film ends with a short plea for financial support. After the film, we discuss why the disaster has not been more in the news. A student raises his hand. "Americans just don't care about others." Another pipes up, "Well, there's been so many disasters recently, I mean,

you lose count, how much can we give? How much can we care?" Sympathy fatigue, I write on the board and the students titter. "It is a natural disaster and not a human created one like 9/11." "Indifference," another student says. "We weigh American lives more." "But what about the Tsunami?" another protests (this is right after the Tsunami that hit the coast of Indonesia which provoked a large flow of support from Americans). Then, one says, "I overheard someone react to the earthquake in Pakistan by saying, 'Now there will be fewer terrorists.'" Another says, "I heard a student say, 'Just a bunch of rag heads.'" Another adds that someone said, "Did they get Osama?" And slowly it dawns on me that it is not just indifference to the suffering of Pakistanis and non-Anglo-Americans. I start to feel sick to my stomach as I realize that some Americans have derived a measure of satisfaction. They get off on the idea of people dying miserably in Pakistan. (Fieldnotes, 2005)

In a similar vein, I wonder about my style of teaching, which rests in part on rehearsing the stories and critiques of people in prison. "Good," a student might think, "those prisoners should suffer." Or the students may take in the stories, shudder, but also demarcate their lives as unconnected or disconnected.

The perils, as well as the futility, of educating for values are quite vivid to me. Since I don't feel that we are making any progress in our local organizing I feel like a bit of a fraud. I feel defeated. My classes are popular enough, but I am not sure at all what the students want, expect, or will tolerate, from me, from the class, from the readings, from themselves or each other.

Training students on how to do interviews with imprisoned people and taking students with me to meetings at the NAACP was useful. The students seemed to awaken to the darker side of the society through this process, but I do not see any way to continue.

The spring, 2013 semester is finally drawing to a close. After class one day, I gripe to Olivia, a teaching assistant, that the students don't seem to be doing the reading as the semester winds down. A student within my hearing says that "the reality is so overwhelming and there's nothing we can do about it." In the past I've tried to create avenues so that students could learn in the community and also channel their response to the problems we learn about (the school-to-prison pipeline, immigration detention and deportation, abominable health care in prisons) into community participation, advocacy, and activism. I didn't set up an infrastructure this semester for that kind of participation, and now I'm regretting it. It's not that I decided not to; it's that all of the community work has fallen apart, fallen by the wayside, due to a number of external, and—why not say it?—personal reasons that made it hard to persevere.

I feel that I've failed the students, the community, and missed an opportunity. (Fieldnotes, 2013)

ABOLITION DEMOCRACY AND HEARTBREAK

I am at a university giving a guest lecture on natal alienation. During the Q&A, a professor asks, with a tone that suggests he wants a direct reply, "So, do you believe in prison abolition or not?" This is a trap, I think. Many regard prison abolition as utopian and unrealistic, and therefore dismissible. However, if we take the long view, we see that institutions, like empires, come into being and then eventually fade away, or at least transform. I tell him that an argument could be made that focusing on abolition is a distraction, insofar as it serves to alienate many who would be otherwise inclined to cooperate in shrinking considerably the number of people who live in cages. "Let's say I support decarceration," I reply, and hope I won't be perceived as hedging. "Having said that, I think that systematic natal alienation is an inevitable consequence of the current structure of incarceration." (Fieldnotes, 2013)

Prison abolition indicates an imagined future. I offer it with a sense of irony. The theologian Paul J. Griffiths has written that irony "is uncanny (we don't know what to make of it); it is erotic (it calls us, with longing, to something whose shape we cannot see); and it breaks apart whichever practical identity it pertains to, showing the repertoire of that identity to be essentially inadequate to its own aspirations" (Griffiths 2012, 22). To aspire to the abolition of the penitentiary is to propose a future from a present where our current identities seem essentially inadequate. The abolition of the prison requires breaking apart those identities; it requires something like a reconstruction of the self.

Meanwhile, in an antiutopian vein, abolition projects are most fruitfully directed toward a process of democratizing the society, rather than fixing on an ideal future. As a project rather than an end point or ideal, perhaps the spirit of the proposal is captured in the words of Derrick Bell: "We must realize, as our slave forebears did, that the struggle for freedom is, at bottom, a manifestation of our humanity which survives and grows stronger through resistance to oppression, even if that oppression is never overcome" (Bell 1995, 308).

Abolition democracy, as W.E.B. Du Bois termed it, is an attempt to rescue the tragically aborted project of Reconstruction (1977 [1935]). Yet the history we work against is not a history of progress or of advance. The changes do not bring us entirely past older paradigms of dehumanization. It's more of a spiral history, a history of return, a history inhabited by ghosts, where old women live to bury their daughters and then are put in the same cell in which those daughters died; where people still invoke slavery as a way to understand contemporary social practices, social relationships, even gestures; where people live a present and a future haunted by the past, hunted, caged, and enchained. In some ways, it's a history of stasis. It is a mistake, and its own kind of conceit or hubris, to think of history as progress.

I have framed this book as an attempt to cross an abyssal divide (Santos 2007, 2014) and end social death. At the risk of sounding grandiose, organizing against the parole office or the jail is a modest attempt, in a nondescript Rust Belt town, to battle against a racialized colonial divide that encompasses the planet. In less grandiose terms, the politics can be measured by the intimate calculus of accompanying a person well or poorly, of staving off despair in oneself or another, in offering a concrete platform for collective engagement.

Abolition democracy means not merely decarceration but social projects and alternatives to incarceration that can overcome the abyssal divide, a means of overcoming a social fragmentation, the cultural and historical forces that make us appear separate and independent of one another. This question of people moving in and out of jail can become the center. The persistent unease it has engendered as I follow the thread through the research has become the touchstone that compels the innermost motion of the work I do, the thoughts I have, the friendships I strike up, my political judgment, my understanding of American history, the theory that makes sense to me, the dreams that inspire me and the nightmares I am haunted by, the small compromises I make as well as the trespasses, the deviations, and the emotional landscape I inhabit. The participatory research, organizing these points of connection and collective reflection, the activism around atrocities in our backyard, occurring as we speak, marks an interweaving of our public and private lives, of the geographies of our days.

NOTES

CHAPTER 1   CROSSING THE ABYSS:
THE STUDY OF SOCIAL DEATH

1. A number of scholars have made the connection between social death and incarceration. Dylan Rodriguez (2008) sees the prison regime as a technology that anchors contemporary white supremacy. Colin Dayan juxtaposes the social death of slaves with the civil death of the felon in order to argue for the legal and historical continuity between them (2011, 39–70, esp. 42–46). Drawing on literary accounts of the American penitentiary, Caleb Smith makes an argument similar to Dayan's (2009, 41–44). In tracing the legacies of slavery, Loïc Wacquant (2002) discusses prisons as social death. Lisa Guenther likens solitary confinement to living death in her phenomenological study (2013). In a different vein, Lisa Marie Cacho's study of social death takes up "how human value is made intelligible" through racialized, sexualized, spatialized, and state-sanctioned violence (2012, 4). Cacho looks at a range of processes and practices that criminalize immigrants and groups racialized as nonwhite, rather than at the consequences of incarceration per se.

2. Orlando Patterson would probably disagree with this formulation, but Patterson is interested in making general comparative claims about the nature of slavery in different times and places.

3. In April 2013, the New York State Attorney General's Office announced an investigation into CMC and the health care it provides to fourteen county jails in New York State. As a result of its investigation, the attorney general required a series of changes to health care delivery at the Broome County Jail. See my discussion in chapter 10.

4. According to the Bureau of Justice Statistics, in 2007 federal and state governments alone spent $74 billion on corrections; given the scale of county and municipal expenditures on corrections, this number is quite conservative. See the Bureau of Justice Statistics, http://bjs.ojp.usdoj.gov/content/glance/tables/exptyptab.cfm, consulted in October 2012.

5. This practice is both common and controversial. As of this writing, it is subject to ongoing legislation. In October 2012, for example, California banned the use of shackles for pregnant women or women in recovery from pregnancy. See California Senate Bill AB 2530. In 2009, New York State banned the use of restraints on women while giving birth (N.Y. Correctional Law § 611); this law allows their use to transport pregnant women only "in extraordinary circumstances."

6. This is not to suggest that all sexual expression by incarcerated people is evidence of their victimization. In other words, not all sex by incarcerated people is necessarily abusive or oppressive. Juanita Diaz (2006) and Brenda Smith (2006) have each studied sexual expression by incarcerated women as an exercise of agency.

7. For example, to be released on parole, people must agree not to "fraternize" with other people convicted of a felony. Parole officers often interpret this to include family members who have been convicted of felonies, including spouses and

children. People on parole also have to agree to have their homes and cars searched at will by parole officers. This right frequently leads family members who are not on parole to feel monitored by parole officers as well.

8. As critical race theorists, feminists, and others have pointed out, university life is hardly civil. To the contrary, sexual violence and racial harassment routinely take place on campuses throughout the country. I am referring here to the outward appearance of normalcy on most campuses.

CHAPTER 2   NATAL ALIENATION

1. I thank Jodie Lawston for comments that helped me clarify this point.
2. I thank Noelle Paley for crucial discussion of these points.

CHAPTER 3   HUMILIATION

1. Moral reflection need not lead to feeling shame. Many drug crimes can be considered morally neutral acts, some women are incarcerated for killing their abusers, which is not necessarily shameful (although many feel shame), political prisoners consider themselves prisoners-of-war, and so on. On the other hand, of course, many acts for which people have been convicted are violent, immoral, and shameful. See the concluding chapter for a discussion of remorse.

2. Margalit would not agree with this analysis because he believes prisons are not necessarily humiliating. Although I will not argue for it here, Margalit's claims about prison nevertheless force one to conclude that prisons may be intrinsically humiliating, even if he wants to argue that they need not be.

3. Previously, a diagnosis of Gender Identity Disorder allowed transgender people to be eligible for consideration for access to hormone replacement therapy. As of May 2013, the American Psychological Association's *Diagnostic and Statistical Manual of Mental Disorders* (often referred to as *DSM-5*) removed "gender identity disorder" and added "gender dysphoria." This change reflects a response to efforts by advocates for transgender people who recognize that a diagnosis of Gender Identity Disorder pathologized transgender people; however, a diagnosis of GID nonetheless provided the opportunity for transgender people to demand "treatment" through hormones administrators can otherwise deny. Issues springing from diagnosing and pathologizing transgender people and the implications for their access to surgery and hormonal treatment are open, and developments are ongoing.

4. In 2012, in *Miller v. Alabama* 567 U.S. ___ and *Jackson v. Hobbs* 567 U.S. ___, the United States Supreme Court ruled against sentencing schemes that mandate life in prison without the possibility of parole for juvenile homicide offenders. As of this writing, several thousand cases nationally are being reviewed for possible resentencing.

CHAPTER 4   DISSEMBLANCE AND
CREATIVITY: TOWARD A METHODOLOGY
FOR STUDYING STATE VIOLENCE

1. I have adapted this phrase from Judith Butler's (2004) thoughtful essay on David Reimer, "Doing Justice to Someone: Sex Reassignment and the Allegories of Transsexuality." I thank Eunjung Kim for this reference.

CHAPTER 5   RACISM, PRISON, AND
THE LEGACIES OF SLAVERY

1. Winthrop Jordan offers a congeries of cognitive and perceptual preconditions that the English used to differentiate the African from the European. "From the first, Englishmen tended to set Negroes over against themselves, to stress what they conceived to be radically contrasting qualities of color, religion, and style of life, as well as animality and a peculiarly potent sexuality. . . . Their geographic location also helped explain other strange characteristics. The Africans the English encountered were 'heathen' which is to say, they were not Christian. Neither did they belong to other religious traditions recognized by the English: Catholicism, Islam, and Judaism were for the British forms of apostasy, it is true. But they were forms of apostasy that were nonetheless familiar."

"The African religions," on the other hand, "were simply defective. The Africans were not just heathens. They were also 'savage.' They lived lives unlike those of the British. Since their homes, diets, manner of eating, daily social and economic practices, dress, language, in short all those practices that make up culture, were largely strange to the British. They were symptoms of African savagery" (1968, 23). Winthrop Jordan's classic account is powerful and convincing. However, it is possible that the British simply used these symptoms of difference to rationalize their devaluation and enslavement of Africans and people of African descent.

2. Sir Edward Coke in 1738: "He that was taken in Battle should remain Bond to his taker for ever, and he to do with him, all that should come of him, his Will and Pleasure, as with his Beast, or any other Cattle, to give, or to sell, or to kill" (cited in Jordan 1968, 32).

CHAPTER 6   THE BIRTH OF THE PENITENTIARY

1. Whether the American penitentiary is religious in origin continues to be a bone of contention. While many historians argue that it is (e.g., Hirsch 1992), one prominent scholar has argued that the prison is a largely secular institution, the product of an increasingly secular state during the Andrew Jackson administration (Rothman 2005 [1971]). The birth of the penitentiary has also been likened to a new penal colony. In this view, the reformers wanted a form of punishment that was hidden from view not out of concern for the dignity of the prisoner, but because they sought a form of banishment. A related interpretation is that rather than seeking to end the brutality of public humiliation, reformers were striving to contain social unrest (Takagi 1975). In the wake of Shay's Rebellion (1786–87), the ruling classes were concerned that the prisoners who were publicly paraded, tortured, and in some cases executed were receiving public commiseration and acts of solidarity rather than derision and abuse from the crowd. It was thought that a penitentiary would squirrel away any transgressor out of sight and, it was hoped, out of mind.

CHAPTER 7   "DOESN'T EVERYONE KNOW
SOMEONE IN PRISON OR ON PAROLE?"

1. Although this is sometimes termed "recidivism," the term is misleading and ambiguous: the recidivism rate does not always measure the reoffense rate; sometimes it measures the rearrest rate, and other times it represents the reconviction rate, or the reincarceration rate. The actual reconviction rate is closer to 45 percent,

and the reincarceration rate is around 25 percent. These rates also vary enormously by offense. Over 70 percent of offenders who have committed property crimes are rearrested, whereas closer to 1 percent of people convicted of homicide are rearrested on average (see Langan and Levin 2002; Pew Center on the States 2011).

2. The appendix includes the rest of our demands.

CHAPTER 9   STATES OF GRACE: SOCIAL
LIFE AGAINST SOCIAL DEATH

1. "This conjunction of an immense military establishment and a large arms industry is new in the American experience. The total influence—economic, political, even spiritual—is felt in every city, every statehouse, every office of the federal government. We recognize the imperative need for this development. Yet we must not fail to comprehend its grave implications. Our toil, resources and livelihood are all involved; so is the very structure of our society. In the councils of government, we must guard against the acquisition of unwarranted influence, whether sought or unsought, by the military-industrial complex. The potential for the disastrous rise of misplaced power exists and will persist. We must never let the weight of this combination endanger our liberties or democratic processes. We should take nothing for granted. Only an alert and knowledgeable citizenry can compel the proper meshing of the huge industrial and military machinery of defense with our peaceful methods and goals so that security and liberty may prosper together" (Eisenhower 1961).

References

Achebe, Chinua. 2009. *The Education of a British-Protected Child*. New York: Alfred A. Knopf.

Agamben, Giorgio. 1998. *Homo Sacer: Sovereign Power and Bare Life*. Translated by Daniel Heller-Roazen. Stanford, CA: Stanford University Press.

Alexander, Michelle. 2010. *The New Jim Crow.* New York: New Press.

Alexander, Philip. 2011. *The Discovery of America 1492–1584*. Cambridge: Cambridge University Press.

Allard, Patricia. 2006. "Crime, Punishment, and Economic Violence." In *Color of Violence: The Incite! Anthology*, edited by Incite! Women of Color Against Violence. Boston: South End Press.

Allard, Patricia, and Marc Mauer. 2000. "Regaining the Vote: An Assessment of Activity Relating to Felon Disenfranchisement Laws." The Sentencing Project. January. http://www.sentencingproject.org/detail/publication.cfm?publication_id=22. Accessed July 2014.

All of Us or None. 2010. *All of Us or None*. Pamphlet on file with the author. More information about *All of Us or None* is available at www.allofusornone.org.

Anonymous. 2001. "The Story of a Black Punk." In *Prison Masculinities*, edited by Don Sabo, Terry A. Kupers, and Willie London, 127–133. Philadelphia: Temple University Press.

Archibald, Joanne. 2010. "Being in Prison." In *Interrupted Life: Experiences of Incarcerated Women in the United States*, edited by Rickie Solinger, Paula Johnson, Martha L. Raimon, Tina Reynolds, and Ruby Tapia, 57–60. Berkeley: University of California Press.

Ayers, Edward L. 1984. *Vengeance and Justice: Crime and Punishment in the 19th-Century American South*. New York: Oxford University Press.

Baldwin, James. 1985. *The Price of a Ticket*. New York: St. Martin's Press.

Baraldini, Silvia, Susan Rosenberg, and Laura Whitehorn. 1992. "Shawnee Unit—A Control Unit for Women." http://www.prisonactivist.org/pps+pows/marilynbuck/Shawnee. Accessed August 26, 2007.

Barrios, Luis, and David Brotherton. 2009. "Displacement and Stigma: The Social-Psychological Crisis of the Deportee." Unpublished manuscript on file with author.

Barry, Tom. 2009. "The New Political Economy of Immigration." *Dollars and Sense* (January–February).

Bauer, Shane. 2012. "Solitary in Iran Nearly Broke Me: Then I Went Inside America's Prisons." *Mother Jones* (November–December). http://www.motherjones.com/politics/2012/10/solitary-confinement-shane-bauer. Accessed June 2013.

Beaumont, Gustave de, and Alexis de Tocqueville. 1979 [1833]. *On the Penitentiary System in the United States: And Its Application in France.* Carbondale: Southern Illinois University Press.

Beck, Allen J., Marcus Berzofsky, Rachel Caspar, and Christopher Krebs. 2013. "Sexual Victimization in Prisons and Jails Reported by Inmates, 2011–12." *National Criminal Justice* 241399. Washington, DC: U.S. Department of Justice, Office of Justice Programs, Bureau of Justice Statistics. May. http://www.bjs.gov/content/pub/pdf/svpjri1112.pdf. Accessed November 2014.

Beck, Allen J., and Candace Johnson. 2012. "Sexual Victimization Reported by Former State Prisoners, 2008." *National Criminal Justice* 237363. Washington, DC: U.S. Department of Justice, Office of Justice Programs, Bureau of Justice Statistics. May. http://www.bjs.gov/content/pub/pdf/svrfsp08.pdf. Accessed November 2014.

Bell, Derrick. 1985. "The Supreme Court, 1984 Term: Foreword: The Civil Rights Chronicles." *Harvard Law Review* 99:4–83.

———. 1995. "Racial Realism." In *Critical Race Theory: The Key Writings That Formed the Movement*, edited by Kimberle Crenshaw et al. New York: New Press.

Bennett, William J., John J. DiIulio Jr., and John P. Walters. 1996. *Body Count.* New York: Simon and Schuster.

Berkman, Alan. 2005. "Engaged in Life: Alan Berkman on Prison Health Care (as told to Susie Day)." In *The New Abolitionists: (Neo)Slave Narratives*, edited by Joy James, 289–294. Albany: State University of New York Press.

Berkman, Alexander. 1912. *Prison Memoirs of an Anarchist.* New York: Mother Earth Press. http://theanarchistlibrary.org/library/alexander-berkman-prison-memoirs-of-an-anarchist#toc155.

Berlin, Isaiah. 1969. *Four Essays on Liberty.* Oxford: Oxford University Press.

Bhatt, Keane. 2014. "The Hypocrisy of Human Rights Watch." *NACLA Report*, February 5.

Bhattacharjee, Anannya. 2002. "Private Fists and Public Force: Race, Gender, and Surveillance." In *Policing the National Body: Race, Gender and Criminalization in the United States*, edited by Annanya Bhattacharjee and Jael Silliman. Cambridge, MA: South End Press.

Bhavnani, Kum-Kum, and Angela Davis. 2000. "Women in Prison: A Three-Nation Study." In *Racing Research, Researching Race*, edited by Frances Windance Twine and Jonathan Warren, 227–245. New York: New York University Press.

Blake, William. 2012. "A Sentence Worse Than Death." 2012 Yale Law Journal Prison Law Writing Contest Honorable Mention. http://solitarywatch.com/2013/03/11/voices-from-solitary-a-sentence-worse-than-death/. Accessed July 2013.

Bond, Michael. 2012. "Does Solitary Confinement Breach the Eighth Amendment?" *New Scientist*, June 29. http://www.newscientist.com/article/dn21992-does-solitary-confinement-breach-the-eighth-amendment.html#.Ub9SsUKlZUR. Accessed June 2013.

Boudin, Chesa. 2007. "From Jail to Yale." http://womenandprison.org/motherhood/chesa-boudin.html. Accessed September 2007.

Boudin, Katherine, and Rozann Greco. 1988. *Parenting Inside/Out: The Voices of Mothers in Prison.* The Children's Center, Bedford Hills Correctional Facility.

Bradley, R. G., and K. M. Davino. 2002. "Women's Perceptions of the Prison Environment: When Prison Is 'the Safest Place I've Ever Been.'" *Psychology of Women Quarterly* 26.

Brodwater, Taryn. 2007. "Mom Faces Prison: Woman Given Probation Had Baby, Then Appeals Court Overruled Judge." *Spokesman-Review* (Spokane, WA), June 20.

Brooks, George. 2004. "Felony Disenfranchisement: Law, History, Policy, and Politics." *Fordham Urban Law Journal* 32, no. 5: 101–148.

Brown, Robbie, and Kim Severson. 2011. "Enlisting Prison Labor to Close Budget Gaps." *New York Times*, February 24.

Browne, Angela, Alissa Cambier, and Suzanne Agha. 2011. "Prisons within Prisons: The Use of Segregation in the United States." *Federal Sentencing Reporter* 24, no. 1 (October): 46–49.

Browne, Angela, Brenda Miller, and Eugene Maguin. 1999. "Prevalence and Severity of Lifetime Physical and Sexual Victimization among Incarcerated Women." *International Journal of Law and Psychiatry* 22, nos. 3–4: 302–322.

Brownridge, Douglas A. 2006. "Violence against Women Post-Separation." *Aggression and Violent Behavior* 11, no. 5 (September–October): 514–530.

Buchanan, Kim Shayo. 2007. "Impunity: Sexual Abuse in Women's Prisons." *Harvard Civil Rights–Civil Liberties Law Review* 42:45–87.

———. 2010. "Our Prisons, Ourselves: Race, Gender and the Rule of Law." *Yale Law and Policy Review* 29:1–82.

Buck, Marilyn. 2001. *Enemies of the State*. Montreal: Abraham Guillen Press; Toronto: Arm the Spirit.

Buck, Marilyn, Laura Whitehorn, and Susan Day. 2005. "Cruel but Not Unusual—The Punishment of Women in U.S. Prisons." In *The New Abolitionsts: (Neo)Slave Narratives and Contemporary Prison Writings*, edited by Joy James. Albany: State University of New York Press.

Bunney, Marcia. 1998. "Finding Self-Respect for Battered Women." In *Frontiers of Justice*, vol. 2, *Coddling or Common Sense?*, edited by Claudia Whitman, Julie Zimmerman, and Tekla Miller. Fort Wayne, IN: Biddle Publishing.

———. 1999. "One Life in Prison: Perception, Reflection, and Empowerment." In *Harsh Punishment: International Experiences of Women's Imprisonment*, edited by Sandy Cook and Susanne Davies. Boston: Northeastern University Press.

Burridge, Andrew, and Jenna M. Loyd. 2007. "*La Gran Marcha*: Anti-Racism and Immigrants Rights in Southern California." *ACME: An International E-Journal for Critical Geographies* 6, no. 1: 1–35.

Butler, Judith. 2001. "Doing Justice to Someone: Sex Reassignment and Allegories of Transsexuality." *GLQ: A Journal of Lesbian and Gay Studies* 7, no. 4: 621–636.

———. 2004. *Undoing Gender*. New York: Routledge.

Cacho, Lisa M. 2012. *Social Death: Racialized Rightlessness and the Criminalization of the Unprotected*. New York: New York University Press.

Cahn, Naomi R. 1993. "Inconsistent Stories." *Georgetown Law Review* 81:2475–2531.

Card, Claudia. 2003. "Genocide and Social Death." *Hypatia* 18, no. 1 (Winter): 63–79.

Carleton, Mark T. 1971. *Politics and Punishment: The History of the Louisiana State Penal System*. Baton Rouge: Louisiana State University Press.

Carol E. 2010. "ASFA, TPR, My Life, My Children, My Motherhood." In *Interrupted Life: Experiences of Incarcerated Women in the United States*, edited by Rickie Solinger, Paula Johnson, Martha L. Raimon, Tina Reynolds, and Ruby Tapia, 83–85. Berkeley: University of California Press.

Carson, E. Ann, and Daniela Golinelli. 2013. "Prisoners in 2012—Advance Counts." *National Criminal Justice* 242467. Washington, DC: U.S. Department of Justice, Office of Justice Programs, Bureau of Justice Statistics. July. http://www.bjs.gov/content/pub/pdf/p12ac.pdf. Accessed November 2014.

Carson, E. Ann, and William J. Sabol. 2012. "Prisoners in 2011." *National Criminal Justice* 239808. Washington, DC: U.S. Department of Justice, Office of Justice Programs, Bureau of Justice Statistics. December. http://www.bjs.gov/content/pub/pdf/p11.pdf. Accessed November 2014.

Casella, Jean, and James Ridgeway. 2012. "How Many Prisoners Are in Solitary Confine-ment in the United States?" Solitary Watch. http://solitarywatch.com/2012/02/01/how -many-prisoners-are-in-solitary-confinement-in-the-united-states/. Accessed November 2014.

Center for Constitutional Rights. 2012. *Ruiz, et al. v. Brown, Jr., et al.* (federal lawsuit, amended). Filed May 31. http://ccrjustice.org/files/Ruiz-Amended-Complaint-May -31–2012.pdf. Accessed September 2013.

Chappell, Cathryn A. 2004. "Post-Secondary Correctional Education and Recidivism: A Meta-Analysis of Research Conducted 1990–1999." *Journal of Correctional Education* 55, no. 2 (June): 148–169.

Chen, Ching-In, Jaui Dulani, and Leah Lakshmi Piepzna-Samarasinha, eds. 2011. *The Revolution Begins at Home: Confronting Intimate Violence within Activist Communities.* Brooklyn, NY: South End Press.

Childs, Dennis. 2003. "Angola, Convict Leasing, and the Annulment of Freedom." In *Violence and the Body: Race, Gender, and the State*, edited by Arturo J. Aldama, 189–208. Bloomington: Indiana University Press.

Cholo. 2011. "Exposure." In *Captive Genders: Trans Embodiment and the Prison Industrial Complex*, edited by Eric A. Stanley and Nat Smith. Oakland, CA: AK Press.

Christianson, Scott. 1998. *With Liberty for Some: 500 Years of Imprisonment in America.* Boston: Northeastern University Press.

Chung, Jean. 2013. "Felony Disenfranchisement: A Primer." The Sentencing Project. http:// www.sentencingproject.org/doc/publications/fd_Felony%20Disenfranchisement%20 Primer.pdf. Accessed July 2014.

Cohen, Stanley. 2001. *States of Denial: Knowing about Atrocities and Suffering.* Cambridge: Polity.

Collins, Patricia Hill. 2000. *Black Feminist Thought: Knowledge, Consciousness, and the Politics of Empowerment.* New York: Routledge.

Columbus, Christopher. 2011. "Letter to Rafael Sanchez, 1493." In *The Discovery of America 1492–1584*, edited by Philip Alexander. Cambridge: Cambridge University Press.

Cook, Charles Orson, and James M. Poteet. 1979. "'Dem Was Black Times, Sure 'Nough': The Slave Narratives of Lydia Jefferson and Stephen Williams." *Louisiana History: Journal of the Louisiana Historical Association* 20, no. 3 (Summer): 281–292.

Cover, Robert. 1995. *Narrative, Violence, and the Law.* Ann Arbor: University of Michigan Press.

Craig, Pamela Barnes. 2001. "Slavery and Indentured Servants." In *American Women: A Library of Congress Guide for the Study of Women's History and Culture in the United States.* Library of Congress. http://memory.loc.gov/ammem/awhhtml/awlaw3/ slavery.html. Accessed July 2013.

Crenshaw, Kimberlé. 1991. "Mapping the Margins: Intersectionality, Identity Politics, and Violence against Women of Color." *Stanford Law Review* 43, no. 6: 1241–1299.

Cruel and Unusual. 2006. DVD. Directed and produced by Janet Baus, Dan Hunt, and Reid Williams.

Curtin, Mary Ellen. 2000. *Black Prisoners and Their World, Alabama, 1865–1900.* Charlottesville: University of Virginia Press.

Dailey, Lige, Jr. 2001. "Reentry: Prospects for Postrelease Success." In *Prison Masculinities*, edited by Don Sabo, Terry A. Kupers, and Willie London, 255–264. Philadelphia: Temple University Press.

Darwish, Mahmoud. 2010. *Journal of Ordinary Grief.* Translated by Ibrahim Muhawi. New York: Archipelago Books.

Davis, Angela. 2003. *Are Prisons Obsolete?* New York: Seven Stories Press.

———. 2005. *Abolition Democracy*. New York: Seven Stories Press.

———. 2009. "Women, Privilege, and Prisons." Speech at Ebenezer Baptist Church, Atlanta, March 24.

Davis, Lois M., Robert Bozick, Jennifer L. Steele, Jessica Saunders, and Jeremy N.V. Miles. 2013. "Evaluating the Effectiveness of Correctional Education: A Meta-Analysis of Programs That Provide Education to Incarcerated Adults." Santa Monica, CA: RAND Corporation.

Davis, Mike. 1995. "Hell Factories in the Field: A Prison-Industrial Complex." *Nation* 260 (February 20): 229.

Davis, Troy. 2008. "The Walking Dead." http://www.troyanthonydavis.org/family-friends.html. Accessed July 2013.

Dayan, Colin. 2007. *The Story of Cruel and Unusual*. Cambridge, MA: MIT Press.

———. 2011. *The Law Is a White Dog*. Princeton, NJ: Princeton University Press.

De Genova, Nicholas, and Nathalie Peutz, eds. 2010. *The Deportation Regime: Sovereignty, Space, and the Freedom of Movement*. Durham, NC: Duke University Press.

Diaz-Cotto, Juanita. 2006. *Chicana Lives and Criminal Justice: Voices from El Barrio*. Austin: University of Texas Press.

Dickens, Charles. 2001 [1842]. *American Notes for General Circulation*. London: Chapman and Hall.

Dignam, Brett. 2008. "Can Feminism Work for Women in Prison?" Conference paper, Women, Incarceration, and Human Rights Conference, Emory School of Law, February 27–28.

Dodge, Mara. 2002. *Whores and Thieves of the Worst Kind: A Study of Women, Crime, and Prisons, 1835–2000*. DeKalb: Northern Illinois University Press.

Douglass, Fredrick. 2008 [1883]. "The Color Line." In *Frederick Douglass: Selected Speeches and Writings*, edited by Philip Sheldon Foner, 648–655. Chicago: Lawrence Hill Books.

Du Bois, W.E.B. 1899. *The Philadelphia Negro: A Social Study*. Philadelphia: University of Pennsylvania Press.

———. 1904 [1901]. "Crime and Slavery" [originally published as "The Spawn of Slavery: The Convict-Lease System in the South"]. In *Some Notes on Negro Crime, Particularly in Georgia*, 2–9. Atlanta: Atlanta University Press.

———. 1977 [1935]. *Black Reconstruction in America*. New York: Atheneum.

Duguid, Stephen. 2000. *Can Prisons Work? The Prisoner as Object and Subject in Modern Corrections*. Toronto: University of Toronto Press.

Dussel, Enrique. 1993. "Eurocentrism and Modernity (Introduction to the Frankfurt Lectures)." *boundary 2* 20, no. 3 (Autumn): 65–76.

———. 2000. "Europe, Modernity, and Eurocentrism." *Nepantla: Views from the South* 1, no. 3: 465–478.

Dworkin, Andrea. 2002. *Heartbreak*. New York: Basic Books.

Eckholm, Eric. 2008. "New Tack on Straying Parolees Offers a Hand Instead of Cuffs." *New York Times*, May 17.

Eisenhower, Dwight D. 1961. "Farewell Address to the Nation." http://www.eisenhower.archives.gov/research/online_documents/farewell_address/Reading_Copy.pdf. Accessed November 2014.

Ellis, Eddie. 2013. "Words Matter: Another Look at the Question of Language." Center for New Leadership on Urban Solutions. http://nationinside.org/images/pdf/Words_Matter_Final_Draft_04.12.13.pdf. Accessed July 2014.

Espiritu, Yen de. 2003. *Home Bound: Filipino American Lives across Cultures, Communities, and Countries.* Berkeley: University of California Press.

Esposito, Barbara, and Lee Wood. 1982. *Prison Slavery.* Edited by Kathryn Bardsley. Washington, DC: Committee to Abolish Prison Slavery.

Ewald, William. 2002. "'Civil Death': The Ideological Paradox of Criminal Disenfranchisement Laws in the United States." *Wisconsin Law Review* no. 5:1045–1137.

The Farm. 1998. Directed by Liz Garbus, Wilbert Rideau, and Jonathan Stack.

Farmer, Paul. 2003. *Pathologies of Power: Health, Human Rights, and the New War on the Poor.* Berkeley: University of California Press.

Feldman, Allen. 1991. *Formations of Violence: The Narrative of the Body and Political Terror in Northern Ireland.* Chicago: University of Chicago Press.

Fellner, Jamie, and Marc Mauer. 1998. *Losing the Vote: The Impact of Felony Disenfranchisement Laws in the United States.* Washington, DC: Human Rights Watch and The Sentencing Project.

Ferreira da Silva, Denise. 2007. *Toward a Global Concept of Race.* Minneapolis: University of Minnesota Press.

Flemke, Kimberly. 2009. "Triggering Rage: Unresolved Trauma in Women's Lives." *Contemporary Family Therapy* 31:123–139.

Flynn, Elizabeth Gurley. 1963. *The Alderson Story: My Life as a Political Prisoner.* New York: International Publishers.

Foner, Eric. 2002. *Reconstruction: America's Unfinished Revolution, 1863–1877.* New York: HarperCollins.

Foucault, Michel. 1995 [1975]. *Discipline and Punish: The Birth of the Prison.* Translated by Alan Sheridan. New York: Vintage Books.

Freedman, Estelle B. 1984. *Their Sisters' Keepers: Women's Prison Reform in America, 1830–1930.* Ann Arbor: University of Michigan Press.

Frosch, Dan. 2007. "Inmates Will Replace Migrants in Colorado Fields." *New York Times,* March 4.

Fry, Elizabeth. 1827. *Observations on the Visiting, Superintendence, and Government of Female Prisoners.* Cornhill, UK: John and Arthur Arch.

Galtung, Johan. 1969. "Violence, Peace, and Peace Research." *Journal of Peace Research* 6, no. 3: 167–191.

Garland, David. 2007. "The Peculiar Forms of American Capital Punishment." *Social Research* 74, no. 2 (Summer): 435–464.

Gawande, Atul. 2009. "Hellhole." *New Yorker,* March 30.

George, Amanda. 1993. "Strip Search: Sexual Assault by the State." In *Without Consent: Confronting Adult Sexual Violence,* edited by Patricia Weiser. Canberra: Australian Institute of Criminology.

Gibbons, John J., and Nicholas deBelleville Katzenbach. 2006. "Confronting Confinement: A Report of The Commission on Safety and Abuse in America's Prisons." *Washington University Journal of Law & Policy* 22:385–562.

Gilmore, Ruth Wilson. 2007. *Golden Gulag: Prisons, Surplus, Crisis, and Opposition in Globalizing California.* Berkeley: University of California Press.

Gilroy, Paul. 1995. *The Black Atlantic: Modernity and Double-Consciousness.* Cambridge, MA: Harvard University Press.

Girshick, Lori B. 2011. "Out of Compliance: Masculine-Identified People in Women's Prisons." In *Captive Genders: Trans Embodiment and the Prison Industrial Complex,* edited by Eric A. Stanley and Nat Smith. Oakland, CA: AK Press.

Glaze, Lauren E. 2011. "Correctional Population in the United States, 2010." *National Criminal Justice* 236319. Washington, DC: U.S. Department of Justice, Office of Justice Programs, Bureau of Justice Statistics. December. http://bjs.ojp.usdoj.gov/content/pub/pdf/cpus10.pdf. Accessed June 2012.

Glaze, Lauren E., and Laura M. Maruschak. 2010. "Parents in Prison and Their Minor Children." *National Criminal Justice* 222984. Washington, DC: U.S. Department of Justice, Office of Justice Programs, Bureau of Justice Statistics. August 2008 (revised 2010). http://www.bjs.gov/content/pub/pdf/pptmc.pdf. Accessed November 2014.

Glaze, Lauren E., and Erika Parks. 2012. "Correctional Populations in the United States, 2011." *National Criminal Justice* 239972. Washington, DC: U.S. Department of Justice, Office of Justice Programs, Bureau of Justice Statistics. November. http://www.bjs.gov/content/pub/pdf/cpus11.pdf. Accessed November 2014.

Goffman, Erving. 1958. "Characteristics of Total Institutions." In *Symposium on Preventive and Social Psychiatry*, 43–84. Washington, DC: Walter Reed Army Institute of Research.

———. 1963. *Stigma: Notes on the Management of Spoiled Identity.* Upper Saddle River, NJ: Prentice-Hall.

Goodman, Amy. 2007. "Sister of Georgia Death Row Prisoner Troy Anthony Davis Leads Campaign to Save His Life: Interview with Martina Correia." *Democracy Now.* October 4. Accessed April 13, 2014.

Gordon, Avery. 2004. "Going Inside: The Prison Research Visit." In *Keeping Good Time*, 35–39. Boulder, CO: Paradigm.

———. 2008. *Ghostly Matters: Haunting and the Sociological Imagination.* Minneapolis: University of Minnesota Press.

Gordon, Linda. 2002. *Heroes of Their Own Lives: The Politics and History of Family Violence—Boston, 1880–1960.* Champaign: University of Illinois Press.

Goring/Sweet (Clifton Goring/Candi Raine Sweet). 2011. "Being an Incarcerated Transperson: Shouldn't People Care?" In *Captive Genders: Trans Embodiment and the Prison Industrial Complex*, edited by Eric A. Stanley and Nat Smith. Oakland, CA: AK Press.

Grandy, Moses. 1843. *Narrative of the Life of Moses Grandy; Late a Slave in the United States of America.* London: C. Gilpin, 5, Bishopsgate-street. http://docsouth.unc.edu/fpn/grandy/grandy.html. Accessed September 2013.

Grant, Jaime M., Lisa A. Mottet, Justin Tanis, Jack Harrison, Jody L. Herman, and Mara Keisling. 2011. *Injustice at Every Turn: A Report of the National Transgender Discrimination Survey.* Washington, DC: National Center for Transgender Equality and National Gay and Lesbian Task Force.

Grassian, Stuart. 2006. "Psychiatric Effects of Solitary Confinement." *Journal of Law & Policy* 22:325–383.

Graves, Anthony C. 2012. "Testimony by Anthony C. Graves." Senate Judiciary Committee Subcommittee on The Constitution, Civil Rights & Human Rights, "Reassessing Solitary Confinement: The Human Rights, Fiscal and Public Safety Consequences." June 19. http://www.judiciary.senate.gov/pdf/12–6–19GravesTestimony.pdf. Accessed June 2013.

Griffiths, Paul J. 2012. "Called to a Halt." Review of J. Lear's *A Case for Irony. Commonweal* (March 9): 22–23.

Guenther, Lisa. 2012. "Fecundity and Natal Alienation: Rethinking Kinship with Levinas and Orlando Patterson." *Levinas Studies* 7:1–19.

———. 2013. *Solitary Confinement: Social Death and Its Afterlives.* Minneapolis: University of Minnesota Press.

Guha, Ranajit. 2001. "Projects of Our Time and Their Convergence." In *The Latin American Subaltern Studies Reader*, edited by Ileana Rodríguez. Durham, NC: Duke University Press.

Han, Sora. 2006. "Bonds of Representation: Vision, Race and Law in Post–Civil Rights America." PhD diss., University of California, Santa Cruz.

Haney, Craig. 2003. "Mental Health Issues in Long-Term Solitary and 'Supermax' Confinement." *Crime and Delinquency* 49, no. 1: 124–156.

———. 2008. "A Culture of Harm: Taming the Dynamics of Cruelty in Supermax Prisons." *Criminal Justice and Behavior* 35:956–984.

Haney-López, Ian. 2006. *White by Law: The Legal Construction of Race*. New York: New York University Press.

Harris, Cheryl I. 1993. "Whiteness as Property." *Harvard Law Review* 106, no. 8: 1707–1791.

Havis, Devonya. 2009. "Arts of Resistance and the Insurrection of Subjugated Knowledges." Conference paper, Association of Feminist Epistemologies, Methodologies, Metaphysics, and Science Studies Conference, University of South Carolina, March 21.

Heffernan, Esther. 2005. "History of Women's Prisons." In *Encyclopedia of Prisons and Correctional Facilities*. Edited by Mary F. Bosworth. Thousand Oaks, CA: Sage Reference.

Heidenreich, Linda. 2011. "Transgender Women, Sexual Violence, and the Rule of Law: An Argument in Favor of Restorative and Transformative Justice." In *Razor Wire Women: Prisoners, Activists, Scholars, and Artists*, edited by Jodie Michelle Lawston and Ashley E. Lucas, 147–165. Albany: State University of New York Press.

Hening, William Walter. 1810. *The Statutes at Large; Being a Collection of All the Laws Of Virginia, from the First Session of the Legislature in the Year 1619*. Vol. 2. Richmond: Samuel Pleasants, Printer to the Commonwealth.

———. 1823. *The Statutes at Large; Being a Collection of All the Laws Of Virginia, from the First Session of the Legislature in the Year 1619*. Vol. 3. Philadelphia: Thomas Desilver.

Henrichson, Christian, and Ruth Delaney. 2012. "The Price of Prisons: What Incarceration Costs Taxpayers." Vera Institute of Justice. July.

Hernández-Truyol, Berta Esperanza. 2002. "Toward a Multicultural Conception of Human Rights." In *Moral Imperialism: A Critical Anthology*, edited by Berta Esperanza Hernández-Truyol. New York: New York University Press.

Hine, Darlene Clark. 1989. "Rape and the Inner Lives of Black Women in the Middle West: Preliminary Thoughts on the Culture of Dissemblance." *Signs* 14 (Summer): 912–920.

Hirsch, Adam J. 1992. *The Rise of the Penitentiary: Prisons and Punishment in Early America*. New Haven, CT: Yale University Press.

Howle, Elaine M. 2014. "Sterilization of Female Inmates: Some Inmates Were Sterilized Unlawfully, and Safeguards Designed to Limit Occurrences of the Procedure Failed." *California State Auditor Report*. June. https://www.auditor.ca.gov/pdfs/reports/ 2013–120.pdf. Accessed June 2014.

Huckleby, Charles, Jr. 2002. "On Being a Nigger." In *Writing as Resistance: The Journal of Prisoners on Prisons Anthology (1988–2002)*, edited by Bob Gaucher. Toronto: Canadian Scholars Press.

Hughes, Timothy, and Doris James Wilson. 2014. "Reentry Trends in the U.S." Bureau of Justice Statistics. http://www.bjs.gov/content/reentry/reentry.cfm. Accessed November 2014.

Human Rights Watch. 1996. "All Too Familiar: Sexual Abuse of Women in US State Prisons." http://www.hrw.org/reports/1996/Us1.htm. Accessed August 20, 2007.

———. 2007. "No Escape: Male Rape in U.S. Prisons." Accessed August 20, 2007.

Hunter, Tera. 1998. *To 'Joy My Freedom*. Cambridge, MA: Harvard University Press.

Huschka, Ryan J. 2006. "Sorry for the Jackass Sentence: A Critical Analysis of the Constitutionality of Contemporary Shaming Punishments." *Kansas Law Review* 54, no. 3 (April): 803–836.

Ignatiev, Noel. 1996. *Race Traitor*. New York: Routledge.

INCITE! Women of Color Against Violence. 2007. *The Revolution Will Not Be Funded: Beyond the Non-Profit Industrial Complex*. Cambridge, MA: South End Press.

Irwin, John. 1987. *The Felon*. Berkeley: University of California Press.

———. 1992. *The Jail*. Berkeley: University of California Press.

———. 2009. *Lifers: Seeking Redemption in Prison*. New York: Routledge.

Itzkowitz, Howard, and Lauren Oldak. 1973. "Note: Restoring the Ex-Offender's Right to Vote: Background and Developments." *American Criminal Law Review* (Spring): 721–722.

Jackson, George. 1970. *Soledad Brother: The Prison Letters of George Jackson*. New York: Coward-McCann.

James, C. L. R. 1989 [1938]. *The Black Jacobins*. New York: Vintage.

James, Doris J., and Lauren E. Glaze. 2006. "Mental Health Problems of Prison and Jail Inmates." *National Criminal Justice* 213600. Washington, DC: U.S. Department of Justice, Office of Justice Programs, Bureau of Justice Statistics. September. http://www.bjs.gov/index.cfm?ty=pbdetail&iid=789 Accessed November 2012.

James, Joy, ed. 2005. *The New Abolitionists: (Neo)Slave Narratives and Contemporary Prison Writings*. Albany: State University of New York Press.

Johnson, Corey G. 2014. "Bill Seeks New Restrictions on Sterilizations in California Prisons." Center for Investigative Reporting. February 20. http://cironline.org/reports/bill-seeks-new-restrictions-sterilizations-california-prisons-5985. Accessed July 2014.

Jordan, Winthrop. 1968. *White over Black: American Attitudes toward the Negro, 1550–1812*. Chapel Hill: University of North Carolina Press.

Kelley, Robin D. G. 1994. *Race Rebels: Culture, Politics, and the Black Working Class*. New York: Free Press.

King, Ryan S., and Marc Mauer. 2004. "The Vanishing Black Electorate: Felony Disenfranchisement in Atlanta, Georgia." http://www.sentencingproject.org/Admin/Documents/publications/fd_vanishingblackelectorate.pdf. Accessed January 28, 2009.

Klein, Donald. C. 1991. "The Humiliation Dynamic: An Overview." *Journal of Primary Prevention* 12, no. 2: 93–121.

Koyami, Emi. 2006. "Disloyal to Feminism: Abuse of Survivors within the Domestic Violence Shelter System." In *Color of Violence: The Incite! Anthology*, edited by the Incite! Women of Color Against Violence. Cambridge, MA: South End Press.

Langan, Patrick A., and David J. Levin. 2002. "Recidivism of Prisoners Released in 1994." *National Criminal Justice* 193427. Washington, DC: U.S. Department of Justice, Office of Justice Programs, Bureau of Justice Statistics Special Report. June. http://www.bjs.gov/content/pub/pdf/rpr94.pdf. Accessed November 2014.

Law, Victoria. 2009. *Resistance behind Bars: The Struggle of Incarcerated Women*. Oakland, CA: PM Press.

———. 2010. "Nor Meekly Serving Her Time: Riots and Resistance in Women's Prisons." *New Politics* (mayfirst.org) 12, no. 4 (Winter): 48.

Lawston, Jodie Michelle. 2009. *Sisters Outside: Radical Activists Working for Women Prisoners*. New York: State University of New York Press.

Lawston, Jodie Michelle, and Ashley E. Lucas. 2011. *Razor Wire Women: Prisoners, Activists, Scholars and Artists*. New York: State University of New York Press.

Lee, Arlene F., Philip M. Genty, and Mimi Laver, Child Welfare League of America. 2010. "The Impact of the Adoption and Safe Families Act on Children of Incarcerated Parents." In *Interrupted Life: Experiences of Incarcerated Women in the United States*, edited by Rickie Solinger, Paula Johnson, Martha L. Raimon, Tina Reynolds, and Ruby Tapia, 77–82. Berkeley: University of California Press.

Levasseur, Raymond Luc. 2005. "Trouble Coming Every Day." In *The New Abolitionists: (Neo)Slave Narratives and Contemporary Prison Writings*, edited by Joy James. Albany: State University of New York Press.

Levi, Robin, and Ayelet Waldman, eds. 2011. *Inside This Place, Not of It: Narratives from Women's Prisons*. San Francisco: McSweeney's.

Lewis, W. David. 1965. *From Newgate to Dannemora: The Rise of the Penitentiary in New York, 1796–1848*. Ithaca, NY: Cornell University Press.

Lichtenstein, Alex. 1996. *Twice the Work of Free Labor: The Political Economy of Convict Labor in the New South*. New York: Verso.

Lindsley, Syd. 2002. "The Gendered Assault on Immigrants." In *Policing the National Body: Race, Gender, and Criminalization in the United States*, edited by Annanya Bhattacharjee and Jael Silliman. Cambridge, MA: South End Press.

Lipsitz, George. 2004. "Abolition Democracy and Global Justice." *Comparative American Studies* 2, no. 3: 271–286.

Lowe, Lisa. 2006. "The Intimacy of Four Continents." In *Haunted by Empire: Geographies of Intimacy in North American History*, edited by Ann Laura Stoler, 191–212. Durham, NC: Duke University Press.

Loyd, Jenna, Matt Mitchelson, and Andrew Burridge. 2012. *Beyond Walls and Cages: Prisons, Borders, and Global Crisis*. Athens: University of Georgia Press.

Lugones, María. 2007. "Heterosexualism and the Modern/Colonial Gender System." *Hypatia* 22, no. 1 (Winter): 186–209.

Lukes, Steven. 1997. "Humiliation and the Politics of Identity." *Social Research* 64, no. 1 (Spring): 36–51.

Macintyre, Ben. 2011. *The Napoleon of Crime: The Life and Times of Adam Worth, Master Thief*. New York: Broadway Books.

Maldonado-Torres, Nelson. 2008. *Against War: Views from the Underside of Modernity*. Durham, NC: Duke University Press.

Mahoney, Martha R. 1991. "Legal Issues of Battered Women: Redefining the Issue of Separation." *Michigan Law Review* 90:1–94.

Mallicoat, Stacy L., and Connie Ireland. 2013. *Women and Crime*. Thousand Oaks, CA: Sage.

Mancini, Matthew. 1996. *One Dies, Get Another: Convict Leasing in the American South, 1866–1928*. Columbia: University of South Carolina Press.

Manware, Melissa. 2007. "Jail Won't Let Mother Pump Milk; Pastor Says Inmate's Baby Spits Up Formula and Cries Constantly." *Charlotte Observer* (November 27): 1A.

Manza, Jeff, Clem Brooks, and Christopher Uggen. 2003. "Civil Death or Civil Rights? Public Attitudes towards Felon Disenfranchisement in the United States." Paper presented at the annual meeting of the American Sociological Association, Atlanta, GA, August 16. http://www.socsci.umn.edu/~uggen/POQ8.pdf. 2007–10–05. Accessed September 5, 2014.

Margalit, Avishai. 1998. *The Decent Society*. Cambridge, MA: Harvard University Press.

Mariner, Joanne. 2012. "A Thousand Years of Solitude." *Aletho News*. http://alethonews.wordpress.com/2012/06/08/a-thousand-years-of-solitude/. Accessed June 2013.

Martinot, Steven. 2007. "Motherhood and the Invention of Race." *Hypatia* 22, no. 2 (Spring): 79–97.

Martinson, Robert. 1976. "California Research at the Crossroads." *Crime and Delinquency* 22:180–181.

Matsuda, Mari. 1989. "When the First Quail Calls: Multiple Consciousness as Jurisprudential Method." *Women's Rights Law Reporter* 11:7–10.

Mauer, Marc. 2006. *Race to Incarcerate*. New York: New Press.

Mbembe, Achille. 2003. "Necropolitics." Translated by Libby Meintjes. *Public Culture* 15, no. 1: 11–40.

McDaniels-Wilson, C., and J. Belknap. 2008. "The Extensive Sexual Violation and Sexual Abuse Histories of Incarcerated Women." *Violence Against Women* 14:1090–1127.

McGreevy, Patrick, and Phil Willon. 2013. "Female Inmate Surgery Broke Law." *Los Angeles Times*, July 13.

McNeill, Fergus, and Kristel Beyens. 2014. "Introduction: Studying Mass Supervision." In *Offender Supervision in Europe*, edited by Fergus McNeill and Kristel Beyens. New York: Palgrave Macmillan.

Mears, Daniel P. 2005. "A Critical Look at Supermax Prisons." *Corrections Compendium* 30, no. 5: 6–7, 45–49.

———. 2009. "Supermax Incarceration and Recidivism." *Criminology* 47, no. 4 (November): 1131–1166.

Mears, Daniel P., and M. D. Reisig. 2006. "The Theory and Practice of Supermax Prisons." *Punishment and Society* 8:33–57.

Méndez, Juan E. 2011. "Interim Report of the Special Rapporteur of the Human Rights Council on Torture and Other Cruel, Inhuman or Degrading Treatment or Punishment." August. United Nations General Assembly. http://daccess-dds-ny.un.org/doc/UNDOC/GEN/N11/445/70/PDF/N1144570.pdf?OpenElement. Accessed June 2013.

Mendible, Myra. 2005. "Visualizing Abjection: Gender, Power, and the Culture of Humiliation." *Genderforum/Imagendering* 11:1–26.

Menschel, David. 2001. "Abolition without Deliverance: The Law of Connecticut Slavery 1784–1848." *Yale Law Journal* 111:183–222.

Mignolo, Walter. 1995. *The Darker Side of the Renaissance: Literacy, Territoriality, and Colonization*. Ann Arbor: University of Michigan Press.

———. 2009. "Dispensable and Bare Lives: Coloniality and the Hidden Political/Economic Agenda of Modernity." *Human Architecture: Journal of the Sociology of Self-Knowledge* 5, no. 2 (Spring): 69–88.

Miller, Reuben. 2014. "Devolving the Carceral State: Race, Prisoner Reentry, and Urban Poverty Management." Lecture, Sociology Department, Binghamton University, February 19.

Miller, Susan B. 1988. "Humiliation and Shame." *Bulletin of the Menninger Clinic* 52:42–51.

Minton, Todd, D. 2012. "Jails in Indian Country, 2011." *National Criminal Justice* 238978. Washington, DC: U.S. Department of Justice, Office of Justice Programs, Bureau of Justice Statistics. September 25. http://www.bjs.gov/content/pub/pdf/jic11.pdf. Accessed November 2014.

Morrison, Toni. 1987. "The Site of Memory." In *Inventing the Truth: The Art and Craft of Memoir*, edited by William Zinnser, 103–124. Boston: Houghton Mifflin Company.

National Clearinghouse for the Defense of Battered Women. 2011. "Abuse History among Incarcerated Women." http://www.ncdsv.org/images/NCDBW_AbuseHistoryAmongIncarceratedWomen_updated_5–20–2011.pdf.

New York State Commission of Correction. 2012. "Final Report of the New York State Commission of Correction in the Matter of the Death of Alvin Rios, an Inmate of

Broome County Jail." http://archive.pressconnects.com/assets/pdf/CB1962191023 .PDF. Accessed July 2014.

New York State Parole Handbook. 2010. Revised. https://www.parole.ny.gov/intro _handbook.html. Accessed July 2013.

Nietzsche, Friedrich. 1989 [1887]. *On the Genealogy of Morals*. Translated and edited by Walter Kaufmann. New York: Vintage.

O'Connor, Flannery. 1961. "On Her Own Work." In *Mystery and Manners: Occasional Prose*, edited by Sally and Robert Fitzgerald. New York: Farrar, Straus & Giroux.

O'Hearn, Denis. 2010. "Imprisonment and Solidary Cultures of Resistance: A Comparison of Political and Supermax Confinement." Paper presented at the annual meeting of the American Sociological Association, Atlanta, GA, August 13. http://www .allacademic.com/meta/p409545_index.html. Accessed November 2014.

Olds, Bruce. 1995. *Raising Holy Hell*. New York: Penguin.

Pager, Devah. 2003. "The Mark of a Criminal Record." *American Journal of Sociology* 108, no. 5: 937–975.

———. 2007. *Marked: Race, Crime, and Finding Work in an Era of Mass Incarceration*. Chicago: University of Chicago Press.

Painter, Nell. 1995. "Soul Murder and Slavery: Toward a Fully Loaded Cost Accounting." In *U.S. History as Women's History: New Feminist Essays*, edited by Linda K. Kerber, Alice Kessler-Harris, and Kathryn Kish Sklar. Chapel Hill: University of North Carolina Press.

Paley, Noelle, and Joshua M. Price. 2010. "Violent Interruptions." In *Interrupted Life: Experiences of Incarcerated Women in the United States*, edited by Rickie Solinger, Paula Johnson, Martha L. Raimon, Tina Reynolds, and Ruby Tapia, 406–411. Berkeley: University of California Press.

Parkes, Debra. 2004. "Ballot Boxes behind Bars: Towards the Repeal of Prisoner Disenfranchisement Laws." *Temple Political & Civil Rights Law Review* (Fall): 71–111.

Patterson, Orlando. 1982. *Slavery and Social Death*. Cambridge, MA: Harvard University Press.

———. 1993. "Slavery, Alienation, and the Female Discovery of Personal Freedom." In *Home: A Place in the World*, edited by Arien Mack. New York: New York University Press.

Pettit, Becky. 2012. *Invisible Men: Mass Incarceration and the Myth of Black Progress*. New York: Russell Sage.

Pew Center on the States. 2008. "One in 100: Behind Bars in America in 2008." February. Washington, DC: Pew Charitable Trusts. http://www.pewcenteronthestates .org/uploadedFiles/8015PCTS_Prison08_FINAL_2-1-1_FORWEB.pdf. Accessed March 31, 2010.

———. 2009. "One in 31: The Long Reach of American Corrections." March. Washington, DC: Pew Charitable Trusts. http://www.pewstates.org/uploadedFiles/PCS _Assets/2009/PSPP_1in31_report_FINAL_WEB_3–26–09.pdf. Accessed July 2013.

———. 2011. "State of Recidivism: The Revolving Door of America's Prisons." March. Washington, DC: Pew Charitable Trusts. http://www.pewtrusts.org/uploadedFiles/ wwwpewtrustsorg/Reports/sentencing_and_corrections/State_Recidivism _Revolving_Door_America_Prisons%20.pdf. Accessed June 2013.

Platt, Anthony M. 1977. *The Child Savers: The Invention of Delinquency*. Chicago: University of Chicago Press.

Poteet, Jennifer. 2001. "Gyn and Bitters." *POZ Magazine*, July.

Powers, Gershom. 1829. "Letter of Gershom Powers, Esq. in answer to a Letter of the Hon. Edward Livingston in relation to the Auburn State Prison." Albany: Croswell and Van Benthuysen.

Price, Joshua. 2008. "Participatory Research as Disruptive? A Report on a Conflict in Social Science Paradigms at a Criminal Justice Agency Promoting Alternatives to Incarceration." *Contemporary Justice Review* 11, no. 4: 387–412.

———. 2012a. "A Politics for Our Time? Organizing against Jails." In *Beyond Cages and Walls: Prisons, Borders, and Global Crisis*, edited by Jenna Loyd, Matt Michelson, and Andrew Burridge. Athens: University of Georgia Press.

———. 2012b. *Structural Violence: Hidden Brutality in the Lives of Women*. New York: State University of New York Press.

Price, Joshua M., and Noelle Paley. 2009. "Violent Interruptions." In *Interrupted Life: Experiences of Incarcerated Women in the United States*, edited by Paula Johnson et al. Berkeley: University of California Press.

Prison Association of New York. 1846. "Prison Discipline." *United States Magazine and Democratic Review* 19, no. 142: 129–140.

Quijano, Aníbal. 2000. "Coloniality of Power and Eurocentrism in Latin America." *International Sociology* 15, no. 2 (June): 215–232.

Rabaka, Reiland. 2010. *Against Epistemic Apartheid: W.E.B. Du Bois and the Disciplinary Decadence of Sociology*. Lanham, MD: Rowman and Littlefield.

Rafter, Nicole Hahn. 1985. "Gender, Prisons, and Prison History." *Social Science History* 9, no. 3 (Summer): 233–247.

Rawick, George. 1972. *The American Slave: A Composite Autobiography*. Westport, CT: Greenwood Press.

Reid, Elizabeth A. 2013. "The Prison Rape Elimination Act (PREA) and the Importance of Litigation in Its Enforcement: Holding Guards Who Rape Accountable." *Yale Law Journal* 122:2082–2097.

Reilly, Steve. 2012. "Report Faults Company in Death of Broome County Jail Inmate." *Press and Sun Bulletin* (Binghamton, NY), October 23.

Reisman, Jeffrey. 2006. *The Rich Get Richer and the Poor Get Prison*. Boston: Allyn & Bacon.

Reuben, William A., and Carlos Norman. 1987. "Brainwashing in America? The Women of Lexington Prison." *Nation* (June 27): 244.

Rhodes, Lorna. 2004. *Total Confinement: Madness and Reason in the Maximum Security Prison*. Berkeley: University of California Press.

———. 2005. "Pathological Effects of the Supermaximum Prison." *American Journal of Public Health* 95, no. 10 (October): 1692.

Richie, Beth. 1996. *Compelled to Crime: The Gender Entrapment of Battered Black Women*. London: Routledge.

———. 2001. "Challenges Incarcerated Women Face as They Return to Their Communities: Findings from Life History Interviews." *Crime and Delinquency* 47, no. 3 (July): 368–389.

———. 2005. "Queering Antiprison Work: African American Lesbians in the Juvenile Justice System." In *Global Lockdown*, edited by Julia Sudbury. New York: Routledge.

Ripstein, Arthur. 1997. "Responses to Humiliation." *Social Research* 64, no. 1 (Spring): 90–112.

Ristroph, Alice. 2008. "State Intentions and the Law of Punishment." *Journal of Criminal Law & Criminology* 98, no. 4 (Summer): 1353–1406.

Roberts, Dorothy. 1998. *Killing the Black Body: Race, Reproduction, and the Meaning of Liberty*. New York: Vintage.

———. 2003. *Shattered Bonds: The Color of Child Welfare*. New York: Basic Books.

Robinson, Gwen, Fergus McNeill, and Shadd Maruna. 2013. "Punishment in Society: The Improbable Persistence of Probation and Other Community Sanctions and

Measures." In *The SAGE Handbook of Punishment and Society*, edited by Jonathan Simon and Richard Sparks. London: Sage.

Rodriguez, Dylan. 2006. *Forced Passages: Imprisoned Radical Intellectuals and the U.S. Prison Regime*. Minneapolis: University of Minnesota Press.

———. 2008. "'I Would Wish Death on You . . .' Race, Gender, and Immigration in the Globality of the U.S. Prison Regime." *Scholar and Feminist Online* 6, no. 3 (Summer). http://sfonline.barnard.edu/immigration/drodriguez_04.htm. Accessed November 2014.

Roediger, David R. 1999. *The Wages of Whiteness: Race and the Making of the American Working Class*. Rev. ed. London: Verso Books.

Rosenberg, Susan. 2005. "Women Casualties of the Drug War." In *The New Abolitionists: (Neo)Slave Narratives and Contemporary Prison Writings*, edited by Joy James. Albany: State University of New York Press.

———. 2011. *An American Radical: Political Prisoner in My Own Country*. New York: Citadel Press.

Ross, Jeffrey Ian, ed. 2013. *The Globalization of Supermax Prisons*. New Brunswick, NJ: Rutgers University Press.

Ross, Loretta. 2008. "Understanding Reproductive Justice." Position paper. 2006. http://www.sistersong.net/publications_and_articles/Understanding_RJ.pdf.

Ross, Luana. 1998. *Inventing the Savage: The Social Construction of Native American Criminality*. Austin: University of Texas Press.

Rothman, David. 2005 [1971]. *The Discovery of the Asylum: Social Order and Disorder in the New Republic*. New Brunswick, NJ: Aldine Transaction.

Sabol, William J., Heather C. West, and Matthew Cooper. 2010. "Prisoners in 2008." *National Criminal Justice 228417*. Washington, DC: U.S. Department of Justice, Office of Justice Programs, Bureau of Justice Statistics. December 2009. Revised June 30. http://bjs.gov/content/pub/pdf/p08.pdf. Accessed November 2014.

Salah-El, Tiyo Attalah. 2005. "A Call for the Abolition of Prisons." In *The New Abolitionists: (Neo)Slave Narratives and Contemporary Prison Writings*, edited by Joy James. Albany: State University of New York Press.

San Francisco Children of Incarcerated Parents Partnership. 2010. "Children of Incarcerated Parents: A Bill of Rights." In *Interrupted Life: Experiences of Incarcerated Women in the United States*, edited by Rickie Solinger, Paula Johnson, Martha L. Raimon, Tina Reynolds, and Ruby Tapia, 37–44. Berkeley: University of California Press.

Santana, Raymond. 2012. "'Central Park Five': New Film on How Police Abuse, Media Frenzy Led to Jailing of Innocent Teens." Interview with Amy Goodman and Nermeen Shaikh. *Democracy Now*. http://www.democracynow.org/2012/11/28/central _park_five_new_film_on. November 28. Accessed August 2014.

Santos, Boaventura de Sousa. 2002. "Toward a Multicultural Conception of Human Rights." In *Moral Imperialism: A Critical Anthology*, edited by Berta Esperanza Hernández-Truyol, 39–62. New York: New York University Press.

———. 2007. "Beyond Abyssal Thinking: From Global Lines to Ecologies of Knowledges." *Review Fernand Braudel Center* 30, no. 1: 45–89.

———. 2014. *Epistemologies of the South: Justice against Epistemicide*. Boulder, CO: Paradigm Publishers.

Scheper-Hughes, Nancy. 1992. *Death without Weeping: The Violence of Everyday Life in Brazil*. Berkeley: University of California Press.

———. 1996. "Small Wars and Invisible Genocides." *Social Science Medicine* 43, no. 5: 889–900.

Scheper-Hughes, Nancy, and Philippe Bourgois. 2004. "Introduction: Making Sense of Violence." In *Violence in War and Peace*, edited by Nancy Scheper-Hughes and Philippe Bourgois. Oxford: Blackwell.

Schlesinger, Traci, and Jodie Lawston. 2011. "Experiences of Interpersonal Violence and Criminal Legal Control." *Sage Open* 1, no. 2: 1–14.

Schlosser, Eric. 1998. "The Prison-Industrial Complex." *Atlantic Monthly* (December).

Schmitt, John, Kris Warner, and Sarika Gupta. 2010. "The High Budgetary Cost of Incarceration." *Center for Economic and Policy Research* (June).

Schorsch, Kathleen, and Robin Levi. 1998. "Human Rights for Women in U.S. Custody." *Women's Institute for Leadership Development (WILD) for Human Rights*. http://www.wildforhumanrights.org/documents/resources/women_in_custody.pdf. Accessed January 15, 2009.

Schulman, Barbara. 2004. "Effective Organizing in Terrible Times: The Strategic Value of Human Rights for Transnational Anti-Racist Feminisms." *Meridians: feminism, race, transnationalism* 4, no. 2: 102–108.

Scott, James C. 1992. *Domination and the Arts of Resistance: Hidden Transcripts*. New Haven: Yale University Press.

Senate Judiciary Committee, Subcommittee on the Constitution, Civil Rights and Human Rights. 2012. "Reassessing Solitary Confinement: The Human Rights, Fiscal and Public Safety Consequences." June 19. http://www.judiciary.senate.gov/hearings/hearing.cfm?id=6517e7d97c06eac4ce9f60b09625ebe8. Accessed June 2013.

The Sentencing Project. 2007. "Felony Disenfranchisement Laws in the United States." Briefing Sheet, April. http://www.sentencingproject.org/Admin/Documents/publications/fd_bs_fdlawsinus.pdf. Accessed September 2007.

Shakur, Assata. 2001. *Assata: An Autobiography*. Chicago: Chicago Review Press.

Shelley, Kristopher "Krystal." 2011. "Krystal Is Kristopher and Vice Versa." In *Captive Genders: Trans Embodiment and the Prison Industrial Complex*, edited by Eric A. Stanley and Nat Smith. Oakland, CA: AK Press.

Shen, Eveline. 2006. "Reproductive Justice: Commentary: How Pro-Choice Activists Can Work to Build a Comprehensive Movement." *Mother Jones*, January 24. http://www.motherjones.com/commentary/columns/2006/01/reproductive_justice.html. Accessed May 30, 2008.

Shengold, Leonard. 1979. "Child Abuse and Deprivation: Soul Murder." *Journal of the American Psychoanalytic Association* 27:533–559.

———. 2000. *Soul Murder Revisited: Thoughts about Therapy, Hate, Love, and Memory*. New Haven, CT: Yale University Press.

Shohat, Ella. 2009. "Orientalism and Cinema." http://www.cccb.org/rcs_gene/ellashohatdef.pdf. Accessed April 15, 2011.

Simon, Jonathan. 2001. "'Entitlement to Cruelty': Neo-liberalism and the Punitive Mentality in the United States," In *Crime, Risk and Justice: The Politics of Crime Control in Liberal Democracies*, edited by Kevin Stenson and Robert Sullivan. Portland, OR: Willan.

Sisters Inside. 2004. "A Campaign to End the Sexual Assault of Women by the State." http://www.sistersinside.com.au/media/AntiStripSearchingInfo.pdf. Accessed April 15, 2011.

Sluiter, Engel. 1997. "New Light on the '20. and Odd Negroes' Arriving in Virginia, August, 1619." *William and Mary Quarterly*, 3rd ser., 54, no. 2 (April): 395–398.

Smith, Andrea. 2004. "Beyond the Politics of Inclusion: Violence against Women of Color and Human Rights." *Meridians: feminism, race, transnationalism* 4, no. 2: 120–124.

———. 2005. *Conquest: Sexual Violence and American Indian Genocide*. Cambridge, MA: South End Press.

————. 2010. "Indigeneity, Settler Colonialism, White Supremacy." *Global Dialogue* 12, no. 2 (Summer–Autumn).

Smith, Brenda. 2003. "Watching You, Watching Me." *Yale Journal of Law and Feminism* 15, no. 2: 225–288.

————. 2005. "Sexual Abuse of Women in Prison: A Modern Corollary of Slavery." *Fordham Urban Law Journal* 33, no. 2: 571–607.

————. 2006. "Rethinking Prison Sex: Self Expression and Safety." *Columbia Journal of Gender and the Law* 15:185–234.

Smith, Caleb. 2009. *The Prison and the American Imagination.* New Haven, CT: Yale University Press.

Smith, John. 2003 [1624]. *The Generall Historie of Virginia.* Vol. 4. Madison, WI: Wisconsin Historical Society.

Smith, Kemba. 2005. "Modern Day Slavery: Inside the Prison-Industrial Complex." In *Global Lockdown: Race, Gender, and the Prison-Industrial Complex,* edited by Julia Sudbury. New York: Routledge.

Smith, Robert L. 2007. "Advocates Decry Breast-Feeding Mom's Arrest." *Cleveland Plain Dealer,* November 8.

Smith, Zadie. 2000. *White Teeth.* New York: Penguin.

Solinger, Rickie. 2009. "Beggars and Choosers." Exhibit curated by Rickie Solinger. Schatten Art Gallery, Woodruff Library, Emory University. January 15–March 12.

Solinger, Rickie, Paula Johnson, Martha L. Raimon, Tina Reynolds, and Ruby Tapia, eds. 2010. *Interrupted Life: Experiences of Incarcerated Women in the United States.* Berkeley: University of California Press.

Spade, Dean. 2011. *Normal Life: Administrative Violence, Critical Trans Politics, and the Limits of the Law.* Brooklyn, NY: South End Press.

Spillers, Hortense. 2003. "Mama's Baby, Papa's Maybe." In *Black, White, and in Color: Essays on American Literature and Culture.* Chicago: University of Chicago Press.

Stanko, Stephen, Wayne Gillespie, and Gordon A. Crews. 2004. *Living in Prison: A History of the Correctional System with an Insider's View.* Westport, CT: Greenwood.

Stone-Manista, Krista. 2009. "Protecting Pregnant Women: A Guide to Successfully Challenging Criminal Child Abuse Prosecutions of Pregnant Drug Addicts." *Journal of Criminal Law and Criminology* 99, no. 3: 823–856.

Szlekovics, Monica. 2007. "1600 Elmwood Avenue." In *A Memory, a Monologue, a Rant, and a Prayer,* edited by Eve Ensler. New York: Villard.

Takagi, Paul. 1975. "The Walnut Street Jail: A Penal Reform to Centralize the Powers of the State." *Federal Probation* 39 (December): 18–26.

Taylor, M. Grayson L. 2000. "Prison Psychosis." *Social Justice* 27, no. 3 (Fall): 50–55.

Terkel, Studs. 2005. *Hard Times: An Oral History of the Great Depression.* New York: New Press.

United States v. Gementera, 379 F.3d 596, 2004.

Wacquant, Loïc. 2002. "From Slavery to Mass Incarceration." *New Left Review* 13 (January–February): 41–60.

Walker, Alice. 1983. "Beyond the Peacock: The Reconstruction of Flannery O'Connor." In *In Search of Our Mothers' Gardens.* New York: Harcourt Brace Jovanovich.

Walters, William. 2010. "Deportation, Expulsion, International Police." In *The Deportation Regime,* edited by Nicholas De Genova and Nathalie Peutz, 69–100. Durham, NC: Duke University Press.

Warner, Kebby. 2010. "Pregnancy, Motherhood, and Loss in Prison: A Personal Story." In *Interrupted Life: Experiences of Incarcerated Women in the United States,* edited by Rickie

Solinger, Paula Johnson, Martha L. Raimon, Tina Reynolds, and Ruby Tapia, 89–93. Berkeley: University of California Press.

Weisberg, Robert, and David Mills. 2003. "Violence Silence: Why No One Really Cares about Prison Rape." *Slate.* October 1. http://www.slate.com/articles/news_and _politics/jurisprudence/2003/10/violence_silence.html. Accessed November 2014.

Wessler, Seth Freed. 2011. "Shattered Families: The Perilous Intersection of Immigration Enforcement and the Child Welfare System." Race Forward: The Center for Racial Justice Innovation. November. https://www.raceforward.org/research/reports/ shattered-families. Accessed November 2014.

Western, Bruce. 2007. "Mass Imprisonment and Economic Inequality." *Social Research* 74, no. 2 (Summer): 509–532.

"The We That Sets Us Free/Building a World without Prisons." 2008. Justice Now!, producer. Compact disc.

When Kids Get Life. 2007. Directed, written, and produced by Ofra Bikel. *PBS/Frontline.* Transcript. http://www.pbs.org/wgbh/pages/frontline/whenkidsgetlife/etc/script .html. Accessed July 2013.

White, Larry. 2009. "The Prisoner's Perspective." *Building Bridges.* Newsletter on file with the author. July.

Whitman, James Q. 2007. "What Happened to Tocqueville's America?" *Social Research* 74, no. 2 (Summer): 251–268.

Williams, Patricia. 1991. *The Alchemy of Race and Rights.* Cambridge, MA: Harvard University Press.

Wilson, Richard Ashby. 2010. "When Humanity Sits In Judgment." In *In the Name of Humanity: The Government of Threat and Care,* edited by Ilana Feldman and Miriam Ticktin, 27–58. Durham, NC: Duke University Press.

Witherspoon, Paula Rae. 2011. "My Story." In *Captive Genders: Trans Embodiment and the Prison Industrial Complex,* edited by Eric A. Stanley and Nat Smith. Oakland, CA: AK Press.

Wood, Erika, and Liz Budnitz, with Garima Malhotra. 2009. "Jim Crow in New York." Brennan Center for Justice. http://www.brennancenter.org/sites/default/files/ legacy/publications/JIMCROWNY_2010.pdf. Accessed April 2013.

Young, Kevin. 2012. *The Grey Album: On the Blackness of Blackness.* Minneapolis: Graywolf Press.

INDEX

About the Author

JOSHUA M. PRICE has engaged in advocacy with and for currently and formerly incarcerated people since 2004. For his efforts, the New York State Assembly has awarded him a citation for Outstanding Contribution to Civil Rights of New Yorkers, and the Broome/Tioga (New York) NAACP has named him "Person of the Year." He is the author of *Structural Violence: Hidden Brutality in the Lives of Women*. He teaches in the Department of Sociology at the State University of New York at Binghamton.